The Future for Palestinian Refugees

The Future for Palestinian Refugees

TOWARD EQUITY AND PEACE

Michael Dumper

LYNNE
RIENNER
PUBLISHERS

BOULDER
LONDON

HV
640.5
.P36
D86
2007

Published in the United States of America in 2007 by
Lynne Rienner Publishers, Inc.
1800 30th Street, Boulder, Colorado 80301
www.rienner.com

and in the United Kingdom by
Lynne Rienner Publishers, Inc.
3 Henrietta Street, Covent Garden, London WC2E 8LU

© 2007 by Lynne Rienner Publishers, Inc. All rights reserved

Library of Congress Cataloging-in-Publication Data
Dumper, Michael.
The future for Palestinian refugees : toward equity and peace / by
    Michael Dumper.
    p. cm.
    Includes bibliographical references and index.
    ISBN-13: 978-1-58826-474-9 (hardcover : alk. paper)
    1. Refugees, Palestinian Arab. 2. Arab-Israeli conflict—Refugees.
I. Title.
HV640.5.P36D86   2007
362.87089'9274—dc22   2006032447

British Cataloguing in Publication Data
A Cataloguing in Publication record for this book
is available from the British Library.

Printed and bound in the United States of America

∞ The paper used in this publication meets the requirements
of the American National Standard for Permanence of
Paper for Printed Library Materials Z39.48-1992.

5 4 3 2 1

To Declan

Contents

List of Illustrations	ix
Acknowledgments	xi
1 Introduction	1
2 Palestinian Refugees: An Overview	21
3 Looking at International Practice	49
4 Local Integration, Resettlement, and Repatriation	77
5 The Role of UNRWA	105
6 The Issue of Reparations	133
7 Truth, Justice, and Reconciliation	157
8 Conclusions	185
Appendix: Sources of Data for Policy Formulation	193
List of Acronyms	203
Bibliography	207
Index	223
About the Book	233

ILLUSTRATIONS

Maps

2.1	The UN Partition Plan and the Rhodes Armistice Line	25
2.2	Territories Held by Israel After 1967	27
2.3	UNRWA Area of Operations	38

Tables

2.1	Palestinian Refugees and Internally Displaced Palestinians	41
2.2	Registered Refugees in UNRWA Area of Operations	44
2.3	Estimated Distribution of Palestinian Refugees by Host Country or Region, 1949 and 2000	46
4.1	Estimated Number of Palestinian Refugees in Areas Not Bordering Palestine, 1998	93
5.1	UNRWA Expenditures by Program, 1950–2001	117
5.2	UNRWA Expenditures (Regular Services) per Refugee, 1994–2001	120
5.3	EU Aid to Palestinians, 1993–1999	128
A.1	Thematic Responsibilities of the Refugee Working Group	194

Acknowledgments

In writing this book, I have been fortunate to receive support, advice, and encouragement from so many colleagues and students. I would like to thank, in particular, my University of Exeter colleagues Iain Hampsher-Monk, former research coordinator in the Department of Politics, and Tim Dunne, current head of department, for providing basic structural support. By arranging for some light teaching terms, bringing forward some sabbatical leave, and directing some university research funds for teaching buy-outs, I was able to complete the book in just over a year. I would also like to thank the GARNET consortium for providing research funds and David Armstrong for arranging this. Part of the research was also funded by a British Academy and Leverhulme Senior Research Fellowship and by the Department of Politics.

I am particularly fortunate to have an excellent team of postgraduate students whose work has overlapped to a considerable degree with my own research. Over the past few years, there have been many fruitful discussions among us, and I am sure I have been the main beneficiary of their insights and arguments. I would like to acknowledge the data collection conscientiously carried out on my behalf by Ghada Ageel, Nerys Irving-Jones, Awad Mansour, Maha Samaan, Shahira Samy, and Claire Yorke. Their efforts brought to my attention a much wider range of material than I would have managed to cover on my own in the time available. Additional thanks must go to Nerys and Claire for their help with the bibliography.

A number of colleagues have provided a wide range of support to this study. I would like to thank Roula el-Rifai at the International Development Research Centre (IDRC), whose interest and support for comparative studies with regard to the Palestinian refugee issue provided the initial impetus for the project. The IDRC's financial support for an international workshop on the comparative study of repatriation programs at Exeter in 2003 resulted in the formation of an important network of scholars whose expertise I was able to draw upon and who provided much of the material on which to base this work. Similarly, I would also like to thank Sari Hanafi of the American University of Beirut, Eyal Benvenisti of Tel Aviv University, and Ingrid Jaradat and Terry Rempel of BADIL for invitations to conferences on the refugee issue in Heidelberg (2003), Ghent (2003), and Geneva (2004), where I met other scholars, encountered new ideas and methodologies, and was able to test my own approach in different ways.

Other support and advice was received from Rosemary Hollis, Awad Mansour, Salim Tamari, Fritz Froelich, Ardi Imseis, Menachem Klein, Michal Reifen, Jaber Suleiman, Raja Awad, Lex Takkenberg, Karen AbuZayd, and Jalal al-Husseini. I would particularly like to thank Michael Fischbach, Rex Brynen, and Terry Rempel for their detailed and at times challenging comments on drafts of the manuscript. Reflecting on and addressing their criticisms has, I am sure, made this book stronger and more coherent. I would also like to thank Shahira Samy, Amneh Badran, and Lena al-Malak for their helpful comments and corrections on some chapters; my father, Tony Dumper, for his advice on structure and legibility; and Chris Jones for the hours he labored to turn my serpentine grammatical constructions into more accessible English. Finally, I would like to thank Ann, my best friend, wife, and partner, for her constant advice, practical support, and encouragement. This work would not have been completed if not for her help.

The Future for Palestinian Refugees

1

INTRODUCTION

From the dilapidated camps of Lebanon to the eye of the storm in Gaza and the West Bank, the Palestinian refugees continue to call on the attention of the world's media and public opinion. Refugees make up over 70 percent of the total Palestinian population, with the *registered* refugee population of over 4 million increasing at approximately 124,000 per annum (UNRWA, 2004b). The issue is probably the most difficult of the outstanding problems in the protracted peace negotiations that erratically have taken place between Israel and the Palestinians. The Palestinian sense of grievance is at the heart of the Arab-Israeli conflict, which in turn permeates the politics of the region. At the same time, running to stand still, the cost of support for refugees is increasing beyond what the host communities and the international donors are willing to withstand. It is clearly an issue that will not fade away over time and further delay only increases the complexity of the problems to be solved.

Despite this urgency, however, a solution seems as remote as when the problem began in 1948. The return of Palestinian refugees and their descendants to their former homes in Israel would alter the character and demographic profile of Israel to the extent that the raison d'être of Israel as a specifically Jewish state would be extinguished. Resolving the refugee issue in line with UN resolutions presents not only enormous political, security, and cultural risks to Israel but also existential ones. At the same time, the quest of the Palestinians to return to their homes has become part of the Palestinian self-identity and an integral part of their state-building activity. Their refusal to be marginalized and absorbed into the region reflects a nationalism that has deepened and consolidated despite fragmentation and exile. Thus a political agreement imposed on the refugees without their consent is likely to create further tensions in the region, while the continuation of the status quo is similarly destabilizing.

Coverage of the issue of Palestinian refugees in both academic and general literature—the genesis of the problem, the role it has played in the

Arab-Israeli conflict and regional dynamics, and its current salience in the Middle East peace process—has been extensive. Why, therefore, another book on the Palestinian refugees? What more can be said, what new insights brought to this subject, when so much has been said before? Simply put, this book intends to offer a broader perspective on the subject than others have. It seeks to contextualize the issue through comparative study and is a deliberate attempt to draw on the experience of the international community in dealing with other refugee situations to see how the insights and lessons learned may apply to the Palestinian case. It builds upon earlier research and collaborative work of the author, which focused on the comparative study of refugee repatriation and its relevance to the Palestinian case (Dumper, 2006). In this previous work, comparative research between different repatriation programs in different parts of the world was conducted in order to probe the notion of Palestinian *exceptionalism,* that is, the view that the Palestinian case is unique and therefore requires solutions based upon its own specificity. The study sought to establish whether the lessons learned in other refugee situations would be relevant to the Palestinian case and the extent to which such policies were transferable.

The broad conclusion was that there was transferability on both the macro and micro levels, but there were also many areas where the Palestinian case was quite unique and this had to be factored into the planning process. (These themes will be explored further in the second section of this chapter.) This new study broadens the area of research from the earlier focus on repatriation alone to encompass a wider range of topics—from the role of external forces in peace agreements, durable solutions such as local integration, resettlement and repatriation, the role of lead agencies in repatriation programs, the issues of reparations, and, finally, the often neglected role of reconciliation.

The study has three main aims. First, these topics will be studied with reference to international practice elsewhere with a view to examining the range of options available to policymakers, the donor community, nongovernmental organizations (NGOs), and activists. Thus its approach is both comparative and prospective, and it advances the argument that international practice has been neglected in formulating proposals in the Middle East peace process. Second, in doing so it also seeks to evaluate the various proposals put forward in both the formal and unofficial, or Track II, arenas of negotiations. It, thus, explores the notion that international benchmarks prevailing in other situations rather than being viewed as obstacles to overcome can facilitate and give guidance as to the practicalities of peacemaking in the Middle East.

Third, it seeks to bridge the gap between those often termed as "realists" and those rooted in the discourse of human rights and international humanitarian law. Stimulated by the challenge of South African politician and international lawyer Qader Asmal, it tries to explore a possible way "beyond the twin traps of naiveté and *realpolitik*" (Asmal, 2000: 19). In essence the study is an argument against the exceptionalism of the Palestinian-Israeli case and for the primacy of international law while recognizing specific differentiating features that make it so intractable.

This introductory chapter will include four sections. The first will be an exposition of the political issues arising from the creation of Israel and the Palestinian refugees and the ongoing lack of resolution of their situation. While highlighting the importance of the refugee issue in the Arab-Israeli conflict and its centrality in any peace negotiations, it will also attempt to unpack the main issues so they may be examined individually. The second section will place into context the main themes addressed by this book. It will discuss the relevance of comparative work to the Palestinian case and elaborate on the elements of international experience that could be transferred. The third section comprises an overview of the research carried out on this question. The final section will introduce the following chapters and summarize the main argument the book intends to advance.

Politics of a Palestinian Return and the Jewishness of Israel

What, then, are the main political issues around a Palestinian return? This section will try to explain why the issue is so intractable and to identify the main elements and secondary issues that have to be addressed. It uses as an organizing tool a series of concentric circles in which some core elements are placed in the center with other elements placed in broader circles around it. This schematic approach recognizes that there are some elements that are more important than others in terms both of the passions they engender and of the way in which they run through or figure in the other elements. However, readers should note that the author is not attempting to construct an argument about which are the most important elements that need to be addressed first or require greater effort on the part of the key actors in the conflict. Some of the more peripheral elements may be more important to one or more of the key actors. For example, "host country integration" is of immense importance to Jordan, which hosts 40 percent of Palestinian refugees outside Israel and the Occupied Palestinian Territories (OPTs). Other elements may figure more importantly at different periods over the fifty-five years under review. The concentric circles structure is intended to give an indication of how the deeper one enters the circle the more intractable the issue appears. To some extent, it is true, the circles reflect a continuum stretching from existential issues through to operational and logistical issues. The more marginal the element the less emotive and the more operational it is. But this is not the aim of the configuration.

"Matter Out of Place": Palestinian and Israeli Self-Identities

At the very core of the Arab-Israeli conflict is the Palestinian sense that the displacement from their homes and enforced exile is unjust and contrary to the natural order of life. There is no doubt that Palestinian national identity has been consolidated by the shared experience of "refugeedom" and of the resistance to both Israeli and international attempts to normalize their exiled condition. Nevertheless, the experience does not sufficiently explain the determination of refugees to reject this status and cling to the notion of a future state that will also be their home. It goes much deeper than the unity-through-adversity dynamic. The sense of being what Mary Douglas has termed "matter out of place" and needing to be put back into place has cut so deeply into the Palestinian psyche that their sense of identity as complete persons is under question (cited in Malkki, 1992).[1] The status of being a refugee, of being displaced, and of being in exile is experienced as a transitional phase, a place in waiting, of being incomplete, even though it has lasted for at least three generations. It casts a shadow over their everyday lives, reaffirmed by every checkpoint and every encounter with officialdom, and it is only by returning to Palestine that they can achieve wholeness as individuals and as a people (Dorai, 2002).

Trying to express the existential basis of being a Palestinian refugee in these terms is not to argue that the Palestinian experience is unique. This sense of incompleteness is shared by many refugee communities across the world (Malkki, 1992; Hammond, 1999: 228). What, however, gives particular force to the Palestinian experience is the great sense of grievance that comes from the fact that the perpetrators of this status are former refugees themselves. As the late Edward Said wrote: "What could be more intransigent than the conflict between Zionist Jews and Arab Palestinians? Palestinians feel that they have been turned into exiles by the proverbial people of exile, the Jews" (Said, 1990: 360).

On top of this, successive Israeli governments have been supported in this act of calumny by powerful members of the international community. Despite a series of UN resolutions and a body of international law that confirms the rights of refugees to return to their homes, the opportunity to lay to rest the sense of being matter out of place is denied to them by the weakness of the international community. At the same time, one cannot deny the fact that their protracted displacement and exile has been exploited by Arab states for their own purposes and that the Palestinian political elite have traded their allegiances to various governments in return for material and diplomatic support. As a result, the simplicity of their claim to return may have been sullied. However, for the Palestinian refugee the fact of displacement remains a personal wound that is not eased by palliatives of compromise and compensation. What comes across as intransigence is in fact a very personal need for completeness.

In addition to this core element in the conflict is the question of the Jewishness of the Israeli state. This is not the mirror image of the Palestinian quest to return: Palestinians are not seeking an exclusively Arab, or Muslim and Christian, state. Nevertheless, the desire for Israel to remain predominantly Jewish—and therefore not accept the return of Palestinians to their homes, which since 1948 have been subsumed in the new Israeli state—is also an existential one and entwined with perceptions of Israeli self-identity. Only by understanding this element can one see the intractability of the conflict.

There are two aspects to this determination to maintain the Jewishness of Israel. The first is derived from the predominantly European Jewish experience of being a religious minority in a largely hostile Christianized West. The experience has ranged from the softer end of marginalization, such as being barred from public office and from military preferment, to the harsher end of persecution, seen in the pogroms of czarist Russia to the Holocaust of Nazi Germany. Despite some notable exceptions, European society exhibited silence, passivity, and at times complicity at such discriminatory policies. This experience left a deep imprint on Jewish perceptions of their relations with non-Jews and provided much of the impetus behind the exclusivity of the Zionist settler movement. The possibility of coexistence with the Palestinian Arabs in Palestine, considered in some Zionist circles, was ultimately dwarfed by the enormity of the slaughter of up to six million European Jews. The establishment of the state of Israel in 1948 was followed by a second experience of hostility and aggression from the Arab states and from the uprooted Palestinians. The wars of 1956, 1967, and 1973 and the low-level guerrilla warfare with the various factions of the Palestine Liberation Organization (PLO), Islamic Resistance Movement (HAMAS), and Hizbollah only resulted in confirming the determination by Israeli Jews to ensure their security and strength by relying on themselves. This sense of self-reliance is very deep, permeating both the domestic and foreign policy of Israel and seen in laws that dispossessed and marginalized Palestinians who remained in the area that became Israel after 1948.

The second aspect of this core element in the Arab-Israeli conflict is the importance to Israeli Jews of living in a society that is Jewish to the core, and not Jewish as an add-on or as a benignly permitted and tolerated minority. The experience of anti-Semitism in Europe and North America and the vicarious anti-Israeli sentiments visited upon Jews in Arab countries prior to their expulsion or migration to Israel led to a determination to safeguard the successful creation of "Jewish" society. Israel is now a society where Judaism provides the framework for both spiritual and social relations: a Rabbinate is the established clerical body supervising laws of personal status (marriage, wills, deaths, etc.); kosher dietary laws are the norm; and the Shabbat is respected and impinges on transportation, entertainment, and public activities. Even secular Israeli Jews who are opposed to the fundamentalist strand that has come to the fore in recent times are deeply attached to the Jewishness that permeates Israeli society. The prospect that this gain of a sense of place, of a specifically Jewish place, being reversed through the absorption of large number of Palestinian refugees is resisted not just at a political level, but existentially as well. Most Israeli Jews will accept that in order to achieve a stable peace, Palestinian grievances have to be addressed to some extent. But to share their society with, or to dismantle the Jewish foundations of the state for the sake of Palestinian refugees—who have been depicted for decades as terrorists and now as suicide bombers—is, in their view, asking much too much. In this context, one can see how the definition of Zionism as a racist ideology is incomprehensible to most Israeli Jews and even smacks of covert anti-Semitism. It can be quite legitimately argued that the construction of a state on an exclusivist ethnicity falls within the definition of racism, but the issue here is that due to their experience of the historic racism of others, Israeli Jews cannot see or experience Zionism in this way.

Mechanisms and Modalities

In the next circle, one can find a cluster of mechanisms and modalities that are commonly present in trying to rectify conflict, communal divisions, and displacement. These will be discussed more fully in later chapters, but they are touched on briefly in this section to give an idea of the complexity of the whole issue of a Palestinian return. There is no particular order of priority. The first mechanism is that of reparation, the intention to repair the damage that has occurred. Reparation comprises many dimensions and components. There are material, moral, and legal reparations, which are manifested in different forms. In this book, I will concentrate on two of the main forms: restitution and compensation.

Restitution of Palestinian refugee property is clearly the most intractable and explosive component in any reparations between Israelis and Palestinians. It is the thing that refugees most want and that Israelis will most resist. While many of the villages and urban areas where Palestinians once lived have either been destroyed, rebuilt, or occupied in some way, studies have shown that a significant proportion can still be identified and in this way can be reallocated to refugees and their descendants (Abu Sitta, 1999). Technically, some restitution may be possible, but the prospect of it occurring in the face of the existential elements outlined above are remote. Given that Jews only owned less than 10 percent of historic Palestine, much of the land of the new Israeli state is refugee property (Fischbach, 2000: 240; Jiryis, 1976: 78; Peretz, 1958: 143, 181). To return this to the original owners and residents would not only allow an influx of new non-Jewish residents, but also, literally, cut the ground from beneath the state. Nevertheless, restitution remains an issue. This is partly because it has some weight in UN resolutions and international law and has successfully occurred in other refugee situations (such as in Bosnia) and is under serious consideration in Cyprus. Partly, also, it remains an issue because it is possible to separate restitution of property from actual physical return to that property, thus refuting Israeli fears of an influx. And finally, the emotions and associations that property evokes through memories and an oral tradition that is kept alive by the work of Palestinian refugee organizations fuel a continuing call for restitution.

The second form of reparation, compensation, comprises a cluster of issues that require agreement, all of which are contentious. In the first place, there has to be an agreement upon who is eligible for compensation. Are all displaced Palestinians eligible or only those who are registered as refugees? As the work of the Refugee Working Group set up by the Madrid Peace Conference in 1991 attests, the issue of who exactly is a refugee and how many of them require a solution is subject to political considerations, with the result that the PLO and Israel have adopted potentially irreconcilable positions. Following on from this difficulty is the question of *what* should be compensated. Is it merely land and building or also movable property? How do we factor in inflation and from what date? Do we include loss of earnings and psychological and emotional traumas experienced, and are there moral and legal liabilities that have to be addressed as well? Then there is the issue of whether compensation be paid to individuals in a lump sum or through indirect forms tied to the development of services and infrastructure, such as training and educational vouchers or public investment through national authorities. In addition, both Israel and the host countries have made claims for compensation: Israel for loss of infrastructure and investment in the OPTs, and Jordan, Syria, and Lebanon for the burden of supporting refugees for over fifty years. Finally, there is the question of financing a compensation scheme. To Palestinians, it is also important that Israel accept some significant financial responsibility as a form of reparation, and judging from discussions with the donor community, there is an expectation that Israel will finance most of the direct compensation. At the same time, there is a broad consensus that the United States, European Union (EU), and some Arab states would be responsible for the greater proportion of the funding of repatriation and resettlement programs and associated developmental costs. Connected with this question are the modalities of distribution. Who will manage an international compensation fund, and what will be the involvement of Palestinian and Israeli representatives?

Also in this second circle is the issue of repatriation. Clearly, the numbers involved and the locality to which a repatriation program is directed will depend upon the nature of the peace agreement between Israelis and Palestinians. If there is some repatriation to their original homes in pre-1967, this will be a very different kind of program from one directed toward the OPTs. Readers should be aware that the term *repatriation* in the Palestinian case is confusing. Until recently repatriation in the literature of forced migrations implied a return to the previous residences or nearby. It was loosely used in the Palestinian case to also mean refugees moving to the OPTs that would become the new Palestinian state. In this sense, it could be called repatriation. However, to Palestinian refugees in Lebanon, Jordan, and Syria, this would often mean in practice a "resettlement," as they were not going back to their homes. The confusion is exacerbated by trends in UN High Commission for Refugees (UNHCR) thinking and practice to redefine the repatriation of refugees as a return to their *homeland* and not specifically to their homes (Refugee Studies Centre, 2005: 90–100; Fagen, 2006: 46).

Nevertheless, whatever the mix of repatriation to pre-1967 Israel or to the OPTs, planning and executing a repatriation program encounters a number of complex issues. These will be explored in greater detail in Chapter 4, but they include the essential but problematic involvement of the international community in ensuring funding, coordination, mobility, and border controls. Another issue is ensuring the cooperation of the refugees themselves, which involves prolonged consultation and possibly new participatory structures. Here it is important to take into account gender issues and to differentiate between the needs of different sectors of the community, whether it be because of age, educational levels, or health requirements. Finally, it also involves issues related to the capacity of local communities and administrative structures to deal with large inflows of refugees, and the directing of funds to ensure a comprehensive development of the society and economy, as opposed to targeting the returned refugees only.

A final issue in this second circle is that of reconciliation and justice. As with the other issues in this circle this is one that both feeds into the peace agreement and yet is also dependent upon the overall nature of the peace agreement. Its importance lies in the fact that without some reconciliation based on a sense of justice, the prospect of a "warm" or cordial peace, rather than simply a cessation of hostilities, is unlikely. In the context of a new Palestinian state coexisting alongside a state of Israel (with the inherent interdependency between the two with regard to economy and resources such as access to air, land, sea, markets, labor, and water), a collective moving on from the trauma of 1948 and the subsequent suffering would be a prerequisite for a stable and prosperous peace. There must be not only a range of mechanisms in place to ensure that positive images of the opposing community are engendered, but also a number of state-to-state activities both on a legal and symbolic level. Practice elsewhere has indicated that for the latter, public declarations of apology, commemorations of particular events, and the setting up of truth and reconciliation commissions offer a way forward. The adoption of some features of a transitional justice regime, with war crime tribunals and amnesties in exchange for public confessions, as in South Africa, seems very remote in the Palestinian-Israeli case, but nevertheless it will constitute an important threshold to cross and a breakthrough to an era of forgiveness, atonement, and cooperation.

Legal and Developmental Issues

In the third and outer concentric circle lie a number of issues that generate perhaps less heat but are certainly contentious, as the earlier issues mentioned. The first is the role of international law in the conflict. This has been both critically important and also problematic. For example, the Palestinian claim for return and/or compensation is based fundamentally upon the UN Declaration of Human Rights. Article 13.2 states that everyone has the right to return to their country. More specifically, it is based upon UN General Assembly Resolution (UNGAR) 194, which has not been implemented. However, the perspective adopted by Israel and many Western governments is that as a nonbinding General Assembly Resolution, 194 confers no legal rights as such, but merely is a recommendation. This argument also observes that the clauses recommending Israel to allow the return of refugees was part of an overall package concerning the division of territory of Palestine and the internationalization of Jerusalem, which were not acceptable to the Palestinians.

One should also note that subsequent agreements between Israel and Egypt, Jordan, and the PLO pay only cursory reference to the main resolutions concerning refugee rights. Instead, the main focus of these agreements is not the rights of refugees but the withdrawal from territories occupied in 1967. Thus, while international law is based upon UN resolutions, it is also based upon bilateral agreements which in practice in the Arab-Israeli conflict have sidestepped some of the more difficult issues concerned with refugees. Furthermore, with respect to the UN Declaration of Human Rights, there is debate as to whether the rights articulated there are multigenerational, that is, that they should be accorded to the descendants of the original Palestinian refugees. Thus, rather than international law providing clear and unambiguous guidelines, all these ambiguities result in the Palestinian refugee "right of return" being an arena for debate over interpretations of international law.

Within this ambiguity lies another legal issue that is tied up with the legitimacy of the PLO. Having finally received recognition from Israel, the PLO, by considering the option of negotiating the refugees' claim to return to their homes, finds its legitimacy being questioned by some of its supporters and opponents alike. In this context, who will sign a treaty with the Israelis dealing with restitution, repatriation, and compensation? Will it be the PLO, the interim government in the OPTs known as the Palestinian National Authority (PNA), or some other representative body of refugees? Will refugees still consider it their right to make individual claims against the Israeli government even after such an agreement is signed? Where does this leave the "end of conflict" clause so sought after by the Israelis, and who will ensure it?

Here we can see how the twin issues of state-building and legitimacy are essential components of a peace agreement involving displaced persons and refugees. This is exacerbated by the role of international funding. For example, the World Bank estimated that simply in order to meet current growth in school enrollments in the OPTs *without* any repatriation, the PNA would need to construct fifty new schools per year (World Bank, 2000a: 90–91). There is no possibility that the PNA can meet these additional costs from its own revenue sources. Thus, to what extent should the World Bank, the UN Development Programme (UNDP), the EU, or the existing Ad Hoc Liaison Committee (AHLC) as the main donors to the PNA recurrent budget have a role in determining development priorities? Nevertheless, putting aside the difficulties of establishing a coordinating structure that meets the accountability requirements of the donor community and the most efficient way of implementing the disbursements of funds, it is clear that a donor presence will be a prerequisite for any implementation of refugee clauses in an agreement. Yet one can imagine the questions raised by refugees over the legitimacy of their institutions in negotiating on their behalf when these same institutions are so dependent upon external support.

There are two further development issues that add to the complexity of the conflict. The first is the question of the integration of refugees into the host countries if they do not wish to return, or repatriate, to the new Palestinian state, or if they are barred from doing so. Integration is not quite so simple. The three main states involved—Lebanon, Syria, and Jordan—have different priorities, including concerns about costs and the transformation of their own internal demographic balances. The second developmental question is the future role of the UN Relief and Works Agency for Palestine Refugees in the Near East (UNRWA). Clearly, following an agreement on the future of the refugees, the various service functions would be transferred to the PNA and the governments of the host states. Yet, should UNRWA play a role in any transitional programs, such as repatriation or integration? Some argue that these additional functions should be taken on by new and specially dedicated agencies, while others contend that as the repository of collective refugee experience and of accumulated expertise on the refugee community, UNRWA can be usefully utilized.

The issues discussed above are clearly not exhaustive. We have not touched on the issues of camp-dwelling ownership, of camp rehabilitation, and of prioritizing different vulnerable or strategic sectors of the refugee community. What must be clear, however, is the complexity of the problems that lie ahead. In dealing with these problems, there will be a long protracted process of give and take between the two main parties and between them and the international community, both as donors and as guarantors of any agreement. This book advances the argument that there also needs to be an input based upon international practice. While there is no single formula in dealing with refugees in conflict situations, the experience of the international community is varied and offers many options that should be seriously considered in dealing with the Palestinian case. The next section will briefly outline how such comparisons can be done and what their advantages and challenges are.

The Comparative Study of Refugee Returns

Despite the growing abundance of literature and the establishment of institutions researching refugee and forced migration situations, the discourse has largely focused on case studies and is uncontextualized.[2] As Richard Black has written: "The core of the field of refugee studies has arguably remained dominated by a policy-led and somewhat exceptionalist view of refugee experience" (Black, 2006: 2).

This is partly due to the fact most research is funded by policy agencies, government departments, and UNHCR. It is true that UNHCR, through its biannual *State of the World's Refugees,* its working paper series *New Issues in Refugee Studies,* and its annual CD-ROM, *RefWorld,* supplies a great deal of data useful for comparative research. But these publications themselves constitute the raw material and do not develop the analytical aspects of comparative research to a significant degree. It is interesting to contrast this lacuna with the corpus of comparative research on transitional state-building, peacemaking, peacekeeping, and peace enforcement, which is much more developed.[3]

Before continuing with this study, it is important to reiterate the opportunities for deeper analysis that comparative research offers. Comparative study allows one to contextualize and classify a range of phenomena that both simplifies discussion and highlights distinctive features that can be held in common. Rebellions and revolutions in different parts of the globe, for example, can be classed according to the social and economic bases of the key actors, whether they be tenant farmer or sharecropper, urban or rural, and so on. Once cases have been contextualized and classified, relationships or correlations between variables (key actors, environmental conditions, socio-economic groupings, etc.) can be suggested and demonstrated. For example, if you wish to demonstrate the hypothesis that voter participation in a democratic political system increases in countries of high per capita gross national product (GNP), this can be tested in groups of culturally mixed countries with different levels of per capita GNPs. Finally, one of the main purposes of such comparative work is to be able to make predictions based upon the generalizations constructed and observed. Correlations can be extrapolated from certain patterns and sequences of activity. Thus, in turning to the field of refugee studies, it is theoretically possible to construct a repatriation program with certain objectives such as durability or a percentage of returned refugees, on the basis of identifying programs that have achieved this.

This is not to be blind to the problems of comparability and its application in policy transfer. Comparing situations so diverse as forced migrations and repatriations, which have such disparate features or are very stretched out over time or involve a large number of variables, is beset with methodological and conceptual problems.

One major shortcoming is known as the inferential problem in which the scholar extrapolates from a restricted number of cases. Not having the time and resources to study more than a handful of cases, scholars resort to making inferences from a small number of cases, which is possibly misleading. Another problem is the transferability of terms from different political, religious, and cultural contexts. For example, the description "class" may not mean the same in a society where family or religious bonds form the basis of an economic unit. A third problem is a bias by scholars in choosing case studies that strengthen their argument. Known as intentionality, in essence, one selects those cases that bear out one's hypothesis. A final acknowledged shortcoming of the comparative method is the possibility of drift in the levels of analysis. Here the problem can be that a study based on one level is then used to draw comparisons with a study based upon another level. For example, a comparative study of foreign policy across many countries may in some cases focus on decisionmaking within the elite group in one country while in other cases the focus is on external constraints on that foreign policy (e.g., superpower interventions) when these are really different levels of analysis.

When applying such comparative research to policy issues, the researcher enters the fields of "lessons drawn" and "policy transfer." However, just as the comparative approach can be problematic, the very notion of "lessons drawn" and "policy transfer" is not free of some debate. This becomes apparent once one starts to seperate out the two terms in order to reach a more precise meaning of the processes that are taking place. Similarly, difficulties become apparent when one tries to identify when such processes are more likely to take place and in what circumstances they can be successful.

Lesson drawing has been summarized as a cause-and-effect description of a set of actions that an agency, government, or supranational body can evaluate to see if they are applicable to another situation (Rose, 1993). Richard Rose has identified five different types of lesson drawing: *copying*, which is implementing a program more or less intact; *adjusting*, where a program is adopted but adapted for contextual differences; *hybridization*, in which elements from two different programs are combined to create a new one; *synthesis*, where elements from several different programs are combined to create a new one; and finally, *inspiration*, where a program provides the intellectual stimulus to develop a new one (Rose, 1993: 27). These processes can be both positive and negative in that they lead to recommendations about what ought or ought not to be done.

Lesson drawing is generally a voluntary process and to a large extent is an integral part of policymaking. Policy transfer, a subset of lesson drawing, on the other hand, can be both voluntary and coercive. It has been defined as "the process by which knowledge of policies, administrative arrangements, institutions, and ideas in one political system (past or present) is used in the development of policies, administrative arrangements, institutions, and ideas in another political system" (Dolowitz, 2000: 3).

An example of the voluntary adoption of policy would be the adoption by the Spanish government of elements of the German constitution relating to the role of the president. An example of coercive transfer would be the structural adjustment programs imposed on less developed countries by the International Monetary Fund. Scholars have tried to identify occasions when the processes are most likely to occur. For example, Rose has suggested several possible situations where a lessons-drawn process is likely to be effective. These involve consideration of the function and structure of the relevant institutions, the equivalence in resources available, the scale of change attempted, jurisdictional features, and the congruity between program values and policymakers (Rose, 1993: 118–142).

However, if a particular policy is successful, there are also problems in determining the extent to which the transferable element is the critical one and thus the degree of success of the policy transfer. Conversely, it is much easier to identify failures. David Dolowitz and David Marsh have suggested there are three types of failure in policy transfer. "Uninformed transfer" is where the borrowing country has insufficient information about the policy that is being transferred, with the result the policy is imperfectly implemented. "Incomplete transfer" is where crucial elements are not transferred. Finally, "inappropriate transfer" is where the social, economic, political, and ideological differences between the borrowing and the transferring country have been given insufficient consideration (Dolowitz and Marsh, 2000: 17).

From the above discussion one can see that the comparative study of refugee returns is not a straightforward exercise. The methodological problems are considerable and the pitfalls of inaccurate hypotheses many. The different elements in the lesson-drawing process and in policy transfer and the diversity and complexity of the case studies themselves make their application to the Palestinian case problematic. This book will be drawing on the experience of UNHCR and other international agencies working with refugees to draw out lessons that can be learned and will be subject to similar challenges. Nevertheless, despite the evolution of the Palestinian refugee situation outside the framework of UNHCR, there are many essential elements that can be instructive. In the Palestinian case, applying the processes of lesson drawing and policy transfer is more, to use Rose's terminology encountered above, a question of "inspiration" and "synthesis" rather than "copying."

It is important to note that comparative work does not necessarily advance the cause of refugees. Contextualizing the Palestinian case can be used to inject a dose of political realism into the debate about, for example, the numbers of likely returnees. UNHCR statistics indicate that in general no more than 25 percent of refugees have returned to their countries of origin. Research into global patterns of return indicate that, despite maintaining their claims for return and restitution, refugees who have spent many years in exile are often wary of returning immediately to their place of origin. Thus in the Palestinian-Israeli context, comparative research can render the cup half full or half empty. In some cases, it can provide tools to advance Palestinian refugee rights, while in others it can reveal that Palestinians will not be unique in failing to achieve their political goals (Dumper, 2006a). As will be discussed in the next section, recent trends in Palestinian refugee research can be loosely divided into two schools of thought—the "political realist" and the "rights-based" school.

While the former attempts to address issues thrown up by a negotiating agenda dominated by Israeli security concerns, the latter emphasizes the importance of adhering to international norms and procedures. This book endeavors to take this debate forward in two ways. It will draw upon the insights gained by the comparative research elements in the rights-based approach by examining international practice across a range of issues that are at the heart of the Palestinian refugee issue. At the same time, it seeks to bridge the gap between the political realist and the rights-based approaches by drawing out possible solutions that can be transferred. The intention will be to explore experience gained elsewhere, to identify what has worked in other refugee situations—and, therefore, what has been politically and logistically feasible—and how this has been absorbed by international agencies concerned with refugees. In this way it aspires to offer a wider range of policy options.

The Study of Palestinian Refugees

It is possible to distinguish two main phases in the recent literature on Palestinian refugees and two significant events—the 1991 Madrid Middle East Peace Conference and the 1993 Oslo Accords between Israel and the PLO—that serve as the watershed between these phases. The first phase was largely characterized by descriptive studies that revealed the socioeconomic conditions of the Palestinian refugees. To some extent, these studies were driven by the close links between researchers and aid and development agencies who were interested in improving the delivery of their services to refugees. Thus, there was a focus on case studies emanating from ad hoc projects that were more directed at humanitarian concerns than at political solutions. To this end, the research of this period was also, in the main, anthropological and historical (Sutcliff, 1974; Smith, 1986; Tibawi, 1963; Plascov, 1981; Morris, 1987; Shlaim, 1986; Kapeliouk, 1987). A significant number of studies in this first phase were also legal, particularly in the field of international law. This reflected the perception in the academic community that, in the light of movement within other areas (such as the acceptance in 1974 of the PLO as having observer status in the UN, and the Israeli-Egyptian peace agreement in 1979), the Palestinian refugees constituted an anomaly that required explaining (Tomeh, 1974; Radley, 1978; Sharif, 1979; Lee, 1986; Mallison and Mallison, 1986; Cattan, 1982). Notable exceptions to this general focus on humanitarian and legal issues were political studies carried out by Rosemary Sayigh on the Palestinian refugees in Lebanon (Sayigh, 1979); the works of Don Peretz on refugees, compensation, and the Palestinians in Israel (Peretz, 1958 and 1993); and the groundbreaking study of Palestinian institution-building outside Palestine by Laurie Brand (Brand, 1988).

Following the 1991 Madrid Peace Conference and the 1993 Oslo Accords, there was a major change and a realignment between the political arena and research. The work of the Refugee Working Group (RWG) set up by the Madrid conference received new impetus as the refugees became a "Permanent Status Issue" in the Oslo Accords, subject to further negotiation during the interim stage of the peace process. As a consequence, there was increased donor and institutional involvement in research on Palestinian refugees. The governments of Canada and Norway and the European Union took on leading roles in sponsoring policy-relevant research. Specific studies were also commissioned by the World Bank, the Ottawa-based International Development Research Centre (IDRC), and the Oslo-based Institute for Applied Social Science (FAFO). These activities culminated in two major international conferences on Palestinian refugee research held in Ottawa, known as Stocktaking I (1997) and Stocktaking II (2003).[4] These were important gatherings of academic researchers, policymakers, and the donor community and resulted in better coordination of research initiatives and the determination of priorities (Brynen and el-Rifai, 2006). Other international conferences and study groups also tried to link a historical understanding of the refugee issue to policy options (Ginat and Perkins, 2001), while others sought to explore Israeli and Palestinian perspectives from a range of disciplinary angles (Benvenisti and Hanafi, 2006; Lesch and Lustick, 2005).

In this second phase, the focus on data collection and case studies continued (Sayigh, 1994), but in general it was more directed toward in-depth studies on Palestinian capacities and solution-orientated studies. The role of UNRWA and the living conditions of the refugee camps, for example, were the subject of major studies (Schiff, 1995; Jacobsen, 2003). In addition, there were important and influential expositions of the positions of the main protagonists, the PLO, and the Israeli government (Gazit, 1995; Tamari, 1996; Zureik, 1996). This new phase was also characterized by a concentration on modalities for implementation (Arzt, 1996; Brynen, 1997; Dumper, 2006a), with a particular focus on the problems of establishing an equitable compensation system (Peretz, 1995; Rempel, 1999; Brynen, 1999; Kubursi, 2001; Lynk, 2001). In this respect, renewed attention was also given to evaluating the utility of archival material (Fischbach, 2003; Tamari and Zureik, 2001; Nasser, 2003; Nathanson, 2003). The links between research and policy options developed, and issues of refugee absorption and camp rehabilitation were especially targeted (Abu Sitta, 1999; Exeter Refugee Study Team 2001; Krafft and Elwan, 2003; Nijem, 2003; World Bank, 2000a, 2000b). It is interesting to note that very little of this work touched on international experience of other refugee situations, although some studies examined the Israeli case (Alterman, 2003). The comparative work that did take place was mainly in the field of international law (Akram, 2002; Lynk, 2001; Boling, 2001; Benvenisti and Zamir, 1995) with useful work commissioned by the grassroots refugee organization BADIL (Resource Centre for Palestinian Residency and Refugee Rights).

In the main, much of the government- and major agency-funded research adopted what could be loosely termed a "political realist" approach. There was a welcome recognition that the future of the refugees constituted an important item on the negotiation agenda, but the emphasis was more on it as a problem that had to be overcome or finessed. There was a consensus that Palestinian refugees would either be absorbed into the new Palestinian state on the West Bank and Gaza Strip or be absorbed by their host communities or by third countries. The fact that a return of Palestinian refugees to their homes was receding from the range of policy options being discussed in the international community was an indication of the dominance of the Israeli security agenda and the interests of the United States and the European Union in preferring regional stability over any consideration of restitution of property. In the late 1990s, and particularly after the Camp David summit in 2000 involving Israel, the PLO, and the United States, there emerged a body of research with a strong human rights agenda. This was largely in response to the indications that many in the leadership of the PLO, supported by the big donor countries, were considering the possibility of trading the rights of Palestinian refugees to return to their homes in exchange for a state in the OPTs.

The main instrument in constructing what can be seen as a distinct new research agenda was a series of seminars and study trips held by BADIL (Ghent, 2003; Geneva, 2003; Cairo, 2004; Haifa, 2004; Bosnia study trip, 2002; South Africa, 2003; Cyprus, 2004) and the coalition of Right of Return groups (London, 2004; Damascus, 2004; Brussels, 2004). Papers were commissioned that examined the international legal basis of a variety of subjects including restitution, temporary protection, compensation, repatriation, relations with host countries, transitional justice, and reconciliation issues. As a result, the rights-based approach to the Palestinian refugees was drawn from the margins of debate into the mainstream. Previously dismissed as being impractical and unrealistic in the face of the Israeli-dominated security agenda for the negotiations, this new work, based upon international law, provided the intellectual underpinnings not only for the justice of the Palestinian case but for the factoring in of refugee concerns (BADIL, 2001; Akram and Rempel, 2003; Welchman, 2003; Prettitore, 2003; Vicente, 2003; Masalha, 2003). So far only a small proportion of this rights-based work has been published in book form (Aruri, 2001).

A noteworthy element in this rights-based approach is the utilization of comparative research. Not all comparative research is rights-based and, as was discussed in the previous section, comparative research can undermine some of the arguments put forward for upholding refugee rights (Dumper, 2006a). Yet as the new body of research initiated by BADIL has shown, comparative research in the Arab-Israeli conflict establishes two very important facts. First, many (though not all) of the problems in the Arab-Israeli conflict have been encountered elsewhere in the world and some of these problems have had a relatively satisfactory resolution based upon a close adherence to refugee rights. Thus, from this perspective, rights-based options are feasible and "do-able" and those who ignore them run the danger of being accused of selecting alternatives that suit the interests of the key power brokers in the region. Second, the participation of refugees in formulating the final outcome of their situation is not merely part of a liberal, idealistic "wish list." Rather it is part of a strategy that will lead to both stability and durability and, as a consequence, have budgetary implications for the donor community in the form of reduced long-term expenditure (Dumper, 2006c: 297). Political realists would take this factor into account if they broadened out their evaluation of peace agreements from the narrow concerns with an (asymmetrical) balance of power. Indeed, one can argue that traditional realist approaches are based upon a restricted view of the range of influences and dynamics at play. Furthermore, as Richard Black has observed, in some cases a rights-based approach is seen as a way of depoliticizing the return issue (Black, 2006: 31). When prescribing policies concerning the lives and livelihoods of refugees, the "soft power" identified by political realists (or more accurately in the lexicon of political science, by neorealists), in the form of the consent and active participation of refugees, is an important factor to be included.

Conclusion

In essence, this book maps out the broad contours of the issue of a Palestinian return with particular reference to wider international practice and its possible bearing on the current debates in the Middle East peace process. It draws upon earlier research by the author on comparative perspectives on Palestinian refugee repatriation to examine a broader range of issues ranging from international involvement in postconflict agreements, to compensation and resettlement issues, to the thorny problem of justice and reconciliation. After giving the background to the Palestinian refugee issue in Chapter 2, the study will focus on five specific issues concerning the future of the Palestinian refugees, a chapter on each. Each chapter adopts approximately the same formula of examining international practice and drawing out its relevance for the Palestinian-Israeli case in order to suggest some concrete policy options.

Chapter 3 will examine the experience of the international community on integrating refugee issues into an overall political settlement of a conflict. Through the examination of UNHCR handbooks and guidelines and some case studies, it will draw out some common features and analyze the possibility of prerequisites in peace agreements dealing with refugees. It will then examine the various peace negotiations between Israelis and the Palestinians and the informal discussions, known as Track II diplomacy, that have taken place on this issue to see if any lessons can be learned from the international experience. Chapter 4 discusses the three "durable solutions" that have evolved in the international humanitarian community: local integration, resettlement to a third country, and repatriation. It attempts to contextualize the issue by examining trends in international practice and identifies important factors to be taken into consideration. The chapter then examines the specific problems associated with Palestinian resettlement in host or third countries and the current debate concerning repatriation. Chapter 5 focuses on the role of a lead agency in carrying out repatriation and resettlement programs and examines the experience of UNHCR in other refugee situations. The unique role of UNRWA is then examined to see if its functions can be enhanced or transformed to take on additional postconflict roles. Various alternatives to UNRWA that are under consideration will also be discussed.

The compensation issue will be examined in Chapter 6. This chapter will examine the extent to which other models of compensation are transferable to the Middle East conflict. Clearly there are important unique features in the dispossession of Palestinian refugees, but some principles based on international law are likely to apply. The chapter will also attempt to draw up a possible compensation model. Chapter 7 examines the related issues of justice and reconciliation in the Middle East conflict. As in other chapters, it examines the evolution of international practice and offers some case studies for consideration. While recognizing the unique features of the Palestinian-Israeli case, it also attempts to pull together essential components in a reconciliation process that may be applicable to the Middle East conflict. The conclusion will discuss some of the key issues that have emerged in this study and relate them to the debate over the future of the refugee issue.

A Note on Definitions

Before continuing it is important to clarify the use of some terms. This book straddles the fields of forced migration studies and refugee studies *and* the study of the Arab-Israeli conflict. As a result, there are a variety of identical terms that mean different things in the different fields. Therefore a number of commonly used terms need to be defined. The term *refugee* is used in the broadest sense of encompassing both those who are registered with UNRWA and those who are not registered but still see themselves as exiled from their homeland and unable to return. As will be explained in later chapters, the narrower UNHCR definition is not used in the Palestinian case due to the circumstances in which Palestinian refugees were created.

The term *displaced persons* is used in three senses in the literature encountered. First, it is used to describe those who have been forced to leave their homes but not necessarily left their countries or crossed any borders. Second, it is used in a narrower and more precise sense to refer to those Palestinians displaced by the 1967 Arab-Israeli War and referred to as such in the Jordan-Israel Peace Agreement of 1994. Finally it is also used to refer to those Palestinians who have left their homes but still reside in the parts of Palestine that became Israel and are more correctly referred to as *internally displaced* Palestinians. Displaced persons who have crossed an international border or ceasefire line are referred to as *refugees*.

In this book, the term *return* is used generically to encompass all elements of a refugee return, including individual returns, "spontaneous" returns, and planned programs of return. It also includes the integration and rehabilitation of returned refugees in the country of origin. In contrast, the term *repatriation* is used as one element of return—the logistical and operational aspects of a large-scale repatriation program. Thus this book refers to a *return process* of which a *repatriation program* is a subset.

The term *resettlement,* or *tawtin* in Arabic, is generally used in the literature of the Arab-Israeli conflict to refer to the integration of refugees into their host countries and not, as is used in the refugee studies field, to resettlement in third countries. In this book, the refugee studies usage is utilized and two terms, *integration* into host countries and *resettlement* to third countries will be employed. The term *returnee,* that is, a refugee who has returned, is avoided as much as possible, not because it is wrong, but because it may cause confusion by adding yet another category. Instead the term *returned refugee* is used, which has the added advantage of conveying the continuity of the experience of refugeedom that many returned refugees have.

The areas of Palestine acquired by Israel in 1967 have been referred to widely as the West Bank and Gaza Strip (or Judea, Samaria, and Azza in some Israeli circles). Since the establishment of an interim Palestinian administration in 1994, the term *Occupied Palestinian Territories* (OPTs) has had increasing circulation. This book adopts this more recent usage, as it more accurately conveys the status of the territories in international law. There are two labels given to the interim Palestinian administrative body: the *Palestinian Authority,* or PA, and the *Palestinian National Authority,* or PNA. This book will employ the PNA, because it reflects its increasing perception as a representative body of the Palestinians and not merely a bureaucratic vehicle with limited service functions.

Notes

1. I am indebted to Laura Hammond (Hammond, 1999: 228), for drawing my attention to this phrase used by the anthropologist Mary Douglas, cited in L. H. Malkki (1992: 35, 40).

2. Some exceptions include articles by Hammond (1999), "Examining the Discourse of Repatriation: Towards a More Proactive Theory of Return Migration"; and Black and Koser, "The End of the Refugee Cycle," in Black and Koser (1999). See also Petrin (2002), "Refugee Return and State Reconstruction: A Comparative Analysis"; Zeager and Bascom (1996), "Strategic Behaviour in Refugee Repatriation: A Game-Theoretic Analysis"; Chimni (2003), "Post Conflict Peace Building and the Return of Refugees: Concepts, Practices and Institutions."

3. For example, Chesterman (2004), Paris (2004), and Wheeler (2000).

4. See Stocktaking I (1997) and Stocktaking II (2003) in bibliography for references to online sources for the conference proceedings.

2

PALESTINIAN REFUGEES: AN OVERVIEW

The Arab-Israeli conflict receives almost daily attention in the media and is well-covered in both general and specialized publications. Most readers will be familiar with the broad outlines of the conflict; however, the central position the refugee issue assumes in the conflict is much less known. How the refugee issue can be taken to be the fundamental cause of the conflict, how the issue affected the failure of the Camp David summit in 2000, and how it has been the final stumbling block in any negotiations. This chapter is designed to provide both an overview of the Arab-Israeli conflict and the role played by the refugee issue in it. The first section will provide an overview of the main historical and political developments in order to provide those unfamiliar with the Palestinian case a firm grasp of the chronology, the key actors involved, the significance of regional factors, and the ideological context. The second section will describe the achievements of the Zionist settlers in transforming territories they acquired into the formidable state that is now Israel, while the third section will focus on the situation of the Palestinian refugees.

Palestinian Refugees: An Overview of Political Developments

It is important to recognize that the State of Israel includes a substantial part of what was called Palestine. Historic Palestine was known in Judaism and by the first Zionist Jewish settlers as *Eretz Israel,* the Land of Israel. Jews consider Palestine to be the promised historical homeland given to them by their deity, Yahweh. However, prior to the arrival of the first Zionist settlers, the geographical area known as Palestine was inhabited almost entirely by Arabs who were subjects of the Ottoman Empire (1517–1918) and ruled from Istanbul. Palestine itself was divided among a number of governorates whose administrative seat changed from Beirut to Damascus over the years. It was not until 1840 that the *mutasarrif* (district) of Jerusalem was established, but even then this did not encompass the whole territory that was finally defined as Palestine by the British when they set up their mandatory government for Palestine in 1920. Indeed, up to this point, the area was known colloquially and in literature as part of Bilad al-Sham, comprising what is today Syria, Lebanon, Jordan, Israel, and the Occupied Palestinian Territories. The point at which a sense of Palestinian identity or national consciousness began is debated, but recent work has pointed to a gradual awareness developing from the early and mid-nineteenth century, rather than the conventional attribution to the arrival of the first Zionist settlers (Kimmerling, 1983; Khalidi, 1992; Muslih, 1998).

As we have seen, Palestinian Arab society in the pre–Israeli state period was forged in and carved out of the Ottoman Empire. Muhammed Muslih writes of the empire as being

> a framework which held together Western Asia, the Balkans, Egypt and the coast of North Africa. In this framework there were different ethnic communities, including Muslims, Christians and Jews. These groups and communities comprised different social orders, including city-dwellers, peasant and nomads, and different religious sects. (Muslih, 1998: 15)

At the end of the Ottoman era, a small segment of wealthy Muslims held key positions and formed the ruling class. While holding large estates, they resided in the main cities of Jerusalem, Nablus, Hebron, Jaffa, and Gaza. The following decades, particularly under the British Mandate for Palestine, saw the emergence of an Arab bourgeoisie and proletariat in the cities. Their progress, however, as Elia Zureik has argued, "was checked by a more advanced and highly efficient Jewish sector which possessed the needed capital, technological know-how, the protection of Mandate authorities, and a well-organised, exclusively Jewish trade union movement, the *Histadrut*" (Zureik, 1979: 52). Palestinians found it difficult to compete with the modern and well-financed ventures of the Jews, and a decline began in local industries.

As well as the need to understand Palestinian Arab society, it is also important to take note of key features in the society and policy that replaced it—the Israeli Jewish society. Until the turn of the twentieth century, one key feature had been the collectivist vision of both state and society. Early Jewish settlers at the end of the nineteenth century were less concerned with ideological objectives on the left-right spectrum, but were inspired by concepts such as "redeeming" the land for Jews. With the second wave of immigration in the early part of the twentieth century, the collectivist approach became more dominant. The last three decades of Ottoman rule of Palestine saw Jews acquiring increasing amounts of land but moving from a plantation form of tenure, which was dependent then on Arab laborers, to self-employment in the cooperative and collective system. Despite this collectivist vision of the early settlers, another key feature of early Jewish society in Palestine was that it was obliged to rely upon external funds in order to initiate and consolidate their ventures.

At the time of the establishment of the British Mandate, and by the end of the second wave of immigration, there were approximately 60,000 Jews living in Palestine. By the end of 1948, the Jewish population in Palestine amounted to around 600,000, composing 35 percent of the total population. Yet, while success may have been achieved in numbers, there was less success in land ownership. At the time of the 1917 Balfour Declaration, a mere 2 percent of the land was Jewish owned in a country with a 90 percent Arab population (Zureik, 1979: 47). By the end of the mandate, this had only increased to 6.59 percent (Fischbach, 2000: 240).

Nevertheless, Zionism was clearly an important defining moment for Palestinian nationalism. Underlying modern-day Zionism was the desire to establish an independent Jewish state, and in 1897 Theodor Herzl founded the Zionist Congress. One of the principal Zionist tenets was that the Jewish people constituted a nation and were entitled to a national homeland. Indeed, Zionism argued that a homeland was imperative in solving the worldwide problem of anti-Semitism. After much debate in the Zionist movement, it was agreed that Palestine would be the focus of their settlement efforts despite the fact that there was already an indigenous population there.

It did not take the Palestinian peasantry long to feel the threat being imposed on them by Zionist settlers. The growing influx of immigrants, the purchase of land, and commercial practices that excluded non-Jews all contributed to a sense of Palestinian alienation. Additionally, the indigenous Arabs could not match the efforts employed by the Zionist Organization in lobbying and gaining external support from abroad, particularly from the UK. The Balfour Declaration issued by the British prime minister in 1917, which was the result of intense Zionist lobbying, was one of the key documents to shape the Middle East. This declaration announced British government support for the development of a Jewish homeland in Palestine with the proviso that the civil and religious rights of the existing non-Jewish communities (i.e., mainly Palestinians) would be respected. The Zionist settler movement interpreted the declaration as a pledge to establish a Jewish state regardless of the obligations to maintain the political and demographic status of the Palestinians.

Following the defeat of the Ottoman Empire by the Allied Powers in 1918, the British government was given permission by the League of Nations to establish a mandate in the area designated as Palestine and Transjordan.[1] Of vital significance was the inclusion of the Balfour Declaration into the Preamble of the Charter of the Mandate. As a result, the World Zionist Organization was given the opportunity to advise on British policies in Palestine, and more importantly, provided for an agency, later called "The Jewish Agency for Palestine," to represent Jewish interests and promote immigration. Naturally, the Palestinian Arabs opposed the prospect of a Jewish homeland, particularly in view of the fact that at this time Jews constituted about 10 percent of the population of Palestine and owned about 2 percent of the land (Masalha, 1992: 14). Resistance mounted through strikes and boycotts culminating in the Great Revolt of 1936–1939, which was put down ruthlessly by the British.

The incompatibility of British promises to both communities in the form of commitments simultaneously to a Jewish "national homeland" and toward Palestinian civil and religious rights as part of its obligations under the mandate system, led to increased intercommunal tensions and open conflict. Unwilling and unable to devote the resources to confront Zionist aspirations, the British government invited the UN to resolve the problem, and in 1947 the UN General Assembly approved the partition of Palestine into a Jewish state and an Arab state with an international enclave around Jerusalem (see Map 2.1). This resolution became the catalyst for a civil war in Palestine. By the time the British withdrew in May 1948, the fighting became widespread.

During the first stages of the war, the local Palestinian forces were reinforced by volunteers from surrounding countries, but despite this support, Jewish forces soon began to overrun Palestinian areas. As a result, there was a major exodus of refugees from Palestinian cities and villages and the refusal of the Zionist forces to allow these refugees to return to their homes became known by the Palestinians as *al Nakba* ("the catastrophe"). A series of armistice agreements between Israeli forces and the Arab states were made in 1949 that established the ceasefire lines and the new borders of the Israeli state. The eastern, mountainous part of Palestine not occupied by Israeli forces was incorporated into the Hashemite Kingdom of Jordan in 1950 while the southern coastal area, known as the Gaza Strip, was temporarily administered by Egypt. At this early stage the fate of refugees was undecided. International concern for their safety and conditions led to the adoption by the General Assembly in December 1948 of UN Resolution 194. While in the main a set of guidelines for the UN mediator and the UN Compensation Commission (UNCC), appointed and set up in the wake of hostilities, it nevertheless became the cornerstone of the Palestinian claim for compensation, restitution, and rehabilitation. It stated that "refugees wishing to return to their homes and live at peace with their neighbours should be permitted to do so at the earliest practicable date, and that compensation should be paid for the property of those choosing not to return and for the loss or damage to property" (UN, 1948).

Map 2.1 The UN Partition Plan and the Rhodes Armistice Line

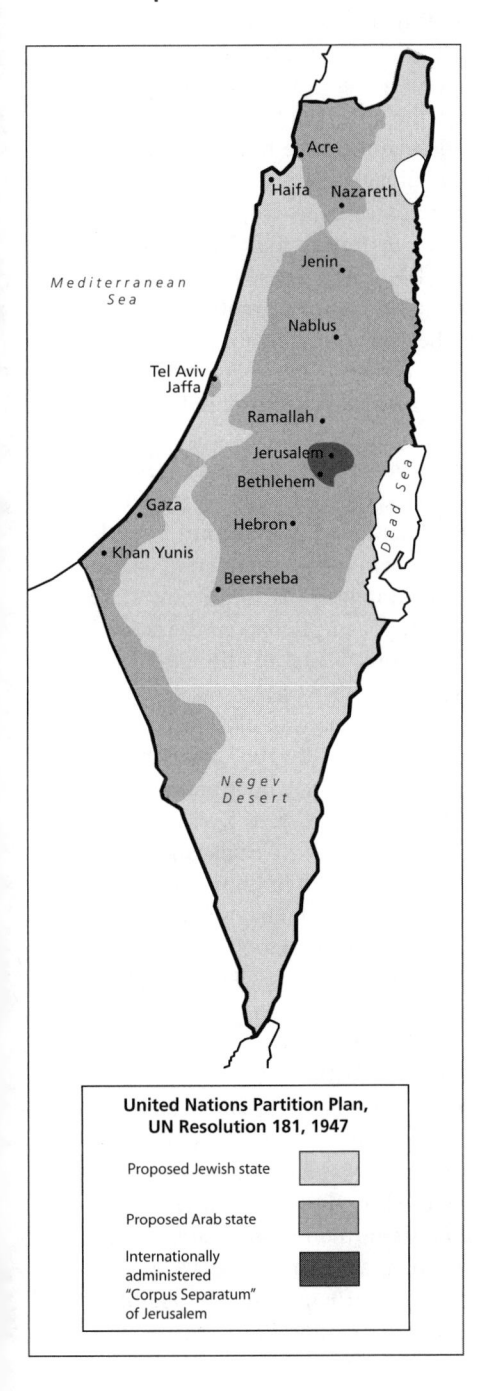

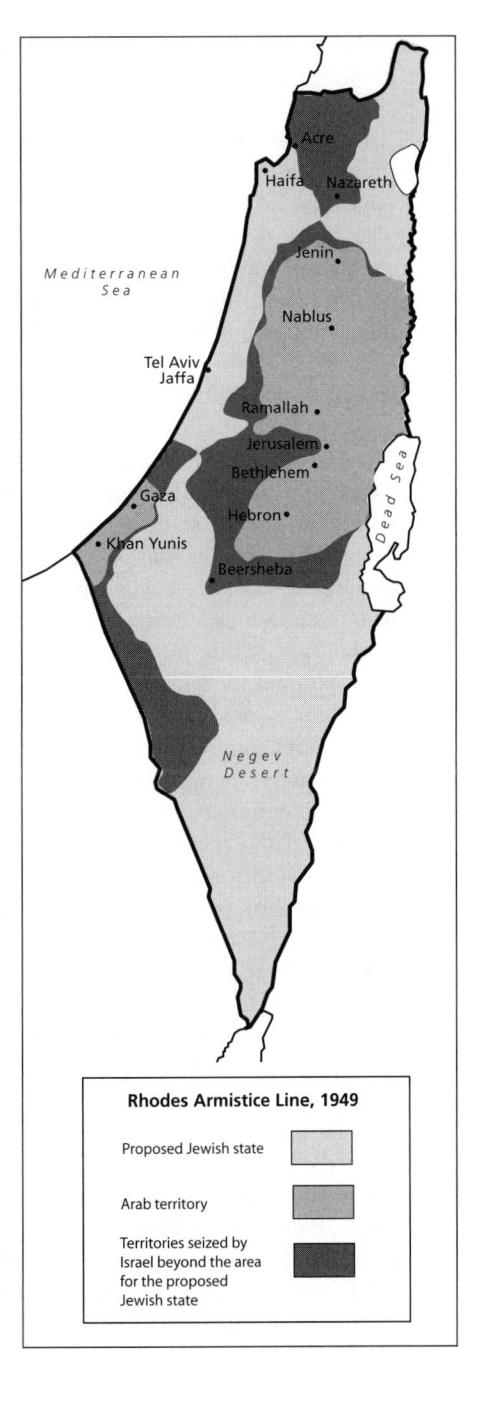

United Nations Partition Plan, UN Resolution 181, 1947

- Proposed Jewish state
- Proposed Arab state
- Internationally administered "Corpus Separatum" of Jerusalem

Rhodes Armistice Line, 1949

- Proposed Jewish state
- Arab territory
- Territories seized by Israel beyond the area for the proposed Jewish state

The Palestinians have always interpreted Resolution 194 as their "right to return" and as a resolution that has the full support of the international community. Israel, on the other hand, has always disagreed with this interpretation, claiming that the resolution is nonbinding. It therefore adopted a policy of noncompliance. At the same time, the new Israeli state viewed the flight of the refugees as a windfall that allowed the state to transfer Palestinian refugee property and land to new Israeli state bodies. A Custodian of Absentee Property was established to manage refugee properties. It was also given the powers to transfer land titles to Jewish and Israeli bodies (Lehn and Davis, 1988: 133–134; Dumper, 1994: 31). These developments allowed Israel to welcome an influx of new Jewish immigrants into abandoned refugee accommodations and thus helped it to consolidate the new state. Henceforth, while Israel was willing to contemplate compensation for refugees (as will be discussed below) it never seriously considered a return program involving restitution.

The period between the 1949 Armistice agreements and the next major event in which the refugee issue was significant, the 1967 War, was a period of great instability for the region. Punctuated by the joint Israeli-French-British invasion of Egypt and Israel's temporary occupation of the Gaza Strip in 1956, it was a period in which Arab hostility to the new state was fueled by the presence of Palestinian refugees in Lebanon, Syria, and Jordan, pressuring their host governments to force Israel to allow their return. Without the support of the superpowers and the Western states in general, their efforts were of no avail and the refugee issue was subsumed under the general attempts to achieve a peace agreement. In 1967, a dramatic change in the balance of power was achieved by Israel. The rapid destruction by Israel of the combined armies of Egypt, Jordan, and Syria and the capture of the remainder of historic Palestine (the West Bank and Gaza Strip) in addition to the Sinai and the Golan left Israel holding territories three times its size. This caused a new wave of Palestinian refugees from the West Bank and Gaza Strip to Jordan and Egypt (see Map 2.2). Palestinians, particularly those in the Jordan valley, fled or were expelled from their villages or refugee camps. It has been estimated that about 335,000 crossed the river into the East Bank of Jordan, two-thirds of whom were refugees for a second time in their lives (McDowell, 1994: 38).

Just prior to the 1967 War, Palestinians had began to despair of any significant support within the region for them to return to their homes. They formed a number of guerrilla groups. Earlier, in 1964, the Arab League had established the PLO as a supine Palestinian body. Following a clash between Palestinian guerrilla forces and Israelis in the refugee camp of al-Karama in March 1968, independent Palestinian action now seemed possible to the refugees, and the dominant guerrilla group known as Harakat al-Tahrir al-Watani al-Filastini (al-FATAH) took over the PLO. Jordan was

Map 2.2 Territories Held by Israel After 1967

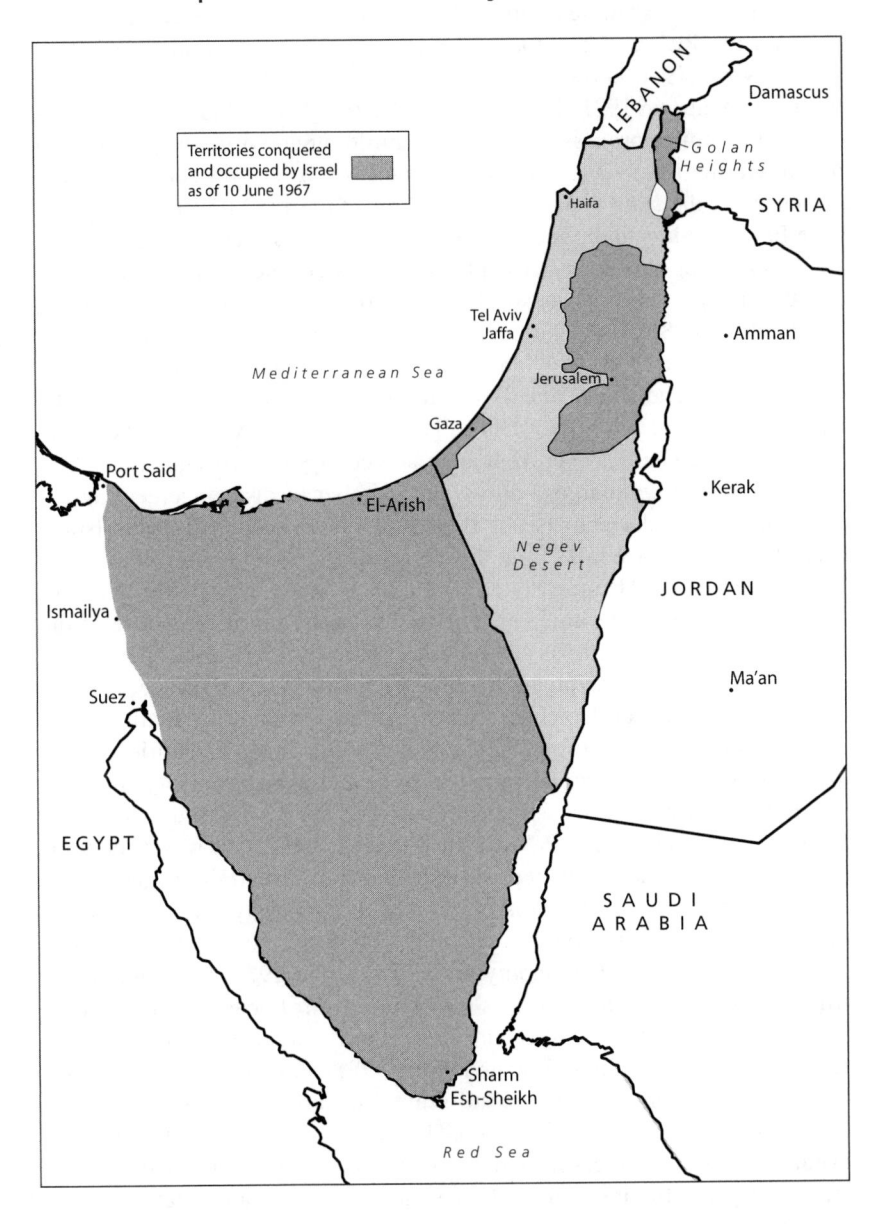

increasingly used by the PLO to carry out operations across the river, to the extent that the Hashemite regime feared for its future. Fierce clashes began between the PLO and the Jordanian army, and after a dramatic military showdown in 1970 known as Black September, Jordan expelled the PLO from the country in 1971. The main hub of activity moved to southern Lebanon and a similar process of institution building and military preparation began. During the 1970s, internal communal divisions in Lebanon and the weakness of the state apparatus itself allowed the PLO to establish quasi-state functions in and around the refugee camps in Lebanon.

Also during this period, Egypt and Syria were increasingly concerned that Israel appeared to be consolidating its control over the territories it had occupied in the Sinai and the Golan because there was no pressure to withdraw. In October 1973, they launched a surprise attack and Israel suffered severe losses. The war officially ended on 22 October, but not before the United States and the Soviet Union had become involved on either side. Strong US intervention to prevent an Israeli collapse provoked a Saudi Arabian–led Arab oil embargo. Following a number of disengagement agreements and a breakthrough visit by President Anwar Sadat of Egypt to Israel, peace talks took place in 1978 in the US president's summer resort at Camp David in Maryland, United States. The talks resulted in two sets of agreements signed the following year. The first set determined the future of the West Bank and Gaza Strip as autonomous Palestinian territories; the second comprised a separate Egyptian-Israeli peace treaty. While Egypt secured the return of the Sinai and Israel secured the neutralization of its southern borders, the clauses concerning the Occupied Palestinian Territories of the West Bank and Gaza Strip fell into abeyance and were never implemented. The Egyptian-Israeli peace agreement outraged the Arab world, who saw it as an abandonment of the Palestinian refugees, and Egypt was diplomatically and economically isolated and expelled from the Arab League.

Nevertheless, the refugee issue refused to fade away. Not only did the Palestinians in the Occupied Palestinian Territories continue to mobilize against settlements and autonomy proposals, but in 1978 Palestinian guerrillas continued to launch attacks into Israel from Lebanon. Israel's next step, therefore, was to try to secure its northern border by invading southern Lebanon. After an initial incursion in 1978, known as the Litani operation, it embarked in 1982 upon a full-scale occupation of southern Lebanon up to and including parts of Beirut. The Israeli siege of Beirut led to the expulsion of PLO fighters from the city. It also led to the massacre of more than 2,000 Palestinians in the refugee camps of Sabra and Shatilla on the outskirts of the city by the allies of Israel in Lebanon, the Christian Phalangists. Israel denied any complicity in the massacre, but its presence in the city as the occupying army indicated a high degree of responsibility. Culpability notwithstanding, the Sabra and Shatilla massacres are an event that is seared into the Palestinian experience of exile and of their relations with Israel. Despite ultimately being forced to retreat in stages culminating in a withdrawal in 2000, and despite replacing PLO hostility with that of radical Islamic groups, such as Hizbollah, Israel was successful in removing the PLO as a military threat.

These events on its three land borders allowed Israel to concentrate on consolidating its control over the OPTs—that is, the West Bank and Gaza Strip—and to neutralize PLO influence over the Palestinians there. The main instrument of consolidation was settlement. Israel's settlement policy began in 1967, and since then Israel has continued to transfer Israeli Jews and new immigrants into strategic parts of the Palestinian territories in contravention of international law. Geographically, Palestinian population centers have been bisected through new road network systems and by land acquisition for Jewish-only residency. In addition, water resources of the territory were integrated into the national grid system. Twenty-five percent of Israel's own water consumption originated in the West Bank. Furthermore, Palestinian water consumption was capped to prevent any increase until 2010 (McDowell, 1994: 88). Israeli control over Palestinians in the OPTs was extended to virtually every aspect of their lives.

As a result of these policies and the lack of attention and support given to the issue in the region, political resistance to the occupation flared up. The first Palestinian intifada (1987–1991) was a defining moment for the Palestinians. It was conducted largely without resort to arms, winning considerable international sympathy for the plight of the Palestinians. The Israelis reacted with overwhelming force but were helpless in repressing the rebellion and were unprepared logistically or psychologically for this type of revolt. At its heart, this was a rebellion of the young and the poor that were organized by an extensive network of committees (Hilterman, 1991; Hunter, 1991; Schiff and Yaari, 1984).

In the midst of the first intifada, tensions in the Gulf region led to the Iraqi invasion of Kuwait. This in turn led to a UN intervention dominated by the United States which ejected Iraq from Kuwait and restricted the use of its military to central areas of Iraq. Partly as an incentive in obtaining Arab support for the coalition, the United States secured the agreement of Israel to participate in an international peace conference. Although Israel benefited from the neutralization of Iraq as a military force, it was economically weakened and more dependent on US economic support at this time because of a new wave of immigration of Russian Jews. Moreover, the war had left the PLO diplomatically isolated and almost bankrupt. Both Israel and the PLO were under pressure for some movement on the political front. The Madrid Peace Conference opened in October 1991, relocated to Washington, and continued for a further nine rounds of negotiations, but very little was actually achieved (Smith, 2004: 419). An initial problem was Israel's refusal to recognize the PLO as a negotiating partner. This led to various diplomatic contortions, such as including Palestinian representatives in the Jordanian delegation. Finally, an impasse was arrived at when models of interim self-government and final status issues were discussed. In terms of refugees, the main contribution of the Madrid Conference was the establishment of a series of multilateral fora, one of which was the Refugee Working Group.

At its first meeting in Ottawa in May 1992, the RWG, chaired by Canada, decided to organize its work on a thematic basis, and countries were allocated as "shepherds" for each theme. The themes primarily addressed humanitarian questions such as family reunification, training and job creation, public health, child welfare, and social and economic infrastructure. Nevertheless, its work soon became mired in controversy as the Palestinians and Israelis failed to agree on either what could be placed on the agenda or definitions of a *refugee* and *displaced persons* (Peters, 1996).

Whereas the so-called Madrid framework failed to produce a breakthrough, secret negotiations had been taking place between Israel and the PLO, culminating in the Declaration of Principles in September 1993, which took the whole world, including the United States, by surprise. Also known as the Oslo Accords, the agreement outlined a process intended to gradually resolve the Israeli-Palestinian conflict. The PLO renounced violence and pledged to fight terrorism. In turn, Israel would withdraw from most of the occupied Gaza Strip, except for Jewish settlements, and from the West Bank city of Jericho. Further redeployments would follow, and a newly established Palestinian National Authority (PNA), sometimes referred to as the Palestinian Authority (PA), would assume control over these areas. The key element to the Oslo framework was the distiction between an interim phase and permanent status phase. Core divisive issues such as the return of refugees, the future of Jerusalem, Israeli settlements, borders, and water were postponed until five years after the establishment of the PNA. The Oslo framework presumed that steps taken during the interim period would build trust and mutual confidence and help therefore to resolve the more intractable issues between them. Instead, the PNA failed to disarm militant organizations, which continued to carry out operations in Israel and the OPTs, while Israel delayed its territorial withdrawals, and even expanded settlements, confiscated land, demolished homes, and imposed restrictions on the movements of Palestinians. The lack of any enforcement mechanisms led both parties to seek advantages where they could and to blame the other side for its failure to adhere to the agreements. A series of additional agreements, such as the Gaza/Jericho Agreement in 1994 (often referred to as Oslo II), the Paris Protocol in 1995 (dealing with economic issues), the Hebron Agreement in 1997 (regarding the withdrawal of Israeli troops from Hebron), and the Wye Memorandum brokered by the United States and Jordan in 1998, was required to keep the process on track.

Despite the ongoing problems, US president Bill Clinton, PLO president Yassir Arafat, and Israeli prime minister Ehud Barak met at Camp David in July 2000 to negotiate a final settlement of the Palestine-Israel conflict. The negotiations ended in failure with neither side being able to agree about the issues of Jerusalem or the fate of the Palestinian refugees (Agha and Malley, 2001). Nevertheless, both sides agreed to continue talks during 2001 at the Egyptian seaside resort of Taba. The talks would utilize the "Clinton parameters," which were the US president's attempt to formulate some general principles around which an agreement could be reached. On refugees, President Clinton suggested the following:

> The solution will have to be consistent with the two-state approach that both sides have accepted as a way to end the Palestinian-Israeli conflict: the state of Palestine as the homeland of the Palestinian people and the state of Israel as the homeland of the Jewish people. Under the two-state solution, the guiding principle should be that the Palestinian state will be the focal point for Palestinians who choose to return to the area without ruling out that Israel will accept some of these refugees. I believe that we need to adopt a formulation on the right of return to Israel itself but that does not negate the aspiration of the Palestinian people to return to the area.
>
> In light of the above, I propose two alternatives: 1. Both sides recognize the right of Palestinian refugees to return to Historic Palestine. Or, 2. Both sides recognize the right of the Palestinian refuges to return to their homeland.
>
> The agreement will define the implementation of this general right in a way that is consistent with the two-state solution. It would list five possible final homes for the refugees:
>
> 1. The state of Palestine
> 2. Areas in Israel being transferred to Palestine in the land swap
> 3. Rehabilitation in a host country
> 4. Resettlement in a third country
> 5. Admission to Israel
>
> In listing these options, the agreement will make clear that the return to the West Bank, Gaza Strip, and the areas acquired in the land swap would be a right to all Palestinian refugees. While rehabilitation in host countries, resettlement in third world countries and absorption into Israel will depend upon the policies of those countries. Israel could indicate in the agreement that it intends to establish a policy so that some of the refugees would be absorbed into Israel consistent with Israel's sovereign decision. I believe that priority should be given to the refugee population in Lebanon. The parties would agree that this implements Resolution 194. I propose that the agreement clearly mark the end of the conflict and its implementation put an end to all its claims. This could be implemented through a UN Security Council Resolution that notes that Resolutions 242 and 338 have been implemented through the release of Palestinian prisoners.
>
> I believe that this is an outline of a fair and lasting agreement. It gives the Palestinian people the ability to determine the future on their own land, a sovereign and viable state recognized by the international

community, Al-Qods as its capital, sovereignty over the Haram, and new lives for the refugees. It gives the people of Israel a genuine end to the conflict, real security, the preservation of sacred religious ties, the incorporation of 80% of the settlers into Israel, and the largest Jewish Jerusalem in history recognized by all as its capital. (Clinton, 2000)

President Clinton's analysis illustrated how the international community finally acknowledged the central role played by the refugee issue. Though he was engagingly frank ("that was a lot of artful language"), he nevertheless sought to work within positions established by the existing balance of power between Israelis and Palestinians rather than deriving his recommendations from international law.

On the basis of these parameters, the Taba talks made significant progress on the refugee issue. These talks will be discussed in greater detail in the following chapters, but we should note here that Israel agreed to accept the return of a limited number of refugees under the rubric of family reunification and that compensation mechanisms were discussed for the first time (Eldar, 2002).

Prior to and even while the Taba talks were being conducted, a new wave of violence and political conflict began in September 2000. Known as the al-Aqsa or second intifada, it was triggered by the visit of the then Israeli opposition party leader, Ariel Sharon, to the Haram al-Sharif in Jerusalem, the third holiest site in Islam. It resulted in violent clashes, and confrontations continued in most of the major towns of the occupied territories. It differed from the first intifada in that the resistance was armed and was quickly monopolized by militant factions rather than simply being a popular protest. While triggered by Sharon's provocative gesture and the failure of the Camp David talks, the underlying cause may perhaps be attributed to the extending interim phase of the Oslo framework where permanent status issues were being postponed indefinitely. As two astute observers of the period have commented: "The deeper backdrop to the current uprising is the actual experience of Oslo on the ground by the population of the West Bank and Gaza. The main features of the extended interim phase have resulted in a situation that is untenable for most and unbearable for hundreds of thousands" (Hammami and Tamari, 2001).

This second intifada was characterized by increased incarceration of Palestinians, severe restriction of movement, escalating violence, suicide bombings, and the reoccupation by Israel of those parts of the West Bank it had withdrawn from under the Oslo Accords. In 2001, the downward spiral was compounded by the al-Qaida attack on the World Trade Center towers and the Pentagon on September 11. Media coverage of the Middle East conflict, especially in the United States, placed it in the larger context of the US war on terrorism and thus obscured the fundamental dynamics of the Palestinian-Israeli conflict.

Partly in an attempt to reverse this trend, the Arab Summit Declaration of March 2002 in Beirut offered Israel security and normal relations in exchange for a withdrawal from occupied Arab territories, creation of an independent Palestinian state with East Jerusalem as its capital, and the return of refugees. The section on refugees called for the "achievement of a just solution to the Palestinian refugee problem to be agreed upon in accordance with UN General Assembly Resolution 194." However, it significantly and deliberately failed to mention the "right of return" as understood by refugees and activists, presumably in an attempt to work within the language of the Clinton parameters and the texts discussed at Taba. Nevertheless, despite this Arab attempt to revive the stalling peace negotiations, the Israeli government did not repond positively.

The continuing deterioration of the situation threatened to destabilize the region, and the European Union, the UN, and Russia attempted to breathe new life into the negotiation process by pressing the United States to take some joint action. Known as the Quartet, it issued a statement regarding a "road map" for peace in September 2002. In October of the same year, US president George W. Bush publicly expressed his support for an independent Palestinian state living in peace beside Israel as the ultimate objective of the road map. Despite this international initiative, tactical actions by both the Palestinians and Israelis on the ground prevented the road map from being implemented.

A number of civil society initiatives or Track II ventures were also launched. The most significant in terms of the backing it received from the political elites was the Geneva Initiative. Sponsored by the Swiss government, the Geneva Initiative was conducted by leading but unofficial Palestinian and Israeli negotiators. Serving as a test run, it amounted to an unofficial blueprint for a final status agreement. It expanded further on concessions Israel offered at Taba and Camp David, such as Israel withdrawing from territories occupied in 1967 and giving up sovereignty of the Temple Mount. The Palestinians would implicitly concede the right of return, although this is not stated explicitly. Both parties agreed that Jerusalem should be the capital of two states (Geneva Accord, 2003). The PNA received the accord with caution and did not come out openly in favor of it, even though many of those involved were close to Arafat and Abbas. On the Israeli side, it was vehemently rejected by the Likud Party and by many in the Labour Party too, who claimed that too many concessions to the Palestinians were being proposed in the accord.

As a result of all these negotiations—the Oslo process, Camp David, Taba, the Beirut and Geneva initiatives, and other official and unofficial negotiations—many refugees have felt that their rights were being traded away in favor of obtaining the basic territorial components of a Palestinian state in the OPTs. A number of groups were formed in the OPTs, the host countries, and the wider diaspora to uphold the rights of Palestinians to return, for compensation, and for restitution of property. These include the London-based al-Awda, the Palestine Right to Return Coalition (www.al-awda.org.uk), and the activist research and information center BADIL (www.badil.org). These bodies point out that compensation is presented as an alternative to a return, and that accepting such a formulation would be a surrender of the right of return, when they insist that the right of return is sacrosanct and must be dealt with separately from compensation and property questions. This explains, as Michael Fischbach writes, "the recent insistence by some Palestinian groups that the refugees obtain justice through property restitution, not compensation" (Fischbach, 2003). While official PLO positions include both concepts, Palestinian NGOs have been more forceful in insisting upon restitution instead of compensation.

Three final events conclude this overview of the main political developments affecting the Palestinian refugee issue. The first is the death of President Arafat. It is too early to say what the long-term effects of his death may bring to the conflict, but because he was a symbol of the Palestinian national identity and a great supporter of refugee rights, it is likely there will be a shift in emphasis in the Palestinian national consensus on the permanent status issues, such as refugees. His successor, President Mahmood Abbas, is himself a refugee from Safad in the Galilee. However, as a result of the latter's clear commitment to the negotiation process, he may be in a stronger position to square the circle between Israeli existential and security concerns and the demands of the refugees for restitution and return. The second event is the Israeli withdrawal or disengagement from the Gaza Strip and some smaller settlements in the northern West Bank. The withdrawal took place August 2005 and included an evacuation of all Israeli settlements in the Strip, leaving no permanent presence of the Israel Defence Forces (IDF) or Israeli settlers in the area. However, Israel continues to maintain exclusive authority over Gaza air space and activity off the coast and exercises control over all the exit points to Israel, with some EU supervision over those with Egypt. The connection with the refugee issue lies in the prospect that by making concessions on those areas that do not affect Israeli interests significantly, Israel is able to consolidate its position on other issues such as the refugee issue. Finally, two elections have dramatically changed the political landscape for negotiations dramatically. The radical Islamic Resistance Movement (HAMAS) was elected as the new PNA government on a platform that does not recognize Israel or any of the agreements signed hitherto. The refusal of Israel or the Quartet to countenance any dealing with the new government has caused a crisis in the peace process and possibly its temporary demise. This is made more likely by the election in Israel of a new party, Kadima, dedicated to former prime minister Sharon's vision of unilateral steps to safeguard Israel's interests such as the continued Israeli withdrawal from parts of the West Bank without negotiations with the PNA.

Palestine into Israel

Before examining the situation of the refugees themselves, it is important to consider exactly what constitutes the Israeli Jewish society that was inserted into the place of Palestinian society. Through an understanding of the main features, we can then more clearly see what was lost and gained, and recognize the passions and politics that the Middle East conflict and the nonreturn of Palestinian refugees has engendered. Following the establishment of the new state, the Israeli government encouraged a rapid program of mass immigration to absorb as many Jews made refugees by World War II and from hostile Arab states as possible. During 1949 and the 1950s, 47,000 Jews were flown to Israel from Yemen. In 1950, 120,000 Jews were flown to Israel from Iraq in two major airlifts known as Operation Ezra and Nehemia. Thus, from May 1948 to late 1951, the Jewish population of Israel doubled with an average of 172,000 new immigrants arriving per year (Peretz and Doron, 1997: 47). Nevertheless, one aspect of this immigration was that Israel's pull factor was weaker than the push factor of anti-Semitism and economic deterioration, with the implication that the Zionist ideology of the state was simply not strong enough to attract immigrants.

Israel has continued to experience considerable demographic changes since its creation. As an immigrant/settler state, population growth and new immigration is constantly changing the ethnic composition of the country (Goldscheider, 2002). At certain times, more than half the population was first-generation immigrants (Dumper, 1996). Jewish society in Israel tends to be divided according to country of origin, and three main groups can be identified, although there is much overlap between them: those born in Israel (Sabras), those born in Asia-Africa (Mizrahim), and those born in Europe-America (Ashkenazim). However, these latter two subgroups are not homogeneous and reflect traditions and the culture in the countries from which they emigrated. For example, the Mizrahim comprise Sephardim, who are descendants of Jews who fled Spain in 1492 who spoke Ladino (a Spanish-Jewish hybrid language) (Peretz and Doron, 1997: 50). Although Israel aspires to be a democratic and egalitarian society, the country is divided among Jews of different ethnic groups, and between orthodox Jews and their more secular counterparts. The most serious rift in Israeli society exists between Jews and those Palestinian Arabs who remained after 1948. Known as Israeli Arabs, they have constituted between one-sixth and one-fifth of the total population of Israel.

These demographic concerns were heightened following the 1967 War in which Israel occupied territory comprising another million Palestinians and other Arabs, thus threatening the Jewish demographic dominance in territory over which Israel had control.

As we have seen in the previous section, one means by which successive Israeli governments have sought to counter Palestinian demographic presence and growth was to encourage the colonization of the OPTs. To many Israelis, the post-1967 settler movement in the OPTs was very much the inheritor of the ideals of the early Zionists. Thus, from the perspective of the refugee question, not only has the creation of a vibrant and strong Israeli state hampered the prospect of Palestinian refugees returning, the ongoing colonization of territory newly acquired in 1967 threatens to create more dispossession and pushes a resolution of the 1948 refugee issue even further away.

It is essential to recognize the strength and relative stability of the Israeli state. Although Zionist pioneers may have hoped to turn Jewish society into an agricultural people, rapid and dramatic industrialization has made Israel one of the most technologically advanced countries in the world. A new generation of technocrats has been created, and thousands of unskilled Israelis have been transformed into sophisticated engineers and technicians. In addition, the security needs of the state have demanded major advances in electronics, communication technology, aviation, and nuclear energy (Avni-Segre, 1969). Thus the conflict has consolidated the supremacy of industrialization over agriculture and led to a militarization of society and politics. Very few Israeli politicians have achieved senior position without also having been very high-ranking in the armed forces.

After 1967 and the occupation of the Golan, West Bank, and Gaza Strip, the Israeli government allowed Palestinian residents in these areas to work inside Israel. Israel experienced a period of growth and required cheap labor, and Palestinians found jobs mainly in construction, agriculture, and service industries. The territories also became an important market for Israeli domestic production. During the first intifada, the supply of Palestinian labor was constantly interrupted and Israel began turning to foreign imported labor from Eastern Europe, the Philippines, and Thailand. In 1989, a new wave of immigration took place with the arrival of Jews from Ethiopia and the Soviet Union. To some extent these developments decreased the need for Palestinian and foreign labor, but only in the short term as the new immigrants were highly skilled and soon moved on to better paid work. Israel responded to the globalization pressures of the late 1990s with a mixture of economic policy reforms. Thus privatization of the major centers of production and the severe pruning of the powers of its powerful trade union federation (Histadrut) transformed the collectivist underpinnings of Israeli society. Nevertheless there is a continuing dependency upon overseas philanthropy and upon economic aid from the United States that has protected some aspects of its welfare and educational systems from market forces.

Profile of Palestinian Refugees

The contrast with the fortunes of Palestinian society could not be starker. By the time of the signing of the armistice agreements in 1949, approximately 750,000 Palestinians had fled to neighboring countries to be temporarily housed in refugee camps or with relatives. Initially, Palestinian refugees received assistance from nongovernmental organizations, such as the American Friends Service Committee (AFSC) and the International Committee of the Red Cross (ICRC), and from a temporary ad hoc UN agency, the UN Relief for Palestine Refugees. However, when it became obvious that the newly founded state of Israel would not agree to the return of all the refugees created by the conflict, the UN decided that a dedicated agency was required to provide emergency relief. Between 1948 and 1949 the UN General Assembly established two separate agencies to provide protection, assistance, and durable solutions to the Palestinian refugees. The first was the UN Relief and Works Agency for Palestine Refugees in the Near East (UNRWA), and the second, the UN Conciliation Committee for Palestine (UNCCP). UNRWA was established as a temporary agency and its mandate was renewed at regular intervals.[2] Most Palestinian refugees were registered with UNRWA, whose role was to maintain the refugee camps, provide education, and to support the communities in four locations: Jordan, Syria, Lebanon, and the West Bank and Gaza (see Map 2.3.) It is important to note that in contrast to the work of the main UN refugee agency set up some months later—the UN High Commission for Refugees (UNHCR)—UNRWA's work did not involve permanent solutions or the provision of international protection to refugees.

Resolution 194 also set up UNCCP in 1949. Among other provisions, its aim was to facilitate the return or resettlement, restitution, and compensation of the refugees based on their individual choices. The role of UNCCP was to act as mediator among Israel, the Arab states, and the Palestinians.

The General Assembly authorized UNCCP to provide protection and facilitate durable solutions for persons displaced as a result of the 1947–1948 conflict in Palestine. This included internally displaced Palestinians inside Israel. In 1950, the Assembly—with Resolution 394(V)—specifically requested UNCCP to protect the rights, properties, and interests of the refugees. Between 1949 and the early 1960s, UNCCP was the main organization dealing with the question of the return of Palestinian refugees. Its work encompassed gathering basic information and seeking solutions to the

Map 2.3 UNRWA Area of Operations

Territories occupied by Israel in June 1967

Number of Palestinian Refugees, by Country and Camp, as of 31 March 2005

Country/Camp	Number of Refugees	Country/Camp	Number of Refugees
Lebanon (12 camps)		**West Bank (19 camps)**	
Mar Elias	612	Aqabat Jabr	5,510
Burj el-Barajneh	15,484	Ein el-Sultan	1,723
Dbayeh	4,002	Shu'fat	10,069
Shatila	8,212	Am'ari	8,805
Ein el-Hilweh	45,004	Kalandia	10,024
Mieh Mieh	4,473	Deir Ammar	2,275
El-Buss	9,287	Jalazone	10,390
Rashidieh	25,745	Fawwar	7,630
Burj el-Shemali	18,625	Arroub	9,859
Nahr el-Bared	30,439	Dheisheh	12,045
Beddawi	15,641	Aida	4,534
Wavell	7,551	Beit Jibrin	2,025
Other camp residents[a]	25,877	Far'a	7,244
Syria (9 camps)		Camp No. 1	6,508
Khan Eshieh	16,108	Askar	14,629
Khan Danoun	8,500	Balata	21,903
Sbeineh	17,261	Tulkarm	17,455
Qabr Essit	19,475	Nur Shams	8,659
Jaramana	3,721	Jenin	15,496
Dera'a	9,306	Other camp residents[a]	4,458
Homs	13,230	**Gaza Strip (8 camps)**	
Hama	7,578	Jabalia	106,691
Neirab	17,703	Beach	78,768
Jordan (10 camps)		Nuseirat	57,120
Amman New Camp	50,703	Bureij	28,770
Irbid	24,351	Deir el-Balah	19,534
Husn	20,988	Maghazi	22,266
Souf	15,882	Khan Younis	63,219
Jabal el-Hussein	29,998	Rafah	95,187
Baqa'a	68,386		
Zarqa	18,004		
Marka	38,425		
Talbieh	871		
Jerash	15,488		
Other camp residents[a]	87		

Note: a. In Lebanon there are 16,282 refugees who were registered in the now destroyed camps of Dikwaneh and Nabatieh and are now living in other camps. In addition there are 9,595 registered refugees who are either UNRWA employees or refugee women married to nonregistered husbands. In Jordan there are 87 women in that latter category. There are also 4,458 refugees who were originally registered in Gaza but who have taken up residence in the West Bank.

Palestine Refugees Registered with UNRWA, as of 31 March 2005

Field	In Camps	Not in Camps	Total
Jordan	283,183	1,497,518	1,780,701
Lebanon	210,952	189,630	400,582
Syria	112,882	311,768	424,650
West Bank	181,241	506,301	687,542
Gaza	471,555	490,090	961,645
Total	1,259,813	2,995,307	4,255,120

Source: United Nations, Public Information Office, UNRWA Headquarters, Gaza, May 2005, www.un.org/unrwa/refugees.

political, legal, and economic aspects of the question. UNCCP developed compensation plans based on both global and individual evaluations of property culminating in studies that identified and valued every parcel of Palestinian- and Arab-owned land in Israel (Fischbach, 2003: 246). In 1966, the agency effectively ceased to operate and existed only on paper. Although negotiations UNCCP failed to resolve the issue of restitution and compensation, these topics were to resurface much later on in 1991 during the Madrid Conference and again during the Oslo Accord negotiations in 1993. In addition, the cessation of UNCCP operations was significant in that it, and not UNRWA, was given the mandate to protect Palestinian refugees, so that when it ceased to function, that role also fell into abeyance, and UNRWA was not formally required or legally permitted to take on that role. As will be shown in Chapter 5, the protection role of UNRWA has gradually built up over the years, largely as a result of the clear need for such a body to take on this role.

One of the most contentious issues in the study and politics of Palestinian refugees is the issue of numbers. Determining who exactly is a refugee is fraught with problems and quite possibly unanswerable. There is no single authoritative source for the global Palestinian refugee, and internally displaced people (IDP) populations, and figures have always been in dispute by both Palestinians and Israelis (see Table 2.1 and notes). Current figures on Palestinian refugees come mainly from UNRWA and the Palestinian Central Bureau of Statistics (www.pcbs.org). There are also other databases to be found in limited formats, including the Institute for Applied Social Science (FAFO) (www.fafo.no). All other data sources depend mostly on the two sources mentioned above.

In June 2004, UNRWA announced the most recent figures of refugees on its books as being 4,188,711 (UNRWA, 2004b). However, the UNRWA definition of a *Palestinian refugee* was meant to work as a definition for the purposes of establishing assistance procedures, and not for determining the legal status of refugees or their rights. It was elaborated for operational ends to determine who was eligible for their services. Its mandate allowed them only to assist bona fide refugees (Schiff, 1995). Registration has financial and social implications for camp-dwelling refugees, as registered refugees are entitled to social and financial services whereas nonregistered refugees are not. Thus registered refugees (RR) who meet the agency's definition of Palestine refugees such as the 1948 refugees are not the total refugee population. The RR figure does not include IDPs in Israel, that is, refugees displaced in 1948 who did not cross any international borders but are now living in a political entity that did not exist in 1947. It does not include those displaced in the 1967 war who are referred to as the 1967 Displaced Persons and were the subject of specific provisions in the Oslo peace process, nor does it include an estimated 1.5 million refugees and

Table 2.1 Palestinian Refugees and Internally Displaced Palestinians

Year	Registered 1948 Refugees[a]	Estimated Nonregistered 1948 Refugees[b]	Estimated 1967 Refugees[c]	Estimated "Other" Refugees[d]	Estimated 1948 Internally Displaced Persons[e]	Estimated 1967 Internally Displaced Persons[f]
1950	914,000	257,021	—	—	23,380	—
1955	905,986	305,260	—	—	40,254	—
1960	1,120,889	362,553	—	—	50,044	—
1965	1,280,823	430,599	—	—	62,215	—
1970	1,425,219	511,417	250,402	37,182	77,346	12,124
1975	1,632,707	607,403	297,400	108,349	96,157	14,205
1980	1,844,318	721,404	352,218	192,875	119,543	16,677
1985	2,093,545	856,802	419,512	293,261	148,616	19,612
1990	2,668,595	1,017,611	498,249	412,491	184,760	23,098
1995	3,172,641	1,208,603	591,763	554,099	229,694	27,239
2000	3,737,494	1,435,441	702,829	722,284	285,557	34,373
2003	4,082,300	1,591,500	779,237	837,991	325,400	38,266

Sources: Figures and notes supplied with permission by BADIL Resource Centre for Residency Rights and Refugee Research. There is no single authoritative source for the global Palestinian refugee and IDP population. The figures above reflect estimates according to the best available sources. Figures are therefore indicative rather than conclusive. Estimates for 1967, "Other Refugees," and IDPs are revised from 2002.

a. Figures from UN Relief and Works Agency for Palestine Refugees (UNRWA). UNRWA figures are based on data voluntarily supplied by registered refugees. Figures as of 30 June each year. UNRWA registration statistics do not claim to be and should not be taken as statistically valid demographic data. They are collected by UNRWA for its own internal management purposes and to facilitate certification of refugees' eligibility to receive education, health, and relief and social services. New information on births, marriages, deaths, and change in place of residence is recorded only when a refugee requests the updating of the family registration card issued by the agency. UNRWA does not carry out a census, house-to-house survey, or any other means to ascertain whether the place of residence is the actual place of residence; refugees will normally report births, deaths, and marriages when they seek a service from the agency. New births, for instance, are reported early if the family avails itself of the UNRWA maternal and child health services, or when the child reaches school age if admission is sought to a UNRWA school, or even later if neither of these services is needed. While families are encouraged to have a separate registration card for each nuclear family (parents and children), this is not obligatory. Family size information may therefore include a mix of nuclear and extended families, in some instances including as many as four generations.

b. Derived from S. H. Abu Sitta, *The Palestinian Nakba 1948: The Register of Depopulated Localities in Palestine*. London: The Palestinian Return Centre, 1998, and the average annual growth rate of the Palestinian refugee population (3.5 percent). The figures do not account for the small number of refugees reunified with family inside Israel.

(continues)

Table 2.1 Continued

c. Derived from Report of the Secretary General under General Assembly Resolution 2252 (EX-V) and Security Council Resolution 237 (1967), UN Doc. A/6797, 15 September 1967 and the average annual growth rate of the Palestinian population (3.5 percent). The figures do not include 1948 refugees displaced for a second time in 1967. The figures for 1967 exclude those refugees who returned under a limited repatriation program in August–September 1967. The figures do not account for Palestinians who were abroad at the time of the 1967 war and unable to return, refugees reunified with family inside the Occupied Palestinian Territories, or those refugees who returned since 1994 under the Oslo political process.

d. Derived from George F. Kossaifi, *The Palestinian Refugees and the Right of Return*. Washington, DC: The Center for Policy Analysis on Palestine, 1996, based on an average forced migration rate of 21,000 persons per year. Includes those Palestinian refugees who are neither 1948 or 1967 refugees and are outside the Palestinian territories occupied by Israel since 1967 and unable due to revocation of residency, denial of family reunification, deportation, etc., or unwilling to return there owing to a well-founded fear of persecution. The figures are based on the percentage of nonrefugee Palestinians in the OPTs (57 percent) and the average annual growth rate of the refugee population (3.5 percent). The figures do not account for family reunification, those refugees who returned to the Occupied Palestinian Territories since 1994 under the Oslo political process and for a small number of Palestinians from inside Israel who have sought refugee asylum.

e. Derived from initial registration figures from UNRWA in *Report of the Director of the United Nations Relief and Works Agency for Palestine Refugees in the Near East*, UN Doc. A/1905, 30 June 1951, and an estimated average annual growth rate of the Palestinian population inside Israel between 1950 and 2001 (4.2 percent). According to the Israeli Central Bureau of Statistics, the Palestinian Muslim population inside Israel (which comprises 82 percent of the total Palestinian population inside Israel) increased annually by 4.4 percent between 1948 and 2001. Israel Central Bureau of Statistics, *Statistical Abstract of Israel*, No. 53 (2002). A significant number of internally displaced Palestinians received assistance from UNRWA until the agency turned over responsibilities for the internally displaced to Israel in 1952. The population estimate for 1950 was likely included as UNRWA registered refugees. The figure does not include those Palestinians internally displaced after 1948, conservatively estimated at 75,000 persons. *Internally Displaced Palestinians, International Protection, and Durable Solutions*. BADIL Information & Discussion Brief No. 9 (November 2002). The annual average growth rate of the IDP population is upgraded by a quarter of a percentage point to allow for further internally displaced after 1948 due to internal transfer, land confiscation, and house demolition.

f. The estimate includes persons internally displaced during the 1967 war from destroyed Palestinian villages in the OPTs. This figure is upgraded by the average annual growth rate of the refugee population (3.5 percent). *Internally Displaced Palestinians, International Protection, and Durable Solutions*. BADIL Information & Discussion Brief No. 9 (November 2002). The figure is upgraded to include the average number of Palestinians displaced by house demolition (1,037) each year between 1967 and 2000. The number of Palestinians affected by house demolition is not upgraded according to the average annual population growth due to the fact that it is unknown how many IDPs return to their home of origin. The number of IDPs in the Occupied Palestinian Territories for 2003 is based on the estimated number of IDPs displaced during the 1967 war and the estimated number of Palestinian homes demolished in 2003 as punitive punishment. Table, "Demolition of Houses by Years in the al-Aqsa Intifada, B'tselem," The Israeli Information Center for Human Rights in the Occupied Territories (www.btselem.org). The number of Palestinians displaced is based on an average household size of 6.4 persons. Table 3.2.14, "Percentage Distribution of Households by Household Size, Average Household Size and Region, 2002," Palestinian Central Bureau of Statistics, 2003. *Statistical Abstract of Palestine No. 4*. The figure does not include the number of Palestinians displaced due to the proximity of their homes to Israeli military checkpoints and colonies (i.e., settlements). The figure also includes the number of persons displaced in 2003 by Israel's separation wall. Palestinian Central Bureau of Statistics, 2003. *Survey on the Impact of Separation Wall on the Localities Where It Passed Through*.

their descendants who did not register with UNRWA as refugees (PLO, 2000: 8). As one can imagine, this has led to a great deal of confusion and despair. In addition to this lack of clarity, Israeli negotiators have disputed the whole notion of the descendants of refugees being regarded as refugees and therefore being part of the totals being discussed. Their argument is that there is little precedent in international law for such a position.

Turning to UNHCR definitions does not clarify the situation. The 1951 Convention Relating to the Status of Refugees refers to a "well-founded fear of persecution" as a basis for being a refugee but does not refer to descendants (Convention Relating to the Status of Refugees, 1951: Art. 1). This is very likely due to the fact that the convention did not anticipate refugee situations lasting for as long as the Palestinian one has. However, the convention does include the children of refugees who are in need of protection within its criteria, so it is possible to argue that there is no requirement for the convention to include a reference to descendants as such. The convention also states that refugees lose their refugee status if they become citizens of, and hence can claim protection of, another state. Under this definition, Palestinian refugees with, say, Jordanian citizenship would lose their status as refugees. The same would apply to refugees in the OPTs once a Palestinian state is established there. Thus, while the convention would provide Palestinian refugees much more international protection than they receive at present, its definitions would create a new set of anomalies in the political resolution of the issue. For the purposes of this book, the term *Palestinian refugee* will refer to all Palestinians and their descendants who were exiled as a result of the 1948 War and who wish to return to their homes, irrespective of their registration status. The reason for this is that whatever the recourse either side makes to international law and conventions, it is the self-definition of the refugees and their descendants that has political consequences and which need to be addressed.

For all this range of views, what is the situation of the Palestinians in exile, whether registered or unregistered? Following 1948 and the flight of Palestinians to the neighboring Arab countries of Transjordan, Lebanon, Egypt, and Syria, there was widespread poverty and unemployment in the refugee camps set up by UNRWA. Recent statistics suggest that one-third of the registered Palestine refugees, about 1.3 million, live in fifty-nine recognized refugee camps in Jordan, Lebanon, the Syrian Arab Republic, the West Bank, and the Gaza Strip (see Table 2.2). The other two-thirds of the registered refugees live in and around the cities and towns of the host countries, and in the West Bank and the Gaza Strip, often in the environs of official camps.

UNRWA has played a pivotal role in the ever-growing humanitarian operation that was constructed around Palestinian refugees. The services and facilities that UNRWA provides are available to all registered Palestinian

Table 2.2 Registered Refugees in UNRWA Area of Operations

Field of Operations	Official Camps	Registered Refugees	Registered Refugees in Camps
Jordan	10	1,740,170	307,785
Lebanon	12	394,532	223,956
Syria	10	413,827	120,865
West Bank	19	665,246	179,541
Gaza Strip	8	922,674	484,563
Agency total	59	4,136,449	1,316,710

Source: UNRWA, *The United Nations Relief Works Agency,* available online at www.un.org/unrwa. Figures as of 31 December 2003.

refugees that reside in its area of operation, and UNRWA remains the sole organization responsible for the majority of Palestinian refugees.[3] Some of the original plans of UNRWA in the 1950s were viewed with suspicion by refugees as they were seen as aimed at absorbing the refugees into the region's economies at the expense of their right to return. From 1957, UNRWA's regular program of activities focused on education, health, relief, and social services. More recently, it has introduced microfinance and microenterprise opportunities to encourage greater economic independence.

UNRWA has played a significant role in the field of primary and preparatory education and vocational and technical training. Education is by far the agency's largest activity with 500,000 pupils in 658 schools in the UNRWA area of operation. Despite some criticisms and concern that its focus on humanitarian activities distracts the international community away from the fundamental political questions at the core of the conflict, in the main, refugee groups have been supportive of the work of UNRWA. As a booklet by BADIL observes: "UNRWA provides the kind of decentralised network, knowledgeable and attentive to local sensitivities, and responsible for some 3.6 million refugees that is capable of responding to the particular needs of refugees not only within each host country but within different regions of the host country" (BADIL, 2000b: 10).

Its central role in supporting Palestinian refugees has led both Israel and the United States to see UNRWA as a major foundation in the growth of Palestinian national consciousness and identity, and because of this have argued that it should be closed down at the earliest opportunity. This was the position taken by the Israelis at the Taba talks and has been accepted by some Palestinian officials eager to extend the role of the PNA and PLO. Clearly, without UNRWA, the onus of providing for the refugees would fall on the host governments in Lebanon, Jordan, and Syria and, since 1993, the PNA. If they were unable or unwilling to do so, it would pose a major challenge to international donors and the international NGOs.

Most Palestinian refugees live in permanent housing, including those in refugee camps. Here the infrastructure has been the responsibility of the host governments, but UNRWA has financed and introduced services. Nearly all camps have electricity, water, and sewerage, but the stability of supply of electricity and drinking water in the camps is often considerably worse than in surrounding areas. Crowding is higher in the camps than elsewhere, and around 30 percent of the households have three or more persons per room. The camps in Jordan and the Gaza Strip are particularly under-resourced, with 40 percent of the households having three persons or more per room (Jacobsen, 2003: 13). Infant mortality is usually an indicator of the general health of a society and its conditions. Among Palestinian refugees, infant mortality ranges between 20 and 30 deaths per 1,000 live births. Camps in Syria show particularly low rates, while the Lebanese rates are the highest. Maternal mortality rates are also highest in Lebanon (240 maternal deaths per 100,000 live births) and lowest in Syria (75). However, due to the special hardship programs of UNRWA, there is little acute malnutrition among children. There is, on the other hand, more reported psychological distress as well as somatic illness among adults in camps than elsewhere in the region, and most of this occurs in Lebanon (Jacobsen, 2003: 10).

Although refugees had the shared experience of flight, camp culture, and the creation of a new life in exile, there were many differences in the conditions experienced by refugees in the different countries. It is not possible in this brief overview to describe the whole range of experiences of refugees who were dispersed throughout the Middle East and other parts of the world (see Table 2.3).

The remainder of this section will provide a brief snapshot of the situation of Palestinian refugees where they are most numerous, namely, the OPTs, Lebanon, Syria, Jordan, and Israel. Apart from Israel, these areas coincide with the area of operations of UNRWA (see Map 2.3 above).

The geographical, political, and social separation of both Gazans and West Bankers produced a very different set of experiences for the refugees. Gaza, initially administered by Egypt until 1967, was characterized mostly by its dense population and its continuous confrontations with the IDF. The residents of the West Bank were more economically and educationally advanced. As a result, there was a tendency for West Bank Palestinians to dominate the political arena and have greater access to external funds. Refugees in the OPTs compose nearly 15 percent of the total Palestinian population and aspire either to return to their homes now in Israel or to be compensated. While treated by the Israeli occupying authorities in exactly the same way as other nonrefugee Palestinians in the OPTs, there are some differences. In addition to their residence in camps, unemployment in the refugee camps is 4 percent higher than the rest of the OPTs. In addition, for every 100 economically active persons in the camps, there are 590 dependants, compared with 530 for the rest of the

Table 2.3 Estimated Distribution of Palestinian Refugees by Host Country or Region, 1949 and 2000

	Percent of Total Palestinian Refugee Population	
Country/Region	1949	2000
Palestine/Israel (1948)	4.1	4.1
West Bank	34.4	9.4
Gaza Strip	26.2	13
Jordan	9.6	42
Lebanon	13.8	6.3
Syria	10.4	6.5
Egypt	1	0.9
Iraq and Libya	0.5	1.6
Saudi Arabia	0	4.6
Kuwait	0	0.6
Other Gulf countries	0	1.8
Other Arab countries	0	1
United States	0	3.6
Other foreign countries	0	4.6

Sources: United Nations Economic Survey Mission for the Middle East, *Final Report of the United Nations Economic Survey Mission for the Middle East (Part 1),* UN Doc. A/AC.25/6, 1949. Palestinan Central Bureau of Statistics, *Statistical Abstract of Palestine,* No. 2, 2001.

Note: Does not include an estimated 31,000 internally displaced Palestinians in Israel.

population. As a result, 32.8 percent of Palestinians living in refugee camps are classified as poor, that is, earning US$2 or below per day. In 1998, despite being just 15 percent of the population, they made up one-quarter of the poor in the OPTs (Palestinian Central Bureau of Statistics, 2002).

An even worse situation has prevailed in Lebanon. Lebanon hosts more than 223,956 registered refugees residing in twelve official camps (UNRWA, 2003a). Some estimates have put the total refugee population, registered and unregistered, as even higher at 350,000 and composing 12 percent of the entire population of Lebanon. The Lebanese government is not a signatory to the Convention Relating to the Status of Refugees (1951) or the Protocol Relating to the Status of Refugees (1967) and extends no special treatment to the refugees, many of whom have resided in Lebanon for over fifty years. In addition, as a result of the Lebanese government's restrictions on employment, conditions have deteriorated drastically in the camps. Until 2005, Palestinians were forbidden to enter the formal Lebanese workforce and were obliged to take low-paid jobs, mostly in agriculture or construction work. Such marginalization forced many to seek work overseas, which further fragmented the community. The Palestinian experience is unique partly due to these restrictions but also because of the civil war in Lebanon and the repeated Israeli incursions. Thus refugees who have been born in exile in Lebanon have also been displaced from camp to camp, which has resulted in many of the communal bonds being disrupted and weakened. As a result of these conditions, the numbers actually resident in Lebanon may be considerably less (Brynen, 2006).

In Syria, the main flow of Palestinian refugees took place between 1948 and 1949 when the State of Israel was being established. A second wave took place after the 1967 War. Palestinian refugees in Syria are largely accepted and helped by the government and share the same duties and responsibilities as Syrian citizens, including joining the Syrian military. They do not require work permits and have the right to own businesses and to enroll in government secondary and university education. A remarkable feature of the Palestinian refugee experience is that adult literacy is much higher among refugees than in the region as a whole, especially for women. Female literacy is most marked in Syria where 90 percent of refugee women over fourteen years old are literate, compared to 60 percent in the national population. However, they have not been completely absorbed; although they can vote for local elections, they cannot vote in parliamentary or presidential elections or run as a candidate for political office (Wadie, 2003; Butenschon, Davis, and Hassassian, 2000: 217–218).

Nearly half of UNRWA registered refugees live in ten camps in Jordan. Their arrival in 1948 virtually doubled the population of Jordan. The government pursued an ambivalent policy in respect to assisting the refugees but did not want to take over the responsibility of UNRWA, whose contribution became a very important part of the government budget (Plascov, 1981: 16). Despite a degree of wariness and hostility by the indigenous population of Transjordanian Arabs, the Hashemite elite offered a full citizenship to all refugees and their descendants. Formally they enjoy the same rights and responsibilities as Jordanians. They are allowed access to most employment except sensitive public service and military positions and have formed an important part of the private sector in the Jordanian economy. An exception to this is the status accorded to Palestinians from the Gaza Strip who were displaced in 1967. These are not considered Jordanian citizens (PLO, 2000: 24).

The position of Palestinians in Israel who were internally displaced as a result of the 1948 War is often forgotten in the literature on Palestinian refugees. Around 30,000 to 40,000 Palestinians currently living in Israel are considered displaced (Bokae'e, 2003). Israel does not recognize IDPs nor their rights, and such displacement and dispossession has had a very visible effect on the socioeconomic status of Palestinian citizens of Israel (Jamal, 2005). Discrimination is rife and IDPs are not recognized as a separate section of society, as refugees or as IDPs. There is no registration system for them, which makes these internally displaced people liable to be ignored in any permanent status negotiations. Finally, there are those who have undergone displacement in the OPTs but are not recognized as refugees.

Their displacement has largely been the result of the ongoing low-level conflict between Palestinians and Israelis. Israel has ordered the demolition of thousands of homes in the OPTs and has confiscated land, such as in East Jerusalem, for security and administrative reasons and to deter militants from suicide bombings and other terrorist attacks on Israel. According to many international organizations and UN human rights bodies, however, these policies violate international humanitarian and human rights law, including protection against arbitrary displacement.

Conclusion

We can see how the Palestinian experience of exile has been varied and yet has many elements in common. While Palestinian refugees in Syria and Jordan have had greater political freedoms and privileges, those in Lebanon and the OPTs and IDPs in Israel have been subject to a range of restrictions. Some refugees have advanced economically, particularly those who have left the region to work in the Gulf or in North and South America and Western Europe. Others have had to contend with extremes of poverty, violence, and repression. What is most definitely held in common, however, is resilience in the face of attempts by both Israel, Western states, and to some extent host governments to constrain and contain the refugees' demand for their rights to be recognized. After nearly sixty years, there is little prospect that these demands will cease, and it remains a dynamic political factor that requires addressing in the politics of the region. At the same time, there also appears little prospect at present or for the foreseeable future of their demands being met. In the chapters following, this study will explore how other refugee situations—both protracted ones like the Palestinian case and others not so protracted—reveal a wealth of experience within the international community and in multilateral agencies that can be utilized. Such an examination offers both a critique of the lack of progress in the Palestinian case and an opportunity to broaden the range of policy options available.

Notes

1. A copy of the Mandate for Palestine is archived on the website of the UN Information System on Palestine (UNISPAL), available online at www.un.org/Depts/dpa/docs/unispal.htm.

2. UNRWA Mandate 302 (IV), Assistance to Palestine Refugees, 8 December 1949, is archived on the website of the UN Information System on Palestine (UNISPAL), available online at http://domino.un.org/unispal.nsf.

3. As of 2000, UNRWA was spending approximately half of its general budget, or about $125 million per year, on the refugee services in the West Bank and Gaza.

3

Looking at International Practice

The fate of refugees has become increasingly central in the negotiations to achieve lasting solutions to conflicts around the world. International practice reveals a growing recognition that peace processes need to take into account the future of people displaced by conflict if the agreements are to have any chance of success. As the former UN High Commissioner for Refugees Ruud Lubbers said, if the international community does not address these issues successfully "then we will pay the bill in political instability later" (Helton, 2002: 7). Indeed the growing refugee crises around the world have extended beyond strictly humanitarian concerns to those of national security demanding protracted foreign policy responses. Writing just months before his untimely death in the bombing of the UN headquarters in Baghdad in 2003, Arthur Helton, a senior research fellow of the Council for Foreign Relations in New York, noted:

> Refugee emergencies have often surprised foreign policy decision makers and military leaders. Crises over the past decade in Bosnia, East Timor, Iraq, Kosovo, and Rwanda are emblematic. . . . It is clear that humanitarian action has become an important feature, indeed sometimes a central aspect, of the new national security agenda. (Helton, 2002: 2)

Thus a nexus focused on the question of refugees has emerged, which combines security concerns and humanitarian impulse. As a result there is much debate, and a new academic field has arisen broadly termed *humanitarian intervention,* where criteria for intervention, the political implications of intervention, and any lessons to be learned are examined (Wheeler, 2000; Chesterman, 2004; Paris, 2004; Stedman, Rothchild, and Cousens, 2002; Darby and MacGinty, 2003).

This chapter focuses on refugees and peace processes. The relocation of the refugee issue from sideshow to center stage can also be seen in peace processes from Namibia, Guatemala, Bosnia, and Cambodia where the ultimate destination of refugees in each case was factored into the agreements themselves. As in many other respects, the Middle East conflict and its own struggling peace process can be seen as an exception to this trend. One reason is because international practice, as embodied in the experience and work of UNHCR, has not impinged upon the Middle East peace process to the extent that it would have if UNHCR had itself been involved. As we have seen, Palestinian refugees are served by a *separate* UN agency, UNRWA, which is outside the administrative and legal framework of UNHCR and has, more importantly, no formal refugee protection element in its mandate, its main focus being on humanitarian assistance. Furthermore, despite any number of UN Security Council and General Assembly resolutions, which have provided the basis of international humanitarian law guidance on Palestinian refugees, Israel has been largely impervious to its obligations under international humanitarian law pertaining to the Palestinian refugees. Nevertheless, the relative absence of the refugee issue from the Middle East peace process to date can be seen as anomalous. If, however, international trends to put more emphasis on the refugee issue continue, they will add to the pressure to include international humanitarian law, international human rights law, and refugee law more fully in the Middle East peace process.

This chapter will examine, therefore, the extent to which the Palestinian refugee question has been included in the Middle East peace process and the extent to which that inclusion conforms to international practice. It consists of five sections. The first will describe the evolution of the international community's involvement in regional peace processes, with a particular focus on the role of UNHCR. The second will look at the agency's operational guides; the Voluntary Repatriation Handbook and the Resettlement Handbook will be examined as a way to illustrate the use of certain legal definitions and concepts and their implementation. In the third section, the role of refugees in peace processes will be discussed, and the impact this relationship has both on what is termed *non-refoulement,* or involuntary repatriation, and on individual choice. The fourth section will examine in greater detail than in the previous chapter the refugee issue in the Middle East peace process. It will focus on the negotiations that have taken place, from the Camp David summit in 2000 to the Track II Geneva Accords in 2004, to identify the extent to which proposals in the Middle East peace process conform both to international law and practice recommended by UNHCR. This section is divided into two subsections: the first will look at macro-level issues, such as international involvement, refugee protection, resettlement, and repatriation, while the second will examine operational issues that have been successfully replicated. The final section will draw up some observations and conclusions.

Evolution of an International Refugee Regime

The flight of populations from conflict is not a new phenomenon. The term *refugee* was coined in an early round of state-building in France when the Huguenots fled from the persecution of Louis XIV in 1658 (Helton, 2002: 8). More recently, the term *international protection regime* for refugees has been adopted. While more fully developed as a legal framework in the post–World War II period, its antecedents can be traced back to the League of Nations and the appointment of a High Commissioner for Refugees in the 1920s (Loescher, 1993: 37). Since this period, more than 100 new states have achieved independence and new tensions and conflicts have arisen, ranging from the collapse of the Soviet Union to the end of the Cold War to regional crises in southern and central Africa, central Asia, and the Balkans. As a result, the number of refugees has grown dramatically and the evolution of UNHCR as *the* global agency responsible for refugees is an example of the growing need for an international framework to manage the flow of refugees and provide solutions to their plight.

Established in 1950, with an initial budget of US$300,000, it focused primarily on the local integration and voluntary repatriation of 400,000 refugees mainly in the European arena. Currently, however, it has 153 offices operating in 69 countries, approximately 5,000 staff, a budget of just under US$1 billion, and assists over 20 million refugees and others "of concern" (Kelley and Durieux, 2004: 8). The increased number of refugees, and the pressure to ensure that solutions proposed for them are effective and durable, have obliged the General Assembly to extend both the mandate and the capacity of UNHCR. The operations for voluntary repatriation, for example, have been extended and now also include the rehabilitation and reintegration of refugees in their countries of origin (Fagen, 2006: 54). During most of the 1980s, UNHCR devoted only 2 percent of its budget to repatriation activities, but as the mass returns and the internationally negotiated peace agreements during the early 1990s transformed UNHCR's traditional approach to integration activities, the way was opened for several large-scale repatriations in which UNHCR and its sister agencies, the UNDP and WFP, played a central role in postconflict missions. Almost all major players accepted the fact that the reintegration of returned refugees was a core component of postconflict peacebuilding, essential both for consolidating peace arrangements and for reconstructing a country's economy and social fabric. Thus, between 1990 and 1996, UNHCR was channeling approximately 14 percent of its budget to activities related to refugee returns. As Jeff Crisp, former director of the UNHCR Policy Evaluation Unit, noted, expenditures for reintegration activities nearly doubled between 1994 and 1996 alone (Crisp, 2001: 8).

UNHCR has two basic and interrelated aims. The first is to protect refugees and the second is to seek ways to help them restart their lives in a normal environment. Experience has shown that the success of return programs requires a raft of interrelated activities that provide both immediate material assistance necessary for initial reintegration and other more sustainable development activities (Kelley and Durieux, 2004). In this context, UNHCR is required "to initiate and strengthen partnerships with development actors and governments, allowing for the inclusion of refugees and returnees in national development plans" (Kurosawa, 2003: 1). It should be noted that UNHCR provides protection and assistance not only to refugees but also to other categories of displaced or needy persons. At the start of 2004, as many as 20 million people were "of concern" to UNHCR—which was approximately "one out of every 300 persons on Earth" (UNHCR, 2003a). UNHCR also assists in organizing the resettlement of refugees to third countries, that is, countries that are not the country of origin or the country known as a host country. Countries frequently designated as third countries are Australia, Canada, the Netherlands, New Zealand, and the United States. Such programs involve close coordination with different actors. For example, in the former Yugoslavia, UNHCR had to bring together refugees and municipal authorities to work on projects, forcing former antagonists to work together.

As a result of the evolving mandate and capacity of UNHCR, it has carried out some of the largest population movements in history. It has also achieved some relative successes in that, during the last decade, it has overseen and often directly administered repatriation programs in over twenty countries. In 1962, UNHCR was involved in the return of some 250,000 Algerian refugees from neighboring countries. In 1973, it organized one of history's largest airborne population exchanges between Bangladesh and Pakistan. In 1978, UNHCR was asked to facilitate the repatriation of 200,000 Bengali people who had taken refuge in Burma, and also to organize the repatriation of 150,000 Zairian refugees living in Angola. The agency also played a fundamental role in the return of refugees to Namibia in 1989, to Cambodia in 1991, and to Bosnia in 1995. At the beginning of this century, UNHCR organized and assisted in possibly the most rapid return movement that has occurred since 1973, namely that which took place in Afghanistan. Between March and September 2002, approximately 1.7 million refugees are estimated to have returned to Afghanistan (Turton and Marsden, 2002).

The credibility of UNHCR's work has been a crucial factor in the protection of refugees and has had two important results. First, it gave the refugee community a voice and a stake in decisions regarding its future. Refugees were encouraged to prepare for repatriation, resettlement, and integration programs by visiting target destinations and by discussing the viability of the locations and resources required. Second, it has often acted to consolidate a peace process; by treating their culture and the religion of the refugee community with respect, the agency enhanced their refugee status and the legitimacy of their requirements (Arzt, 2001: 131).

Because the assistance side of the agency's work is so massive, it is easy to overlook the fact that the primary function of UNHCR is refugee protection. The mandate is gradually evolving and has been quite flexible. The agency derives its mandate from a number of international instruments of law, such as the 1951 Refugee Convention, the 1967 Protocol, and the various General Assembly Resolutions and Executive Committee conclusions (see the section "International Practice, Refugees, and Peace Processes" below). These stress both the fundamental nature of the international protection function and the fundamental rights of those "of concern" to UNHCR. Thus, UNHCR is an operational agency with very specific responsibilities to provide international protection. However, the lack of experience and of mechanisms for dealing with conflict and ethnic cleansing within UNHCR threatened to overwhelm the office. This was succinctly put by UNHCR special envoy in Sarajevo Jose Maria Mendiluce during the Bosnian crisis of the mid-1990s. Referring to the standard field officers' manual, he remarked "we are going to have to throw away the Blue Book" (Cunliffe and Pugh, 1996: 5). As repatriation and reintegration-related activities have grown, UNHCR has faced unprecedented challenges to its longstanding modus operandi.

These challenges have pushed UNHCR to actively promote debate about the nature of its work and to consider how to enhance it in areas not addressed by the 1951 Convention and the 1967 Protocol. Thus another development in the international refugee regime and in UNHCR's work can be seen in the renewal process known as Global Consultations on International Protection (GCIP), which has been followed by the "UNHCR 2004" process. A particular focus of this process has been the question of how to mobilize increased international support for the agency's work in promoting durable solutions for refugees. These developments will be covered in greater detail when we consider ways of achieving the notion of durable solutions and the experience of the international community.

Operational Parameters and International Practice: The UNHCR Handbooks

In order to obtain a clearer idea of the operational framework of UNHCR and thus international practice in general, we will examine the two main handbooks that have been issued to field staff: the Voluntary Repatriation Handbook and the Resettlement Handbook (UNHCR, 1996; UNHCR, 2002).

These two handbooks will also be analyzed to ascertain the extent to which the Middle East peace process is informed by the structural and operational parameters of UNHCR. The Voluntary Repatriation Handbook (VRH), which I will consider first, is mainly concerned with large-scale refugee situations and is an attempt to outline a variety of practical approaches to protection issues and involuntary repatriation operations. As the preface spells out, the suggested courses of action may not be relevant to, or feasible in, every UNHCR operation, and users of the handbook are therefore "encouraged to look at it with a view to selecting actions according to their specific requirements, while ensuring that the fundamental principles are observed" (UNHCR, 1996: vi). The term *refugee,* as used in the VRH, denotes all persons who are outside their country of origin for reasons of feared persecution, armed conflict, generalized violence, or gross violations of human rights and who, as a result, need international protection. For purely practical reasons, other categories of persons who may need UNHCR assistance to return home are not covered. The VRH is intended to promote consistency in international refugee protection and in the practice of agencies working in repatriation. It was designed to be used with the UNHCR "Training Module on Voluntary Repatriation" and to provide field staff and UNHCR partners with practical guidelines for action and management.

The VRH is composed of nine chapters, which cover topics such as UNHCR's mandate for voluntary repatriation, and refers to relevant UN resolutions and UNHCR Executive Committee conclusions. It also covers the protection aspects of voluntary repatriation, international human rights instruments, and the responsibilities of both the host country and the country of origin. Operational issues are covered by chapters on UNHCR's role in voluntary repatriation, such as profiling the refugee community and the country of origin, and how to be prepared for both organized and spontaneous repatriation. The VRH also considers the purpose and content of repatriation negotiations and agreements, and how to deal with residual caseloads of refugees who may decide not to repatriate. Practical logistical guidelines regarding "voluntariness," such as the conduct of information campaigns, interviews, counseling, registration, and computerization, are also given. Finally, the VRH outlines UNHCR's role in the country of origin; the importance of ascertaining the education, health, and security of the refugee community; of ascertaining the character of individual cases; and of the need for interagency and NGO cooperation. There are, in addition, numerous annexes that provide checklists for repatriation procedures, some international and regional instruments as well as samples of a voluntary repatriation, a prototype tripartite agreement, cross-border travel authorization, and other UNHCR guidelines. The final two annexes are some international guidelines adopted by UNHCR known as POP, or People-Oriented Planning, and QIPs, or Quick Impact Projects for work in refugee situations.

The Resettlement Handbook (RH) is, like the VRH, a substantial document. Like the VRH, it is a comprehensive review of the practical aspects of resettlement. These include guidance on determining what the resettlement policies of some countries are and, very usefully, how they compare with the resettlement profile of the RH. After establishing how important resettlement is in international protection, the RH outlines the resettlement process from ascertaining eligibility to UNHCR criteria for determining resettlement as the appropriate solution to the legal and physical needs of particular groups of resettled refugees. These groups include the survivors of violence and torture, those with specific medical conditions, women-at-risk, family reunification groups, children and adolescents, elderly refugees, and other refugees without local integration prospects. Several chapters also provide guidance on procedures for field-workers and how to cooperate effectively with other agencies, NGOs, and the media. Space is also devoted to establishing the importance of training of staff on resettlement. These practical aspects are followed by chapters that include a description of the resettlement of the main receiving countries. The last section of the handbook provides annexes on the Executive Committee's Conclusions relating to resettlement, selected provisions from Universal Instruments, a toolkit or checklist of activities, an organizational structure of the Resettlement and Special Cases Section, resettlement statistics, guidance for the assessment of cases of women refugees, and women-at-risk programs.

Combined, the two handbooks provide a fairly comprehensive armory of practical information and general principles that can be adopted to organize the repatriation or resettlement of refugees in a safe and dignified manner. What is clear is that the experience and know-how exists for this to be achieved but nevertheless depends on the political circumstances as well as the political will of the key actors. In terms of its applicability to the Palestinian case, one should note that in most of the cases dealt with by UNHCR, the causes of refugeedom are wars between states or within states. In such cases, it is necessary to hold the state accountable for how it treats its own citizens and those of other states. It becomes more complicated when a new state of a different people has been established on the homeland of the people who have become refugees. In the Palestinian case, the homeland to be returned to and the state created upon it are not synonymous and the handbooks do not make this crucial distinction. The VRH states that "the Country of origin should allow *its nationals* to return without harassment, discrimination and *restore full national protection* [emphasis added]" (UNHCR, 1996: 14). In the case of Palestinian refugees, they are not regarded by Israel as nationals, and therefore upon their eventual return, the question of restoring full national protection may not be straightforward because protection of the exiled Palestinians was never part of the Israeli state system. They are regarded either as enemies or "absentees." It follows that, should the Palestinian refugees return to their homeland, they may wish to do so as returned refugees in the spirit of the UNHCR handbook, but under the Israeli legal system they would be putative immigrants to the new Israeli state.

Although the VRH is founded on the principles of "a basic right to return voluntarily to country of origin" and the "urge for international cooperation to achieve this solution," the operational aspects of the handbook refer to existing states dealing with their own nationals or with other nationals, but not those who have had their nationality taken away by the creation of a new state (UNHCR, 1996: A11). Thus, in the case of the Palestinian refugees, the handbooks are very useful when they deal with the prerequisites for a political settlement and for program implementation, but they fail to address the cause of the refugeedom in the Palestinian case. Therefore, the meaning of terms in the handbooks, such as *return, repatriation,* and *resettlement,* are not fully applicable here and even detract from their usefulness as a practical guide. Nevertheless, by setting out some clear benchmarks of good practice, both handbooks serve a valuable function in providing the basis for the evaluation of how refugees should be dealt with in peace agreements.

International Practice, Refugees, and Peace Processes

In turning to the actual frameworks in which refugee issues are addressed, we can see that peace processes and agreements have increasingly acknowledged the significance of refugees, particularly with regard to repatriation. Terminating the Cambodian civil war, the Paris Agreement of 1991 provided international guarantees to ensure that Cambodian refugees and displaced persons had "the rights to return to the country, to live in safety, security, and dignity, free from intimidation and coercion of any kind" (Part 5). In Mozambique, the 1992 General Peace Agreement between the government of Mozambique and Renamo stipulated the return of refugees and displaced persons. In Rwanda, the 1993 Arusha Accords included a protocol on the inalienable rights of refugees to return home. In the former Republic of Yugoslavia, the Dayton Peace Accords of 1995 made provision for the repatriation of all refugees and displaced persons to their homes. Clearly, the experience of the international community in managing and shepherding peace processes is very mixed, and the wide variety of peace processes themselves make any attempt to identify a formulaic response very difficult. Nevertheless, there are a number of studies that offer both an overview of the key issues and useful examples of the challenges and pitfalls (Wheeler, 2000; Helton, 2002; Chesterman, 2004; Stedman, Rothchild, and Cousens, 2002; Paris, 2004).

Two different types of conflict can be distinguished resulting in refugee crises. The first type is wars in which refugees are not a core issue. Many conflicts are concerned with governance issues, that is, with control over government institutions, over land, and over the allocation of other resources. In these kinds of wars, refugees are a by-product of the violence. The second kind of conflicts are those over people and their exclusion not only from power and resources but from the very body politic itself, often resulting in dispossession and "ethnic cleansing." These will have, ab initio, the status of refugees as a core issue. As Howard Adelman of York University, Toronto, and former editor of the journal *Refuge*, states:

> In wars of exclusion, a specific war aim is the elimination of some people as part of the polity by creating separate uni-ethnic states or ethnic enclaves, or undertaking ethnic cleansing and genocide. In anti-people and pro-people civil wars, refugees are a direct consequence of the violent conflict rather than merely a by-product. *A central war aim is to produce the refugees* [emphasis added]. (Adelman, 2002: 285)

Nevertheless, in both types of conflict, addressing the refugee issue is an essential part of any postconflict agreement and of peacebuilding. In newly independent or secessionist states, such as East Timor, Eritrea, and Palestine, refugees are key players in state-building as well. As we have seen, international practice and international law recommend a number of options to help find what is known in UNHCR circles and refugee studies as "durable solutions" to refugee crises. UNHCR has recognized there to be three durable solutions: repatriation, integration into the host country, and resettlement to a third country. The 1990s saw the repatriation solution come to the fore as the preferred option of the international community for the reasons we have already indicated. However, some scholars, Adelman in particular, have also argued that repatriation is not always an essential part of a postconflict agreement, and international practice suggests that a range of options including integration and resettlement with compensation packages can also produce a peace agreement (Adelman, 2002: 276–278). His implication is that repatriation is therefore not always necessary. This analysis could be called into question by highlighting his rather serendipitous selection of data from the case studies he presents and his narrow focus on agreements themselves rather than the overall peace process. Some of the examples where an agreement was reached without repatriation were where repatriation had either taken place spontaneously (as in Mozambique) or took place prior to or independently of an agreement (Guatemala) so that the issue did not need to be addressed in the peace agreement. This does not entail the conclusion that repatriation is not an essential part of an overall postconflict agreement. Indeed, as has been noted elsewhere, in a post–September 11 world, the fear of terrorism and subversion will ensure that repatriation will continue to be the preferred option for most of the international community as population mobility is increasingly restricted (Dumper, 2006b: 12).

However, the inclusion of refugee issues into peace agreements is double-edged in terms of promoting the interests of refugees. On the one hand, if the rights of refugees are not an integral part of a political settlement, the likely result is instability on the borders of the state concerned and ongoing conflict (Fagen, 2006). Indeed as Adelman has also observed, this lack of inclusion can lead to what he has dubbed the "warrior refugee" who perpetuates the cycle of violence (Adelman, 2002: 275). Conversely, if the refugee issue is too closely enmeshed with the peace agreements, pressure will be placed upon international agencies and refugee leaders themselves to accept an agreement whose provisions and timetable of implementation are not necessarily in their interests. The principle of *non-refoulement* may be compromised, with refugees being pressured to return before conditions are safe or economically feasible. Furthermore, the principle of individual refugee choice of which of the durable options to adopt may also be marginalized.

International experience suggests that a number of issues are repeated in peace processes involving refugees. These include the right of return to the place of origin, refugee participation, the absorptive capacity of the country of origin and host countries, and the role of the international community and will be addressed in greater detail in the next section and in subsequent chapters.

The first issue is that of the right of return. While not explicitly incorporated in the 1951 Convention Relating to the Status of Refugees, the right of refugees to return to their country or home is based upon customary international law, the four Geneva Conventions, and the Universal Declaration of Human Rights (Takkenberg, 1998: 232–234). Complementing this principle is the formal mandate given to UNHCR in its statute adopted by the UN General Assembly in 1950, which calls on governments to assist the High Commissioner in efforts "to promote the voluntary repatriation of refugees" (UNHCR, 1996: 1). The Paris Agreement in the Cambodian case and the Dayton Peace Agreement in the case of the Former Republic of Yugoslavia (FRY) both include clauses recognizing this right. However, international experience has shown that unless this right is fully accepted by the government of the country of origin and backed up with credible regional or international force, refugees can be left in a state of limbo. Because of the very recognition of the right of return, they are neither officially integrated into their host countries, nor resettled to a third country, nor permitted to exercise their right of return. This is a recipe for ongoing instability and sporadic eruptions of conflict until the matter is resolved.

This issue can be highlighted by the case of Bosnia-Herzegovina. During the conflict with Serbia and Croatia, the country became divided along ethnic lines, and by 1995 4.4 million people were displaced, of which over 1.2 million fled to neighboring countries and Western Europe. The Dayton

Peace Agreement created the Office of the High Representative to coordinate the activities of organizations involved in the civilian aspects of the agreement, including the return of refugees, and it received political guidance from the Peace Implementation Council (PIC), which consisted of fifty-five countries and international organizations that support the peace process. By May 1996, significant progress had been made on the military provisions of the agreement (Bagshaw, 1997: 573–574). The authors of the Dayton Peace Agreement were well aware that the repatriation of refugees would only take place under safe conditions, and in Annex 6 they laid down stringent "benchmarks" for human rights and established mechanisms such as the Commission on Human Rights and the Commission for Displaced Persons and Refugees. In contrast to the provisions regarding the cessation of hostilities, these benchmarks were slow to be met. This had a direct bearing upon the implementation of the provisions relating to the repatriation of refugees contained in Annex 7.

Annex 7 institutionalized the role of UNHCR in the return and repatriation process and mandated it to organize an "early, peaceful, orderly and phased return of refugees and displaced persons." While the peace agreement specified that all refugees had a right to return to their homes of origin, no specific provision was made, however, to ensure that such returns could take place. It relied, instead, upon the signatories of the Dayton Peace Agreement to cooperate in creating the conditions for safe returns. As a result, by 2000, only 10 percent of the Serbs from Croatia, 5 percent of Muslims and Croats from western Bosnia-Herzegovina, and only 1 percent of those expelled by Serbs from eastern Bosnia-Herzegovina (Republika Srpska) returned to their homes (UNHCR, 2000: 231). More recent figures suggest that out of a total of 4.4 million, some 425,000 refugees and 500,000 displaced persons have returned to their prewar homes (Prettitore, 2003: 5)

The point to consider here is that the crisis in Bosnia-Herzegovina was characterized by a high degree of external involvement. UNHCR was involved from the outset; the Office of the High Representative, the Peace Implementation Council, the UN Protection Force (UNPROFOR), a NATO-led Implementation Force (IFOR), and the UN International Peace Task Force created a virtual international protectorate of the state with increasing interventions in legislation concerning property and the appointment of officials and jurists. The EU was involved in attempting to create a regional framework for reconciliation, multi-ethnic democratic processes, and reconstruction through the promotion in 1999 of the Stability Pact for South Eastern Europe. Despite this extensive external involvement, the availability of military force, and assistance in creating a safe environment, the right of return has encountered many difficulties.

A second issue here is that of refugee participation. While in international law there is no *explicit* right of refugee participation in the decision-making process, through provisions guaranteeing freedom of movement, opinion, and assembly, refugee participation is implied. Indeed, a review of UNHCR material, particularly the handbooks already mentioned, indicates that this implication has taken on some operational aspects. Field staff are encouraged to provide information and to consult with refugee representatives (UNHCR, 1996: 26; UNHCR, 2002: 16). Clearly, refugee participation is also achieved through their involvement in negotiations as part of the coalition of exiles that form the opposition. Examples can be seen in the Sri Lanka Eelam Liberation Front, the Rwanda Liberation Army, the African National Conference, and in the Permanent Commissions set up in the Guatemalan camps in Mexico. The attempt to formalize refugee participation is seen most clearly in peace agreements that provide for their participation in elections for a new, more representative government. While desirable in terms of promoting national reconciliation and an inclusive policy, refugee participation in elections, however, also introduces problems. The election timetable can set the development agenda and countries may be obliged to absorb returned refugees before the countries are ready (Fagen, 2006: 48). Good examples of this can be seen in Namibia, Cambodia (Rodicio, 2006), and East Timor (Chesterman, 2004: 210).

A final issue to be considered is that although the role of the international community in bringing about an agreement is usually essential, its ongoing commitment to implementation is often inadequate and temporary. The consequence is that distress is caused to the returnees and host population alike, and as a result the program may not last. This is likely to sow the seeds of further conflict. In order to be effective, international involvement needs to extend beyond the agreement to broader development assistance that encompasses the transition from repatriation to integration. This has been recognized by UNHCR with its development of the concept of the 4Rs—repatriation, reintegration, rehabilitation, and reconstruction—and will be discussed in greater detail in Chapter 4 (Refugee Studies Centre, 2005: 99; Fagen, 2006: 58).

An additional point to be emphasized here is that the donor community is driven by budgetary issues and what is regarded as a built-in bias toward neoliberal assistance programs. Programs are often devised to accommodate the ideological preferences of the donors, but these ideologies are not always in sympathy with the needs and cultural norms of the recipients. There is, for example, a common tendency to encourage the creation of a "civil society" irrespective of whether this undermines the traditional patriarchal or clan structures that may prevail in many refugee communities. Such programs may not only increase a refugee's sense of deracination but also aggravate the social and political tensions arising from exile. Thus, such neoliberal programs can result in new problems unrelated to the original exile or displacement.

The Middle East Peace Process and International Practice

This section will examine the constituent parts that make up the Middle East peace process to assess the extent to which they have conformed to international practice as illustrated by the VRH and the RH. The various milestones along the way have been described in Chapter 2; this section will not describe the political events that led up to each of the negotiations but discuss the contents of the discussions and, where relevant, the agreements themselves. The negotiations referred to are Camp David 2000, also known as Camp David II; the Taba Talks in 2001 as summarized in the Moratinos Papers; the Beirut Declaration of 2002; the Ayalon-Nusseibeh Plan or People's Initiative of 2003; and the Geneva Accord of 2003. This analysis is presented in two parts: macro-level and micro-level. The first will cover general and more conceptual issues, such as the differing approaches to refugeedom and achieving the durable solutions of reintegration, resettlement, and repatriation. The second will examine specific issues concerned with implementation, such as the role of a lead agency, interagency cooperation, and local absorptive capacity.

Macro-Level Issues

International law. The role of international law and the overarching framework that it provides for conflict resolution is an essential feature of the work of the UN and its involvement in peace processes. The work of UNHCR is closely constrained by international law, and it functions in clearly defined parameters. Both handbooks explicitly refer to international instruments as legal reference points. The Voluntary Repatriation Handbook, for example, is guided by UNGAR 428(V), 1672(XVI); the 1951 Convention on the Status of Refugees; UNHCR Executive Committee Conclusions 18(XXXI), 40(XXXVI), 65(XLII), 69(XLIII), and 75(XLV); the 1948 Universal Declaration of Human Rights Article 13(2); the International Covenant on Civil and Political Rights Article 12(4); the International Convention on the Elimination of All Forms of Racial Discrimination Article 5(d)(ii); and the Fourth Geneva Convention Article 3 Protocol II. For its part, the Resettlement Handbook is based upon the 1991 UNHCR Executive Committee decisions, the 1951 Convention on the Status of Refugees and the 1967 Protocol, the 1969 OAU Convention, and the 1984

Cartagena Declaration on Refugees. In contrast, the Taba Talks and the Beirut Declaration only refer to UNGAR 194 (the General Assembly resolution that declared that Palestinians should be allowed to return to their homes) and UNSCR 242 (the Security Council resolution that called on Israel to withdraw from territories occupied in 1967). The Ayalon-Nusseibeh Plan refers to UN resolutions in a general sense. The Geneva Accord uses more international instruments than the other proposals in that it refers to UNSCRs 242, 338, and 1397; UNGAR 194; the UN Charter; and rules of international law (Geneva Accord, 2003: Preamble). Nevertheless, the lack of reference to the main international legal instruments concerning refugees in the Geneva Accord is glaring. The reasons for this can be attributed to realpolitik. As Christine Bell has observed: "To put it starkly, human rights are an integral part of the DPA [Dayton Peace Agreement] and an absent part of the DoP [declaration of Principles], in part because in BiH [Bosnia-Herzegovina] the United States required their inclusion, while in the Israeli/Palestinian process it did not" (Bell, 2000: 313).

The right of return. One of the fundamental issues that require clarification at the outset of the peace negotiations is the cause of conflict, as this frames the international community's response to the issue and the solutions proposed. The UNHCR VRH states that refugeedom can be rectified by implementing the right to return and that the international community should cooperate to realize this solution (UNHCR, 1996: A11). At the Camp David summit, Israel refused to accept responsibility for Palestinian displacement, and the gap between the two sides on this issue was one of the causes of the collapse of the talks. Progress was made some months later in the Taba Talks, where both sides agreed on the need for a joint narrative on the events of 1948, but no actual narrative was agreed upon. The VRH states that the country of origin is responsible for the refugees, who should be allowed to return in safety and dignity (UNHCR, 1996: 12, 14). Repatriation that is voluntary enhances durable solutions and should be lasting and sustainable, while involuntary return amounts to *refoulment* (UNHCR, 1996: 10–11). The Resettlement Handbook, while clearly focused on resettlement as a possible solution, is clear that this is only an option in particular circumstances: when refugees need a durable solution to protect them or when they cannot repatriate and are at risk in their country of origin (UNHCR, 2002: II/1). While Camp David called for a comprehensive, just, and lasting peace as well as a settlement of the refugee issue according to UNSCR 242 and UNGAR 194, Palestinian refugee return was limited to around 100,000 persons and effectively subject to Israeli interpretation of family reunification (MidEastWeb, 2000a, 2000b: 2). At Taba, both sides agreed to a just settlement of the refugee problem based on UNSCR 242 and UNGAR 194. However, in a semantic sleight of hand, the right of return would be subject to the total number of refugees that would be allowed to return that were not specified but by implication were limited. In addition, the right of return would cease once an agreement was achieved. A similar approach was adopted in both the Ayalon-Nusseibeh Plan and the Geneva Accord. In the former, the right becomes void with the implementation of the agreement, while in the latter it is nullified when the permanent place of residence of the refugee is determined by an International Commission that the accord proposes. In trying to work within the Clinton parameters and the progress achieved in Taba, the Beirut Declaration resulted in being largely rhetorical on this subject. It reiterated the attainment of a just solution to the Palestinian refugee problem based on the same UN resolutions but without the slightest suggestion of mechanisms for its implementation.

Timing. The VRH states that "[m]ost UNHCR-organized repatriations, in particular those following wars or decolonization, take place *after political settlements* [emphasis added]" (UNHCR, 1996: 61). This suggests a *sequential approach* in which the political settlement precedes repatriations. The various proposals suggested in Palestinian-Israeli negotiations link together a political settlement and the matter of refugees and their repatriation. This *compound approach* has its drawbacks in that, in the absence of any actual refugee involvement in the political settlement process, undue weight is placed on arriving at a political settlement and not enough on repatriation of the Palestinian refugees. Furthermore, in the Ayalon-Nusseibeh Plan and the Geneva Accord, repatriation is compromised (a sharp contrast from the UNHCR VRH and RH profiles) in favor of achieving a settlement. In the absence of a UN-sponsored settlement, this compound approach becomes more detrimental to the Palestinian refugees' voluntary repatriation and risks transforming a political settlement from being a conflict resolution process to conflict management.

The international community. One of the major roles of UNHCR is to ensure that security in the country of origin has improved sufficiently to absorb returning refugees and that guarantees and amnesties provided by the country of origin are implemented (UNHCR, 1996: 61). Thus, international practice points to the important role that can be played by major powers, regional powers, and UN agencies. In contrast, both the Ayalon-Nusseibeh Plan and Geneva Initiative call for an international role not in shaping the agreement but post facto and for specific tasks. In the former agreement, this role is mainly the financing of payments, while in the latter agreement, international bodies are to take part in resolving the refugee problem but only within the parameters of the agreement itself and not as laid out in the UNHCR handbooks. Neither Camp David nor the Beirut Declaration provides for international involvement; they emphasize instead a bilateral approach of formulating a resolution between the Palestinians and the Israelis without any mechanism of mustering international guarantees at all or any forms of support toward a sustained solution. Taba, on the other hand, included extensive detail of the role of the international community in the composition of an "International Commission for Palestinian Refugees." However, as we discuss below, it, like the Geneva Initiative, is post facto and does not offer the international input that can be seen from other refugee situations.

This lack of international involvement also means that the international consensus that has built up around the attempts to resolve refugee crises is sidestepped. For example, the VRH refers to two regional agreements that provide for return of refugees to their country of origin and that have become part of the instruments in international law. The first is the 1969 Organization for African Unity (OAU) Convention, which stipulated that the country of asylum in collaboration with country of origin should arrange for the safe return of refugees who request repatriation. Some of the provisions of this convention emphasized the voluntary character of repatriation, that is, that the country of origin should facilitate the resettlement of returning refugees and grant them the rights and privileges of nationals of the country, and that "[r]efugees who freely decide to return to their homeland . . . shall be given every possible assistance by the country of asylum, the country of origin, voluntary agencies and intergovernmental organizations, to facilitate their return" (UNHCR, 1996: Annex 3, A15). The second regional instrument is the 1989 International Conference on Central American Refugees (CIREFCA). The states that were represented in the conference "made specific commitments to respect and promote . . . basic principles of voluntary repatriation" (UNHCR, 1996: A16). Some of the principles were the right of refugees to return to country of origin, UNHCR's access to returned refugees, and citizenship for foreign-born children of returned refugees and their foreign spouses. In contrast, only the Geneva Accord considers a regional instrument, that is, the Beirut Declaration, which is based on UNGAR 194 and UNSC Resolution 242. Although strictly not comparable, it is relevant to note that in respect to the specific commitments and instruments, such as those stipulated in the OAU Convention and the CIREFCA Conference, the Beirut Declaration looks quite threadbare with regard to the practicalities of return and repatriation.

UNHCR. As we have seen, since the mid-1980s, UNHCR has acquired a great deal of experience in peacekeeping and negotiations agreements. As a result, it is quite clear about its role in having an input in those parts of agreements that pertain to voluntary repatriation. The VRH proposes a Tripartite Commission composed of the country of origin, the country of asylum, and UNHCR, which represents the refugees (UNHCR, 1996: 33). None of the negotiations under scrutiny seek to draw in the UN, and certainly no consideration whatsoever has been given such a Tripartite Commission. In Taba, UNRWA was to be part of the proposed commission, but it is unclear if its role, particularly relating to refugee protection, would be similar to that of UNHCR. The agreements proposed are bilateral between the two parties of the conflict. Neither the countries of asylum nor the refugees are represented in the negotiations. One result of this is to leave the country of origin, Israel, in a dominant position in relation to other parties and therefore has the power to influence an outcome favorable to its interests. A greater contrast could hardy be imagined to the balancing of interests that are intrinsic in a Tripartite Commission.

Refugee participation. This lack of UNHCR or any other concerned party's involvement raises an important issue of refugee representation. In addition to UNHCR's mandate to consult with refugees in finding durable solutions, and to secure the cooperation of both the country of origin and the international community, the VRH has a section that elucidates refugees' involvement in voluntary repatriation. It states that

> refugee participation in both design and implementation of programmes that serve them can increase the effectiveness and efficiency of those programmes. . . . [R]efugee participation makes assistance work. In-depth knowledge of refugee population and their home country will greatly assist to ensure consultation and participation of refugee women and men in all phases of the repatriation process. (UNHCR, 1996: 19)

As we saw in Chapter 2, the Oslo Accords of 1993 established an interim authority in the OPTs, the PNA. One result of this has been the demise of the PLO outside the OPTs, and with it, the direct channel of representation for Palestinian refugees in Lebanon, Jordan, Syria, and in the diaspora has in effect withered. The extensive consultative process established by Civitas, under the direction of Karma Nabulsi, is an attempt to halt this decline and to provide a platform for the voices of refugees (Nabulsi, 2006). (The election of a HAMAS interim government in 2006 may lead to attempts to revive the PLO.) It is for this reason that there has been a mobilization of refugee groups outside the PLO umbrella. The lack of a body specifically representing the interests of refugees has meant that negotiations are conducted outside the profile suggested by international guidelines in the UNHCR handbooks. In addition, none of the Israeli-Palestinian proposals involve the refugees in the task of finding durable solutions; when their involvement is considered, as in the Geneva Accord, it is limited to their use of the proposed compensation fund. The accord states that "[r]efugees shall have the right to appeal [against] decisions affecting them according to mechanisms established by this Agreement and detailed in Annex X" (Geneva Accord, 2003: 7.11, iii, f).

Non-refoulement. Another major issue expounded at length in the VRH is the very question of voluntariness, or *non-refoulement,* in repatriation. The handbook states that repatriation should be voluntary, which in practice means "not only the absence of measures which push the refugee to repatriate but also he or she should not be prevented from returning" (UNHCR, 1996: 10). In addition, as we have seen, specific conditions are attached to the alternative of resettlement. And when Palestinian refugees are given a free choice to exercise their right to return, there are, as one can imagine, some additional factors to be considered.

Under international law, Palestinian refugees, like all refugees, have the right to return to their country of origin, which, in their case, was Mandatory Palestine prior to the establishment of the Israeli state in 1948. However, for most refugees, their country of origin or homeland exists only as a geographical territory and not as a state. Thus, a return to the homeland entails an adoption of a new national status, that is, an Israeli one. But for a Palestinian refugee to return to a homeland that is now the Israeli state using the guidelines of the VRH, the Israeli state would have to adopt a new classification of its nationals, that is, Palestinian-Israelis with equal human and national rights irrespective of whether or not they were Jews or whether they had left their homes in 1948. In this context, we can see how the imbalances in power relations have mitigated the application of these guidelines. The Palestinian-Israeli peace proposals under scrutiny illustrate the extent to which the Palestinian leadership has contemplated a "return" to a new Palestinian state in one part of the original pre-1948 homeland, the West Bank and Gaza Strip. In essence, the discussions and proposals have explored the feasibility of exchanging the return to their "homes," as stated in UNGAR 194, for a more limited "return" to the new Palestinian state on part of the original homeland, that is, the West Bank and Gaza Strip. At the Taba Talks, the Palestinian negotiators tried to get agreement on the individual free choice of the refugees and their right to return to their homes in accordance with its interpretation of UNGAR 194. Instead, the agreement that appeared was for the Palestinian refugees to be given a set of choices: either return and repatriation to either Israel or to territory ceded by Israel in exchange for occupied land or to the Palestine state, or rehabilitation and relocation in host country or relocation to third country (Eldar, 2002: 3.2). The Ayalon-Nusseibeh Plan and the Geneva Accord go further in circumscribing refugee choice. The former states that Palestinian refugees will return only to the state of Palestine, while the latter discusses only a limited migration to either the Israeli or Palestinian state. In both, however, the meaning of *return* does not correspond to the guidelines of the UNHCR handbooks, which uphold the right to return to a country of origin as a basic human right.

Repatriation. As already indicated, international practice in striving for durable solutions to refugee crises is centered on three options: repatriation to country of origin, integration in host country, and resettlement to third country. These three options will be discussed in greater detail in Chapter 4, and we refer to them here only briefly as they relate to our discussion on UNHCR guidelines and the role of refugees in peace processes. The VRH lays out steps that need to be taken to best ensure voluntary repatriation. The emphasis here is on *non-refoulement*—that reintegration in conditions of "safety and dignity" is key to repatriation (UNHCR, 1996: 78). For example, a first step is the production of a profile of the country of origin. This should provide the refugees with the most accurate information necessary for making an informed choice. The VRH states that the "significance of individual choice is an important safeguard against forced return of a refugee" (UNHCR, 1996: 41). The handbook gives guidelines on how to conduct information campaigns and how to deal with disinformation in order for repatriation to be properly voluntary. It provides a Voluntary Repatriation Form, details on how to prepare for organized repatriations, and instructions on how to deal with spontaneous returns—particularly during conflict situations, which consequently requires safe areas—and how to handle repatriation of individuals.

In contrast, one report of the Camp David discussions suggests that no more than 100,000 Palestinian refugees would be allowed to immigrate to Israel on "humanitarian" grounds (MidEastWeb, 2000a, 200b: 2). At Taba, the Israelis suggested a three-track, fifteen-year absorption program, which was discussed but was not agreed upon. In addition, the Israeli negotiators rejected restitution of the property of the Palestinian refugees. The Ayalon-Nusseibeh Plan stated the Palestinian refugees could return only to the State of Palestine (Ayalon-Nusseibeh Plan, 2004: 4). In the Geneva Accord, the Palestinian team gave up the right of return of Palestinian refugees (Geneva Accord, 2003: Introduction). From this pattern, one can see that since the start of the negotiations in the Middle East peace process in 1991, repatriation has not been regarded as the primary option in addressing the Palestinian refugee issue.

Local integration. The second of the three durable solutions is local integration, and is one that has clearly been espoused by the Israeli side but is held less in favor by the Palestinians, Syria, Jordan, and certainly Lebanon. International practice, as illustrated by the RH, considers local integration as a particular solution to the problem of refugees, when voluntary repatriation does not seem probable (UNHCR, 2002: II/4). The role of UNHCR is, in these circumstances, to assist in the regularization of the legal status of refugees under its protection mandate. One caveat expressed by the RH that limits the option of local integration in the Palestinian case is that the host countries are signatories to universal or regional instruments concerning refugees, and that integration should not be socially, politically, and economically destabilizing (UNHCR, 2002: II/5). At the Taba Talks, rehabilitation in the host country was one of the options for the refugees. In the Ayalon-Nusseibeh Plan, the focus was on compensating the refugees who gave up their right to return and were willing to remain in their present country of residence. For its part, the Geneva Accord called for comprehensive development and rehabilitation programs for Palestinian refugee communities in their host countries.

Resettlement. The third option of resettlement has to be further defined in the Palestinian context. As stated in Chapter 1, the term *resettlement* is not used in the same way in the Arab-Israeli conflict as in the lexicon of refugees studies. *Tawtiin* in Arabic is generally used to refer to the integration of refugees into their host countries and not to resettlement in third countries. In addition, it is also used to refer to a return to the OPTs and the proposed Palestinian state, in order to distinguish from the return of refugees to their homes and to underline the point that directing refugees to the OPTs is not actually a repatriation but a migration to a new state. The RH states that third country resettlement involves the transfer of refugees from the country where they have sought refuge to another state that had agreed to admit these persons (UNHCR, 2002: I/2). The decision to resettle a refugee is made only when other options, such as voluntary repatriation and local integration, are not available and the picture the handbook paints is quite positive:

> [T]hird country resettlement often entails taking refugees from their country of first refuge, transporting them thousands of miles across the world, and helping them to adapt to societies where the culture, climate, language and social structure are unfamiliar. In spite of all efforts, refugees may face problems adapting to such different circumstances. Nevertheless, it is the experience of many Governments and non-governmental organizations that the overwhelming number of refugees successfully overcome such challenges in order to establish themselves in their new country and community. Many resettled refugees, particularly younger family members, have made an astonishing success of their new lives. (UNHCR, 2002: I/7)

The goal is to enhance, not diminish, asylum and protection prospects for refugee populations. Individuals in need of resettlement are usually submitted to one of fourteen main resettlement countries: Australia, Benin, Burkina Faso, Canada, Chile, Denmark, Finland, Iceland, Ireland, the Netherlands, New Zealand, Norway, Sweden, and the United States. The handbook sets criteria for determining whether resettlement is an appropriate solution and identifies basic procedures to be followed in field-office resettlement operations. Priority should be given to refugees with acute physical and legal protection needs, particularly women-at-risk and unaccompanied children (UNHCR, 2002: IV/3).

The Middle East peace proposals under consideration do not refer to resettlement in the accepted UNHCR lexicon. Taba uses the term *relocation* rather than resettlement and consequently it is not clear whether it intended to adopt UNHCR procedures and criteria. This circumlocution may be deliberate to avoid the confusion referred to above with regard to the ambiguous use of the term *resettlement* in Arabic. Taba does prioritize in that there is an agreement to give preferential treatment to the Palestinian refugees in Lebanon who, in accordance with criteria set by the RH, would be a priority. The Ayalon-Nusseibeh Plan addresses the issue of resettlement or relocation to a third country primarily as a compensation matter. The most important weakness of the proposals with regard to this issue, however, lies in the absence of a mechanism to translate any bilateral agreement into a regional and international one. This would require a comprehensive and multilateral approach in resettlement, which all the proposals lack.

Reconciliation and reparation. Two final issues that are fundamental to the achievement of lasting solutions to refugee crises are those of reconciliation and reparation. They are discussed in greater detail in Chapters 6 and 7. It is significant that neither receive much attention in the handbooks under discussion. The VRH considers reconciliation as part of the overall political settlement but does not explore the theme in any detail. It states:

> Most UNHCR-organized repatriation, in particular those following wars or decolonization, take place after political settlements. There may be a delicate balance between parties seeking to control the pace of return movements for political reasons, and government of asylum [sic] favouring rapid return as a solution to the refugee problem. In other instances, return and reintegration, and the assistance associated with it, are themselves foreseen as elements in national reconciliation. (UNHCR, 1996: 61)

It is also significant to note that neither of the handbooks under analysis mention reparations or compensation. In marked contrast to the other options available to refugees in international practice, the option of compensation receives extensive attention in the Palestinian and Israeli proposals under discussion. For example, at the Camp David II summit, Israel proposed the establishment of an international fund to compensate refugees in which Israel, the United States, and Europe would contribute (MidEastWeb, 2000a, 2000b: 2). At the Taba Talks, while the Israeli side rejected restitution of Palestinian refugees' property, it did go further than Camp David by agreeing that a "small-sum" compensation would be paid to refugees in the "fast-track" procedure, which would cover claims of compensation for property losses below a certain amount (Eldar, 2002: 3). The Ayalon-Nusseibeh Plan stated that the international community would compensate those who wished to immigrate to third-party countries and that a Host State Remuneration Committee would be established for remuneration of host states (Ayalon-Nusseibeh Plan, 2004: 4). The Geneva Accord had the greatest amount of detail on compensation. It proposed a framework not only for property loss resulting from the displacement of refugees, but for refugeehood itself (Geneva Accord, 2003: 7).

It is important to note that in these areas the VRH falls behind current thinking in UNHCR. The Convention Plus consultations recognize that reconciliation and durable refugee returns are intrinsically connected and should not be seen as an optional add-on (Refugee Studies Centre, 2005: 97). Ana Garcia Rodicio has argued "that voluntary repatriation is an integral part of the post-conflict reconciliation process and should be understood as such in order to be a durable solution for refugees when they go back to their country of origin" (Rodicio, 2006: 217). The notion of national reconciliation through return is completely absent in the Palestinian-Israeli proposals under scrutiny. Refugee return is treated as an outcome of the political agreement sought and not as part of any reconciliation process. One exception to this pattern is the Geneva Accord, which recognizes that reconciliation involves a process of ongoing engagement between the two sides. It includes provision for reconciliation programs ranging from the exchange and dissemination of historical narratives to cultural programs commemorating Palestinian villages that existed prior to 1949. As will be discussed in Chapter 7, while this is a step forward from previous proposals, it is inadequate in that it is different from the broader and more far-reaching process of reconciliation envisaged by UNHCR.

Micro-Level Issues

This section examines international practice in terms of its micro-level implementation and compares this practice to the way the issues identified are dealt with in the Palestinian-Israeli proposals under scrutiny. To this end, four issues are discussed: the role of a lead agency, holistic or broad-based development, interagency cooperation, and, finally, monitoring and evaluation procedures.

Role of a lead agency. One of the primary mechanisms that the international community and the UNHCR have adopted is that of identifying a lead agency to deal with the refugee problem. This issue vis-à-vis the role of UNRWA will be discussed in greater detail in Chapter 4. At this point, I wish simply to delineate the broad outline of the concept with reference to our two main documents, the VRH and RH. The VRH stipulates that the mandate of UNHCR includes promoting solutions and facilitating repatriation by contributing "to national, regional and international efforts to deal with and resolve the root causes of population displacement within the practical and political limits presented by a particular situation" (UNHCR, 1996: 15).

It is also mandated to consult and engage with refugees in finding durable solutions, secure the political goodwill of the refugees' country of origin and the international community, facilitate voluntary repatriation when refugees desire this, as well as to monitor repatriation to their country of origin. The RH identifies the role of UNHCR as providing alternative solutions for refugees unable to return home or to remain in their country of refuge (UNHCR, 2002: I/2). As the lead agency, its job is to function as a clearinghouse for applications for resettlement, to establish the eligibility of the applicant, to coordinate with third country governments in their resettlement programs, and to evaluate the effectiveness and the protection afforded to refugees by those programs.

As we have seen, because other UN agencies concerned with Palestinian refugees were already in place before the creation of the UNHCR, it is understandable that it is not mentioned in any of the Palestinian-Israeli proposals. Indeed, there is no explicit reference to the role of any lead agency at all. Instead there are frequent references to UNRWA in both the Taba Talks and the Geneva Accord, where it is agreed that UNRWA should be phased out over a period of five years, after which it would cease to exist. To replace UNRWA, both Taba and the Geneva Accord called for the establishment of an International Commission and an International Fund as a mechanism for dealing with compensation in all its aspects. Indeed the impression gained from the Geneva Accord is that the International Commission would function as a lead agency, though not named as such. It would have international support from the UN, UNRWA, the World Bank, as well as other countries such as the United States, the Arab host countries, the EU, Switzerland, Canada, Norway, Japan, the Russian Federation, and others. The work of the International Commission would be carried out by various committees—Technical Committees, Status-Determination Committees, a Host State Remuneration Committee, a Compensation Committee, a Permanent Place of Residence Committee (PPR Committee), a Refugeehood Fund Committee, and a Rehabilitation and Development Committee. It is noteworthy how these proposals in effect recreate the functions of UNHCR as a lead agency without calling upon UNHCR to provide those functions, deliberately sidestepping its involvement! A possible consideration in this formulation of what was effectively a lead agency was to avoid the imposition of UNHCR's protection mandate and legal terms of reference, which would bring into question many of the positions held by both Israel and those Arab states that also oppose UNHCR involvement and are not signatories of the 1951 Refugee Convention.

Holistic development. Over the years, the experience of finding durable solutions to refugee crises has led the international community to recognize the need to avoid "exilic bias" and to ensure that aid and development are directed in such a way as to include the broader community as well as refugees (Black, 2006: 28; Fagen, 2006: 54; Refugee Studies Centre, 2005: 90–100). This particularly has been the case following a civil war or conflict, such as in Bosnia-Herzegovina and Croatia where refugees of an ethnic group may have received assistance packages that caused resentment in members of a different ethnic group who were not refugees. But resentment and accusations of discrimination has also occured between refugees and nonrefugees of the same ethnic group or national group. The VRH is clear that, in general, it is neither possible nor desirable to make distinctions between the displaced and the other affected persons in the same area except on the basis of actual need (UNHCR, 1996: 75). The only proposal under scrutiny that appears to reflect some sensitivity toward this is the Geneva Accord, but it does so in reference to what is known as the capacity building in host countries, that is, in the logistics and expertise, in developing a program of local integration. The proposed Rehabilitation and Development Committee has the goal of pursuing refugee rehabilitation and community development in Palestine, the host countries, and third countries through programs for personal and communal development, housing, education, healthcare, retraining, and other needs. The accord clearly states that such capacity building should be integrated in the general development plans for the region (Geneva Accord, 2003: 7.11, ix). The creation of an International Fund proposed in Camp David, Taba, the Ayalon-Nusseibeh Plan, and the Geneva Accord has been designed specifically to compensate the refugees rather than fulfilling the needs of a development program. One should also note that the VRH identifies vulnerable groups that need special care. These include unaccompanied children; the elderly, handicapped, and chronically ill; unaccompanied women; and single heads of households (UNHCR, 1996: 85). None of these groups are identified in the proposals under review.

Interagency coordination. Another valuable experience of the international community has been the importance of intergovernmental, interagency, and NGO coordination, not only in the strategic direction of agreeing on a solution as described in the section above, but also in the implementation of the programs themselves. Such coordination includes cross-border coordination as well as program delivery coordination with NGOs and local and municipal institutions. The VRH suggests that cross-border coordination is necessary for security considerations, travel arrangements, and movement of belongings (UNHCR, 1996: 99). Cross-border coordination is also necessary in resettlement activities. The RH states that regional resettlement officers have a vital role to play in coordinating resettlement activities and in making sure that consistent resettlement criteria are maintained to avoid imbalances (UNHCR, 2002: VII/15). Of the proposals under review, only the Geneva Accord recognized the need for such cross-border coordination, which would be undertaken by the proposed International Commission.

In turning to interagency coordination, the VRH stresses that cooperation with other NGOs is an important aspect of repatriation activities (UNHCR, 1996: 32, A8). Cooperation should encompass an extensive range of agencies, such as the UN Department of Humanitarian Affairs for intra-UN coordination; the UNDP for rehabilitation and long-term integration; the ICRC for prisoners of war, war wounded, detainees, deportees, separated families, and IDPs; and CARE and GTZ for handling transportation and logistics of refugees. The RH refers to the Working Group on Resettlement, which meets on a regular basis and comprises the UNHCR, the International Organization for Migration (IOM), and governments of resettlement countries (UNHCR, 2002: II/7). In contrast, of the proposals under review, only the Geneva Accord mentions some aspect of coordination, but this is limited largely to UNCCP and UNRWA in requesting relevant documentary records and archival materials in their possession necessary for the functioning of the commission and its committees.

In addition to intergovernmental and interagency coordination, the VRH specifies coordination with local institutions. For example, there should be coordination with the Education Ministry of the country of origin to arrange for recognition of the documentation of students and teachers, which should be provided to them before their return (UNHCR, 1996: 97). Another aspect of coordination with official bodies in the country of origin concerns a declaration of amnesties and the provision of guarantees, which UNHCR may find it necessary to insist on before voter registration to prevent misuse of information. Other studies have shown the importance of capacity building of local and municipal governments prior to any program of repatriation, integration, or resettlement. The Palestinian-Israeli proposals refer to coordination with government but solely in the context of host and third countries. None of these proposals refer to local and municipal government. The Palestinian-Israeli proposals do reflect an appreciation of the role of various NGOs and international bodies in terms of funding purposes, but none in respect to implementing the proposals.

Evaluation and monitoring. A final element of international experience in implementing the three durable solutions to refugee crises is monitoring and evaluating the protection of returned refugees. UNHCR regards its returnee monitoring role as limited and as a final safety net. The VRH states that the

> UNHCR's returnee monitoring role alone will never provide a mechanism for ensuring the safety of returnees and respect for human rights standards in the country of return. It can be a helpful influence to enhance respect for amnesties, guarantees, the rule of law and human rights but should never be seen as a substitute for state responsibility. (UNHCR, 1996: 74)

The VRH goes on to suggest some basic guidelines for acquiring information and documentation, moving and reintegrating refugees, dealing with returnee women, following the rule of law, protecting human rights and witnesses, and building confidence. UNHCR is also concerned with the monitoring of amnesties and guarantees, access to land, demobilization of combatants, and removal of land mines. Of the Palestinian-Israeli proposals, the Geneva Accord allocates some monitoring functions allocated to the various committees that are proposed, but these deal more with the implementation of the agreement rather than the well-being of the refugees themselves and their conditions in their place of permanent residence.

Conclusion

From this comparison of those aspects of peace agreements that have sought to address the refugee issue, we can see that the proposals put forward in both the official and Track II arenas in the Middle East peace process sadly fail to meet the guidelines developed by UNHCR. A number of key areas are sidestepped, such as international law in reference to refugees and the participation of refugee communities in crafting solutions, while in other areas the proposals are weak and undeveloped. This clearly has implications for the permanence of any agreements established in the Middle East. A possible weakness of this analysis is the inconsistency in evaluating the Middle East peace process by the standards set by UNHCR when at the same time the UNHCR definition of what is a refugee is not being employed in that process. The more limited definition of who is a refugee would make the numbers more manageable and an Israeli accommodation may therefore be more forthcoming. However, there is the counterargument that the handbooks are drawn from a wider body of international law than just the convention, so whether or not the Palestinian refugees fall under the convention definition is irrelevant as it is the wider body of law that is applicable. But even allowing for this more limited definition of refugee, and therefore smaller numbers of returning refugees, the existential nature of Israel as a specifically Jewish state (discussed in Chapter 1) would still be threatened. And the repatriation of those (now few and aged) refugees who were actually born in Palestine before 1948 would in no way solve the problem of Palestinian self-determination, which is tied up with the right of return of all (or at least most) refugees, including the children, grandchildren, and. by now, great-grandchildren of those who left in 1948.

In addition, the argument of this study is that international experience suggests that short-cuts do not work and that tailoring agreements solely to meet political exigencies can lead to instability and fresh rounds of tension and conflict. With these considerations in mind, this study proceeds to examine what it has identified as critical issues in the formulation of feasible and durable solutions, that is, the options of local integration, resettlement, and repatriation; the role of a lead agency in repatriation and resettlement; the issue of reparation and compensation; and finally, the growing recognition of the role of reconciliation in making an agreement work.

4

LOCAL INTEGRATION, RESETTLEMENT, AND REPATRIATION

Protracted as it has been, the current situation of the Palestinian refugees cannot continue indefinitely. It is an injustice to be addressed and a wrong that requires righting. In addition, as has already been noted, the refugee population continues to increase dramatically, which greatly adds to the political instability in the region. The argument of this book is that serious consideration should be given to the experience that the international community already possesses in formulating policy options to tackle this ever-worsening situation. UN agencies, international NGOs, and donor countries have acquired valuable experience in dealing with refugee situations, and new policies and institutions are being established in order to meet new challenges arising from forced migration flows. Those concerned with the Arab-Israeli conflict, and with the Middle East peace process in particular, may not always be aware of these ideas, practices, and resources or may not have thought them especially relevant. This, I believe, has been erroneous. That is not to say, however, that we have here a model that can be implemented in the Arab-Israeli case. Indeed, this case has its own uniqueness. Rather, the argument of the book is more nuanced and asserts that certain legal, institutional, and policy instruments can be utilized to suggest a broader range of policy options than are currently recognized that may flesh out the present proposals. It may even be seen that some aspects of the impasse need not actually be matters for dispute. Thus, the range of policies may be increased, which in turn should allow for greater flexibility and more possibilities for compromise.

This chapter will examine the three main traditional alternatives that have been considered during the past few decades as presenting—in the lexicon of the humanitarian assitance field—durable solutions for forced migration and refugees: local integration into the host country, resettlement to a third country, and repatriation to the country of origin. The objective is to draw out from the experience of the international community those elements that may be of assistance in framing policy options in the Middle East peace process. I will try to establish if there are tools available that can help reframe the debate or help clarify the key sticking points.

The first section will describe the main trends in international practice and the evolution of ideas and institutions designed to deal with forced migration. Some of this has been touched upon in Chapter 3 and will be explored from a different angle in Chapter 5 when we consider the role of lead agencies in tackling refugee crises. This chapter will focus more specifically on the three durable solutions to refugee crises and how they have been debated and operationalized.

The next section will go on to examine the first two of the durable solutions—local integration and resettlement—and consider how they have been dealt with in the Middle East peace process. As was mentioned in Chapter 1, there has been ambiguity throughout the literature with different definitions of the term *resettlement*. To some authors, particularly those in the field of forced migration and refugee studies, the term applies to resettlement in a third country following a transfer from the initial country of asylum; to others, mainly those in the field of Arab-Israeli conflict studies, the word refers to resettlement in the current host country or the initial country of asylum. In the field of forced migration studies and refugee studies, resettlement is also known as local integration, but also sometimes as assimilation. The focus of this section will be both host country integration and third country resettlement. The term *host country* refers, in this instance, to that of first asylum, that is, the place where the refugees initially reside after leaving their country of origin; *third country* refers to another country that agrees to resettle refugees from a host country. For the purposes of this discussion, I have adopted the terminology of forced migration and refugee studies in order to connect up with comparative work, but also because it seems to clarify the processes that are taking place and that need to take place. In studying the Arab-Israeli conflict, there is a tendency to get submerged in specifics and fail to see the patterns that broader disciplines can reveal.

In the third section, I will examine the third durable solution—that of repatriation. As we have already seen, the idea of repatriation to the country of origin cannot apply to the Palestinian refugee case as it does to other refugee situations. The country of origin, Palestine, never existed as a modern state and the putative nature of it under the British Mandate has been partially replaced by another country altogether, Israel, and the remaining parts have been annexed and temporarily administered by Jordan and Egypt. Thus, the term *repatriation* has also to be qualified when applied to the Middle East peace process. Here we need to use it in the territorial sense and as country of origin rather than as state of origin. Despite this qualification, the section will seek to demonstrate that a consideration of international practice can still be useful both in framing the operational aspects of a refugee program and in "de-demonizing" some of the anxieties around repatriation per se.

The final section will draw together these discussions to assess the usefulness of this exercise and to consider a number of other related issues that have to be taken into account, including that of reparations and compensation, which will be the subject for the following chapter.

The Evolution of International Practice for Durable Solutions

Local Integration and Resettlement

One of the dilemmas facing international relief efforts with regard to refugee situations is what is known as the relief-development gap. On the one hand, the provision of emergency assistance programs is the most frequent response to forced migration flows; on the other hand, what is required in the long term is continuity, development, self-sufficiency, and stability. Refugees often find themselves recipients of emergency assistance and relief aid, which allows them to survive, but then also find that they are kept in a state of limbo indefinitely with the danger of being dropped at the end of a budgetary cycle without a clear resolution of their situation. Local integration and resettlement have been the options put forward in planning a way out of the immediate crisis on a more sustainable basis. The intention of resettlement has not been only to alleviate the situation for refugees, but also was designed to assist the countries of asylum and to encourage local support for the refugees (UNHCR, 2002: I/2). However, as we shall see, the more the UN agencies and NGOs attempted to put such policies into practice, the more it became apparent that these policies had knock-on effects that also had to be confronted. Local integration could be politically and economically destabilizing; resettlement broke up supportive communities and left the weak and unqualified behind; and, furthermore, the causes of the forced migration may not have been addressed, thus causing more refugee flows. Aid agencies realized that trying to put into practice durable solutions required a comprehensive package of measures involving relief, development, conflict resolution, and rehabilitation.

It was not until the 1960s and 1970s, in response to several large refugee crises, that the policy of resettlement became an established practice (Stein, 1983: 187–201; UNHCR, 2002: I/8). During the Cold War, resettlement was a preferred option as the capitalist West sought to accommodate those fleeing the Communist bloc. Refugees from Eastern Europe after 1952, followed by the Cubans and the Chinese in the 1960s, and then refugees from Tibet, Uganda, and Latin America during the 1970s were all permitted to resettle in the West (UNHCR, 2000: 84-85; Helton, 2002: 271). As Fagen notes, resettlement was "commonly understood to be the only acceptable durable solution," though in reality, it resulted in "a continuing outflow" to the receiving nations (Fagen, 2006: 5). Charles Keely also points out that a dual refugee regime emerged with a "southern" regime for developing countries based on emergency assistance and the "warehousing" of refugees and a "northern" regime for developed countries that was in essence an asylum regime (Keely, 2001: 303–314). With the end of the Cold War, the southern regime of warehousing refugees in huge camps became in itself a humanitarian disaster. A UNHCR report stated that due to their impoverished conditions, lack of opportunities, and the absence of participatory rights, camps wasted the potential of refugees to live productive lives. Furthermore, such conditions could "serve as incubators for future problems," which could lead to dissatisfaction, disillusion, violence, instability, and even conflict (UNHCR, 2004). Resettlement provided an alternative and more stable environment for refugees and reduced the host country's security fears. As Joanne Van Selm asserts, resettlement was about "giving refugees the chance to get their lives back" (Van Selm, 2004: 41). At the same time, opening up the borders of communist Europe, cheap air travel, and developing road infrastructures had an impact upon the "northern" refugee regime of resettlement. In essence, it faced collapse as the flow of asylum seekers increased to encompass flows from Eastern Europe, Asia, Africa, and Latin America at a time when economic downturn and employment protection was heightening domestic anxieties (Refugee Studies Centre, 2005: 72–73).

Other problems began to emerge. Although influxes of refugees are more easily accommodated in more developed countries, they can still strain its political, social, and economic climate. There are therefore limits on what is known as the "local community's absorption capacity" (Jacobsen, 1996: 666). Indeed, refugees can face many difficulties in resettling and integrating in another country, having to confront competition over employment opportunities, housing, and welfare conditions, as well as general hostility (Stein, 1983: 199; UNHCR, 2000: 281; UNHCR, 2002: I/15–I/16). In addition, resettlement can be seen as being guided by the foreign policy interests of donor countries offering cooperation with allies of the receiving country (Helton, 2002: 253). Finally, resettlement has also been resisted both by the receiving countries and by the refugees themselves, who in many cases prefer repatriation (Jacobsen, 1996: 658). As Karen Jacobsen explains, resettlement has been an important response to refugee situations in Southeast Asian countries but has been less "vigorously pursued" in African countries, primarily due to the lack of support that has been shown for it by the refugees themselves (Jacobsen, 1996: 662–663).

As we have seen, the main guardian of refugee interests is UNHCR, which has had to consider the efficacy of the resettlement option. UNHCR has put forward the three main aims of resettlement as international protection, the provision of a durable solution, and a means of burden-sharing with host countries (UNHCR, 2002: I/1; Van Selm, 2004: 40). These aims are echoed in many of the works on resettlement and are often used as a framework to assist resettlement policies. In practice, UNHCR has advocated a flexible and complementary response, often in conjunction with the other durable solutions, in order to meet the diverse needs of the refugee populations (UNHCR, 2001: 1–2). As I noted in Chapter 3, it has also highlighted the importance of prioritizing those refugees who have special needs, including women-at-risk, children, adolescents, those with medical requirements, those who are victims of violence and torture, and the elderly.

However, because the challenges confronting the international community with regard to forced migration do not remain the same, UNHCR has had to reevaluate its work. There has been a growing awareness that traditional solutions were insufficient to deal with the new responsibilities being thrust or urged upon it. These included the need for greater cooperation with other UN agencies and humanitarian organizations such as UNDP, the UN World Food Programme (WFP), the UN Children's Fund (UNICEF), the World Bank, the International Organization for Migration (IOM), and the International Labour Organization (ILO); the need to engage with UN-mandated peacekeeping forces; and the need to respond to the legal and institutional vacuum surrounding IDPs and returned refugees in postconflict situations (Refugee Studies Centre, 2005: 89). In addition, there was a growing awareness that security concerns of developed countries were at odds with, and even overriding, the resettlement option. As a result, UNHCR embarked upon a number of "global consultations" leading to some new and interconnected initiatives, which are relevant here.

The Global Consultations on International Protection launched in 2000 led to the Agenda for Protection, which identified a number of key objectives that strengthened the link between development and refugee protection (Refugee Studies Centre, 2005: 91). This in turn led to the Convention Plus initiative, which sought to operationalize the Agenda for Protection by establishing multilateral agreements between governments and humanitarian agencies and developing Comprehensive Plans of Action to deal with new refugee situations. In 2003, a special unit was established in UNHCR headquarters in Geneva to carry forward the initiative. There were three main elements in Convention Plus: the renewed commitment to resettlement as a means of protection, the targeting of development assistance to support durable solutions for refugees through local integration or repatriation, and a clarification of actions to be taken resulting from secondary migrations. In order to bridge the relief-development divide and to target development assistance to refugees, UNHCR also launched its Framework for Durable Solutions, which had three elements: Development Assistance for Refugees (DAR), Development through Local Integration (DLI), and Repatriation, Reintegration, Rehabilitation, and Reconstruction (4Rs).

These initiatives were designed to enhance the structures laid down by the 1951 Convention, hence were collectively given the term *Convention Plus*. The objective was to make attaining durable solutions for refugees more feasible through a mix of burden sharing and capacity building. Nevertheless, while Convention Plus included the strategic use of resettlement as a tool for protection and as a concrete form of burden sharing, one can argue that in the main these initiatives were partly a response to the collapse of the northern refugee regime and in part driven by the increased security fears of the donor countries. Thus, the main target was seen in some circles as "burden shifting," that is, absolving the West of its responsibilities through an emphasis on reintegration and repatriation with some resettlement thrown in to ensure some burden sharing. Statistics to support this view are too early to be conclusive, but there is some indication that while there is a decline in asylum applications to the West and refugee numbers, there is a rise in IDP numbers (Refugee Studies Centre, 2005: 28). If this trend is to continue, it would indicate that Western countries have been successful in containing the flow of refugees to their borders.

Repatriation

From the above discussion we can see how, quite naturally, repatriation has remained a constant theme running through the debate over durable options for refugees. Indeed, the focus on repatriation has increased over the past fifteen years. Even before the increased security fears arising from September 11, which have decreased the willingness of the developed world to consider the resettlement option, repatriation was acknowledged to be the "most preferred option" of the international community's assistance to refugees. The former High Commissioner of UNHCR Sadoka Ogata declared the 1990s to be the "decade of repatriation" (cited in Black, 2006: 25). What the international community has learned, however, is that repatriation does not consist simply of constructing the political and legal conditions so that refugees can return to their former homes. The process is far more complex than that, and each case requires a raft of specific measures to deal not only with the logistics of return but also with the reintegration of returned refugees and their host community. Nevertheless, it is possible to identify three main elements that can be described as prerequisites for repatriation to be a durable solution: international involvement, refugee participation, and the consolidation of local and regional structures. Many of the points outlined below are derived from my previously published work (Dumper, 2006c). A fourth equally important element is that of justice and reconciliation, and this is dealt with in more detail in Chapter 7.

In turning to the first element, that is, of international involvement, one can see how this in turn comprises at least three main aspects: the involvement of UNHCR, of key regional actors, and of the humanitarian and donor community. Since the 1990s, most repatriation programs are supported by trilateral agreements with either UNHCR or a regional body, the countries of origin and of asylum, and guarantees from key international players. The extent to which this is recognized can be seen in UNHCR's VRH, discussed in Chapter 3, where detailed sections suggest the contents of clauses to be included in any peace agreement, including the repatriation of refugees; the formation of a "tripartite commission" composed of the country of origin, the country of asylum, and UNHCR (or another lead agency); and the participation of refugees in the formulation of a repatriation program. It argues that tripartite commissions are

> a good way to build confidence, resolve differences, and secure a level of agreement and commitment to the basic principles of voluntary repatriation. Such commissions and their technical ad hoc or sub-committees also have a role to play concerning the practical aspects of planning, implementing and monitoring voluntary repatriation operations. (UNHCR, 1996: 33)

Repatriation is *not* a bilateral activity but is backed up by key actors in the international community and necessitates a great deal of intergovernmental coordination. Indeed the VRH contains further sections on the importance of cross-border and cross-agency communication (UNHCR, 1996: 15–40).

By the very act of seeking asylum, refugees inevitably involve neighboring countries. Neighbors may have played a role in the conflict that brought about the exile and displacement in the first place but they would have an interest in the final settlement, which would have implications for them in terms of the stability of their governance, the future of the refugees they are hosting, and their role as a transit country. The roles of Pakistan, Thailand, Mexico, and Kenya in their neighboring conflicts are examples of this. International experience has shown that a regional framework that allows for consultation and input in the planned repatriation therefore is an important factor in the viability of a repatriation program. The role of CIREFCA in the Guatemalan case, NATO and the EU in the Bosnian case, and Australia and the United States in the East Timor case are examples. International involvement is also apparent in the establishment of a lead agency to manage the logistics and funding of return, whether it be UNHCR, IOM, or other NGOs. Coordinating donor contributions and harmonizing their impact upon the development plans of the country of origin are vital processes for avoiding duplication and wastage. Thus, international involvement offers political guarantees and a measure of enforcement, financial support, and possibilities for enhanced cooperation and coordination.

The second element of refugee participation also comprises three main aspects: the nature of the choices available to refugees, the mechanisms of refugee involvement, and capacity building. There is a debate within the UN and other refugee agencies over voluntary repatriation. There are cases in Cambodia, Afghanistan, and Guatemala where choices were restricted to such an extent that there was in effect very little choice. Nevertheless, as we saw in Chapter 3, international practice indicates a clear commitment to the principle of transparency and refugee choice. In addition, accurate and up-to-date information is also essential in providing refugees with informed choices about conditions and options in their country of origin and countering the pattern of "imagined return communities" based on folklore and oral tradition (Black and Koser, 1999: 6–10; Stepputat, 2006: 128). UNHCR's experience, therefore, suggests that informed choices enable refugees to be actors in rather than recipients of repatriation programs. One should emphasize that international experience suggests that refugee participation is more than mere idealism, but more importantly, a shrewd use of scarce resources. The cooperation of the intended beneficiaries—the refugees themselves—engenders dynamism and energy and avoids wastage through noncooperation.

In turning to the actual mechanisms for refugee participation in constructing a repatriation program, one finds that while most large-scale returns are centrally organized by UNHCR and IOM, it is increasingly recognized that a sense of ownership in the process (a "bottom-up" approach) is an important element in ensuring that a repatriation program is acceptable to refugees (Stepputat, 2006: 129; Rodicio, 2006: 229). The VRH clearly stresses the importance of including refugee voices in the formulation of a repatriation program.

> The refugee community should be kept informed of the progress of repatriation negotiations. Formal representation of the refugee community can be considered. Whenever the refugee community is not directly involved in repatriation negotiations, UNHCR must develop and maintain regular communications with the refugees throughout the process. (UNHCR, 1996: 34)

Third, it is also recognized that the development of appropriate human resources and capacity building is essential. It is important to provide refugees with the necessary employment and organizational skills for a return. There is little point in refugees returning to a changed economic environment only to find there is no demand for the skills and training they have acquired in exile. It is clear from UNHCR's experience that it is essential to introduce gender, age, and disability perspectives into repatriation programs at an early stage of planning. The involvement of women and the elderly and other categories of the population in preparing the details of return is critical. If, for example, assistance packages for families are conveyed soley through the male head of the household, this is likely to result in the exclusion of less powerful members of the household.

As we have seen in the previous section, UN and other agencies have acknowledged that repatriation also needs to be fed into the postagreement phase, that is, into the program planning and implementation phase. Repatriation encompasses the transition from actual physical return to reintegration. This has been recognized by UNHCR with its development of the concept of the 4Rs. In this context, a repatriation program has little chance of being implemented if there are not appropriate local and regional structures in place. As a comprehensive Refugee Studies Centre report highlighted:

> Repatriation is often very complex and expensive and still frequently underestimated by the international community, which prefers to assume that the refugee "problem" ends once the refugees have been returned to their country of origin. Providers of humanitarian assistance could draw useful lessons from development actors, who often have a stronger record of employing community-based approaches to their programming. (Refugee Studies Centre, 2005: 52)

In most cases, the burden of a return process falls on the local and municipal administrative structures in the country of origin And international experience has shown that many local governments and municipal authorities do not have the training or resources to absorb large numbers of returned refugees. Moreover, a large repatriation program supported by the international community often brings with it demands from the donors for transparency and the introduction of new administrative procedures, which they simply do not have. As Finn Stepputat has argued, a repatriation program should include the upgrading of personnel skills, administrative capacity, and infrastructure, particularly of the local and municipal authorities (Stepputat, 2006: 129). Connected to this aspect of capacity building is what is known in the literature of forced migration as "exilic bias." The focus on refugees as a target population can distort the development planning of the country of origin (Refugee Studies Centre, 2005: 50). Repatriation packages frequently comprise a mixture of finance, tools, building materials, land grants, and support services to assist the returned refugees in establishing new homes and livelihoods. However, repatriation packages, developmental assistance, and compensation, directed exclusively to returned refugees, have been shown to cause resentment by the host communities and have encouraged refugees to become dependent. A holistic development approach that benefits the broader community in which the refugees are being settled is known to assist reintegration. Through the 4Rs, UNHCR can be seen as expressing a new consensus that repatriation should be incorporated into a national program of development and community assistance (Refugee Studies Centre, 2005: 99–100).

A final aspect of capacity building is connected to the element of refugee participation. Recent research recognizes that exile has meant that in many cases refugees become part of a transnational community establishing new political and social networks and economic exchanges (Black, 2006:

37; Refugee Studies Centre, 2005: 101; van Hear, 2003). This recognizes that refugees have entered a regional labor market, which has an impact on the local economy. Refugees may have actually achieved a higher standard of living in exile and acquired new skills and social and economic ties. Particularly after long periods of exile, refugees are less likely to want to repatriate unless there is the possibility of employment. There is a growing understanding that postconflict repatriation programs need to reflect the greater economic status that refugees may have achieved during their period of exile.

Local Integration and Resettlement in the Middle East Conflict

With expectations wearing thin on the part of Palestinian refugees that a return home was simply a matter of waiting for hostilities to cease, international efforts turned to longer-term alternatives. Despite the very clear terms of UN Resolution 194 calling in 1948 for the refugees to be permitted to return to their homes, many of the early efforts of the international community were actually to encourage them to integrate into the local communities or to resettle in other parts of the Middle East. As Benjamin Schiff has observed in writing of UNRWA, this had a long-term impact on how refugees viewed international interventions.

> The Palestinian refugees had been dubious about UNRWA's intentions from the very beginning—and justifiably so: the agency's top administration, representatives of the most important donor country (the United States), and some officials in the host states decided that repatriation and compensation were neither reasonable expectations nor feasible, and they wished the refugees would quietly assimilate. . . . Perhaps worse than the failure of ambitious water plans, from UNRWA's standpoint, was the sapping of refugee confidence in the organisation caused by the hypocrisy of proclaiming repatriation while planning resettlement. (Schiff, 1995: 46)

In the absence of repatriation, the principal aim in the early 1950s was to ensure the "economic and social rehabilitation" and the self-sufficiency of the refugees (Peretz, 1993: 92). To this end, a number of projects were proposed to resettle the refugees in neighboring countries. Information was gathered by UNCCP's Technical Committee on Refugees to put forward recommendations, and the result was an approach encompassing short-term and long-term plans for the whole region. One project, entitled "Palestine Refugee Problem: Financing Repatriation and Resettlement of Palestine Refugees," was also known as the McGhee Plan after the US assistant secretary of state for Near Eastern affairs. This plan involved Israel accepting the return of 200,000 refugees and relinquishing some territorial claims in exchange for the resettlement of the large part of refugees by Arab states (Peretz, 1993: 93; Schiff, 1995: 18). Although the McGhee Plan was rejected by all sides at the Lausanne Conference in 1949, further attempts were made by the UN General Assembly to encourage the neighboring Arab states to accept and rehabilitate many refugees, and initially Jordan, Egypt, and Syria were willing to cooperate (Khasan, 1994). Incentives were offered in the form of large-scale proposals for economic and social development. The most well-known of these, the UN Economic Survey Mission for the Middle East (popularly known as the Clapp Mission, after its head, Gordon R. Clapp), was based around the experience of the Tennessee Valley Authority in the United States and was a plan to improve water resources and availability to provide adequate irrigation, employment, and self-sufficient land for the refugees (Peretz, 1993, 95; Schiff, 1995: 35–46).

These efforts at alleviating the situation were rejected by the refugees because they feared the efforts were designed to deprive them of their right to return to their homes in Palestine. Even the transition from tented accommodation to shacks and concrete dwellings was resisted for many years and refugees referred to their homes as *malja'* (shelter) rather than *bayt* (home) (Schulz, 2003, 116; Bisharat, 1994: 174). It was not until the late 1960s that the activity of improving their living conditions was separated from their resistance to local integration or resettlement. As a result, by the end of the 1950s, UNRWA ceased its attempts at resettlement and concentrated more on humanitarian efforts (Schiff, 1995: 48ff). Formal relations were established setting out the parameters of UNRWA's operations with Egypt in 1950, with Jordan in 1951, with Lebanon in 1954, and with Syria in 1967 (Takkenberg, 1998: 32).

Apart from these instances of cooperation, resistance to integration and resettlement was supported in the main by the host Arab states. These options were seen as legitimizing Israeli gains and the dispossession of the Palestinians and as a step toward a de facto normalization of Israel in the region. Thus, it was not until 1965 that the host Arab states became signatories to the Arab League–sponsored Casablanca Protocol, in which Palestinian refugees were granted the right to work, reside, and have freedom of movement within the signatory states (Shiblak, 1997: 263). Even then, implementation did not always take place. As Hilal Khasan observes, many Arab states were reluctant to appear to be cooperating with Israel over local integration and resettlement, particularly during a period of increasing Arab nationalism (Khasan, 1994). Nevertheless, limited integration took place partly by default as refugees took the initiative by finding jobs and better housing for their families, making use of kinship ties that had remarkably stayed intact following their flight from Palestine, and in part (in the case of Jordan) deliberately (but discreetly) because the host country saw the advantages of the refugees' contribution to their economy.

In Chapter 2 it was shown how the degree of integration into host countries varied, with Jordanian- and Syrian-based Palestinian refugees being better accommodated than those in Lebanon. Integration and assimilation depended to a large extent on the legal and political framework in which refugees found themselves. Here we will briefly review the main issues with regard to the attitudes and policies of host countries toward local integration. The important point to emphasize, however, is that local integration has not taken place as part of a deliberate policy option but incrementally, in most cases unwillingly, and certainly by default. Thus, the preparation, investment, monitoring, and evaluation all envisaged by the formal UNHCR process set out in the RH is sadly absent in the Palestinian case.

Lebanon is the most hostile state to Palestinian refugees. The political, social, and ethnic makeup of Lebanon has determined its reaction to the refugees, and the instability within the country is largely attributed to them (Sayigh, 1995: 37–53). As an authoritative report by the BADIL Resource Centre concludes, "the situation of the nearly 400,000 Palestinian refugees in Lebanon is distinct from the situation of other Palestinian refugee communities" because Lebanese legislation is aimed at the "marginalization of Palestinian refugees in order to prevent their integration into the Lebanese social and economic fabric" (BADIL, 2000a: 19). Rebecca Roberts describes how the Lebanese authorities see the Palestinians as a destabilizing factor and consequently pursue policies against them (Roberts, 2005: 26). Between 1982, the departure of the PLO from Beirut, and 2005, the Palestinian refugee situation greatly deteriorated. There were increased restrictions on employment, housing, and health care. Palestinians were forbidden from working in over sixty professions and were subject to limitations in the labor market (Sayigh, 1995: 50; BADIL, 2000a: 20). The US Committee for Refugees reported that in 1994 all Palestinian NGOs relating to health care and education, with the exception of the Palestinian Red Crescent Society, were no longer permitted to function unless registered as Lebanese and therefore with a predominantly Lebanese workforce (US Committee for Refugees, 1999: 12–13). The Lebanese government also prevented the reconstruction of those camps destroyed as a result of the Sabra and Shatilla massacres in 1982 and the internecine war that followed. They prohibited the construction of any new camps as well as extensions to existing camps (Sayigh, 1995: 43). As a result, the Palestinian refugees have had little security and little protection of their basic rights. Indeed, the BADIL report concludes that the "Lebanese government policy aims to prevent resettlement and encourage emigration by isolating the Palestinian community" (BADIL, 2000a: 20; Sayigh, 1995: 43; El Khazen, 1997: 275). The rejection of *tawtiin*, or assimilation of refugees, has broad support across the Lebanese political spectrum. As late prime minister Rafiq al-Hariri declared in an interview in 1998,

> The Palestinian refugees currently constitute a problem for Israel as they do for the Palestinians in Lebanon. Lebanon will not help Israel solve this problem. Naturally Israel would be delighted if Lebanon assimilated them under humanitarian slogans. (cited in Bowker, 2003: 75)

As a result of all these pressures secondary Palestinian migration from Lebanon has occurred with some researchers believing that the figures for registered refugees are higher than those actually still residing in Lebanon.

In 2005, the Lebanese government eased restrictions on Palestinian employment opportunities and reconstruction and on access to welfare, but continued to advocate the overriding necessity of repatriation. Indeed, local integration continues to be contingent on "the delicate sectarian balance" within the Lebanese polity and hence is an unlikely durable solution (Salam, 1994: 18–27). In addition, as Rex Brynen has observed:

> International incentives (for example, aid to Lebanon) and disincentives (pressure on the Lebanese government to respect the rights of its Palestinian residents) may play a key role in shaping government policy. Lebanese assessments of the economic advantages (through local expenditure of compensation payments) and disadvantages (through an increased service burden caused by the eventual wind-down of UNRWA) will also play a role, as will Lebanese fears of a large-scale "implantation." (Brynen, 1997: 12)

As a result, policymakers and negotiators have recognized that the refugees in Lebanon should be prioritized in any resettlement or repatriation scheme.

The degree of integration in Jordan is much greater. Refugees enjoy more extensive rights and are a significant component of Jordanian society and the economy. Those who came to Jordan before 1954 were granted automatic citizenship and therefore enjoy the same rights, as well as the same obligations, as Jordanian citizens. From 1988, when King Hussein renounced the annexation of the West Bank, to the present, Palestinians have been allowed to apply for passports, although they have limited validity (Bowker, 2003: 74). The Jordanian government has implemented measures specifically relating to the Palestinians and established a Department for Palestinian Affairs to address their concerns and requirements and a Camp Service Improvement Committee to represent the refugees and look after the maintenance and improvement of infrastructure and services. Furthermore, Palestinians have equal access to social and economic support systems, were subject initially to military conscription, and share an educational curriculum with their East Bank counterparts (Bowker, 2003: 74).

Despite this, there are still restrictions and Palestinians often encounter difficulties in employment, the allocation of public services, and in the sphere of their political activities. While there is not anything like the same level of alienation as in Lebanon, refugees in Jordan are still committed to the right of return (Brand, 1995: 46–61). Their relation to the Jordanian government is one of requiring assistance rather than governance or representation (BADIL, 2000a: 27). Nevertheless, the issue of integration into Jordan remains both very real and very sensitive. A major project, carried out by UNRWA and the Jordanian government to improve infrastructure and services in the camps, is viewed in some quarters with suspicion and concern that it is simultaneously a sign that repatriation has disappeared as an option and that it will undermine their own will to mobilize for their right to return.

In many respects the Jordanian government finds itself placed upon the horns of a dilemma, and local integration is an option it must handle very carefully. With Palestinians making up an estimated 43 percent of the population, formal large-scale integration would prejudice the dominant role of the East Bankers in the government and the military. Thus, in the short term, integration is unlikely to be accompanied by greater political participation as the regime and its main allies seek to consolidate power. At the same time, a mass repatriation to the new Palestinian state would have a serious deleterious effect upon the Jordanian economy, particularly the private sector and government service. Due to its proximity to the West Bank and longstanding kinship and historical ties, the best option for Jordan would be to have a phased repatriation and open borders in an economic framework that allowed refugees to continue to contribute to the Jordanian economy without threatening East Banker domination.

The integration of refugees into Syria has probably proceeded the furthest, although again, not as a result of a formal policy, but more out of solidarity and support to the Palestinian cause. As was shown in Chapter 2, refugees in Syria have been given equal rights in employment, trade, and commerce, with only some exceptions, such as property ownership. A specific body addressing Palestinian affairs was established in 1949, the Palestine Arab Refugee Institution (PARI), which was later replaced by the Syrian General Authority for Palestine Arab Refugee Affairs (GAPAR). Despite early resettlement attempts in Syria in the 1950s, notably in the area bordering Iraq and Turkey, they were all rejected by the refugees (BADIL, 2000a: 35). While easing the situation for Palestinians on a humanitarian basis, Syria has frequently demonstrated in its foreign policy that repatriation is the preferred solution. In fact, as a BADIL report notes, Syria's policy with regard to Palestinian refugees

> confirms that secure civil and social rights in the host countries can protect refugees from falling victim to the dangers of resettlement and loss of their national identity. (BADIL, 2000a: 31)

One illustration of this balanced state of affairs is the rehabilitation of the Neirab refugee camp. The upgrading of accommodation and major infrastructural improvements carried out jointly by UNRWA and the Syrian government has not led to the militant rejection characteristic of the early 1950s (UNRWA, 2003a). However, it should be noted that Syria was not faced with the same demographic challenge that Lebanon or Jordan were. With one of the smallest refugee populations, the service burden was much less and therefore it was much easier for the refugees to be absorbed into the state.

It would be easy to overlook the attempts at local integration in two other areas of refugee residence: the OPTs of the West Bank and Gaza Strip. Clearly, local integration takes on a slightly different meaning here in the sense that since 1967 to all intents and purposes refugees have been integrated by being treated the same as nonrefugees by the occupying power, Israel. However, in the light of discussions that these areas should become the territory of the new Palestinian state, it is not only technically correct but also instructive to examine ways in which refugees have in fact been integrated: the extent to which their camp identities and status as refugees have been maintained, and the nature of their access to employment, housing services, and representation. Once again, the point has to be made that while there was a degree of de facto integration through the passage of time and the playing out of survival strategies by refugees, there has been no deliberate policy of integration by UNRWA or by refugee organizations. There have, however, been a series of attempts by Israeli authorities to achieve integration by dispersing the camp population.

Prior to these attempts, during the earlier period between 1948 and 1967, Palestinian refugees in the West Bank were treated by the government of Jordan in the same way as it treated those settling on the East Bank. In the Gaza Strip, however, during the adminstration of the Egyptian government, plans were drawn up to allow refugees to resettle in the Sinai Peninsula, where water would be diverted from the Nile to permit significant irrigation systems. Egypt signed a rehabilitation agreement with UNRWA in 1953, but the plans were abandoned in the wake of Abdel Nasser taking power and the Israeli invasion of the Gaza Strip in 1956 (Peretz, 1993: 96). Following the Israeli invasion of the West Bank and Gaza Strip in 1967, Israel and UNRWA exchanged letters setting out operational arrangements between them, but it soon became clear that Israel's approach to the refugee camps would be very different from that of the Arab host countries (Schiff, 1995: 195; Takkenberg, 1998: 32). As Schiff observes:

> Starting in 1967, Israeli government officials generated long-run plans for the territories. . . . Israeli objectives generally have been to isolate Palestinian communities, intersperse Israeli settlements, integrate the territories'

water and power networks into the Israeli system, and create incentives for refugees to move out of the camps into housing developments. (Schiff, 1995: 214)

Thus, partly as a result of Palestinian resistance in the early years and partly due to a longer-term strategic objective of dispersing the camp population, a mixture of incentives and unilateral measures were undertaken. For example, the army bulldozed hundreds of refugee shelters in order to build wide boulevards through the middle of the camps as a means of improving their control over resistance activities (Lesch, 1984). In addition, refugees from Rafah and Khan Yunis camps were offered homes in new housing projects but on the condition that they agreed to demolish their refugee shacks. These initiatives evolved into what became known as the "Ben Porat Plan for refugee resettlement" and envisaged the "comprehensive reconstruction" of the refugee camps. Between 1973 and 1985, some 70,000 refugees were relocated. However, by the mid-1980s, Israeli officials acknowledged that these numbers were not matching the rate of increase in the refugee population, and the camps remained as densely populated as before (Schiff, 1995: 215–218). These efforts were swept aside by the intifada in 1987.

With the arrival of the PLO in 1994 and the setting up of the PNA, a new phase began for the refugee population in the OPTs. The issue of integration remained as sensitive as ever. One should note, for example, that despite close collaboration between UNRWA and PNA ministries over capital projects and educational investment, the relationship remained the same as that between UNRWA and other host countries. The PNA was formally treated as a host government by UNRWA, and an exchange of letters constituting an agreement between UNRWA and the PLO was signed in June 1994 (Takkenberg, 1998: 32). During the 1990s, with much discussion about the future of refugees appearing in the public discourse, the question of camp rehabilitation became less of a taboo subject. It is as if the more the question of the right of return is discussed openly in all its political, social, and legal ramifications, the more refugees are able to separate out improving their living conditions from protecting their political rights. For example, following the destruction of the greater part of the Jenin refugee camp by the Israeli army in 2002, reconstruction schemes that ensured a much higher living standard were welcomed by the residents of the camp.

This focus on local integration does not mean that there have not been any other forms of Palestinian migration. Palestinians have migrated in large numbers throughout the Arab world and elsewhere. Prior to the 1991 Gulf War, there were over 350,000 Palestinians living in Kuwait. According to statistics compiled by the PLO Department of Refugee Affairs, in 1998, 10 percent of refugees resided in the non-neighboring states of the Arab world and 8 percent elsewhere (see Table 4.1.)

Table 4.1. Estimated Number of Palestinian Refugees in Areas Not Bordering Palestine, 1998

Country of Residence	Total Number of Refugees	Percentage of Refugee Population
Saudi Arabia	274,762	5.4
Other Arab Gulf countries	139,948	2.7
Iraq and Libya	73,284	1.4
Other Arab countries	5,544	0.1
Total refugees in Arab world	493,538	9.6
Rest of the world	393,411	7.7

Sources: Amended from Palestine Liberation Organization, Department of Refugee Affairs, cited in H. Abu Libdeh, "Statistical Data on Palestinian Refugees: Propects for Contribution to Final Settlement," paper presented at the 2nd International Stocktaking Conference on Palestinian Refugee Research, International Development Research Centre, Ottawa, 17–20 June 2003, p. 2; and from S. Abu Sitta, *The Palestinian Nakba 1948: The Register of Depopulated Localities in Palestine* (London: Palestinian Return Centre, 2000), p. 24.

However, this should be regarded as a form of secondary migration and cannot be strictly construed as resettlement in the sense of a durable option as defined in the literature and by UNHCR. These are spontaneous, autonomous decisions taken largely for economic reasons and do not constitute a formal solution. They are not accompanied, in the main, by the granting of citizenship and other rights.

Repatriation and the Middle East Peace Process

The issue of Palestinian repatriation in the Middle East peace process is clearly tied up with the right of return and with Israeli objections to the refugees exercising this right. As we have established already, repatriation to their homes and country of origin in the Palestinian refugee case is not the same as Afghanis returning from Pakistan or Guatemalans from Mexico. The country of origin, Palestine, has been replaced by another state, and repatriation has complex legal and existential problems for the State of Israel. As a result, no significant repatriation has taken place and is not a likely prospect in the short to medium term. In the current political conditions, as Brynen suggests, it is unlikely that there will be any significant repatriation to any part of historic Palestine for at least another ten years (Brynen, 2006: 81). Nevertheless, it is necessary to discuss the issue for a number of reasons: some repatriation has taken place in the form of family reunification; the issue has been discussed in the early days of negotiations and during more recent negotiations in Taba; and, as a result of heightened security fears of receiving countries, the decline of the option of resettlement in a third country leaves repatriation to an area within historic Palestine as one of the two alternative durable solutions available. In this sense, repatriation is still an issue requiring debate and planning. This section focuses on what can be learned from international practice and how this may be relevant to the Middle East peace process. Repatriation to Israel and to the new state of Palestine is then considered.

If we turn to the three basic elements of any repatriation program, outlined above, we can see how experience in the world community can be utilized to examine the Middle East peace process. In the first place, any peace agreement incorporating the repatriation of Palestinian refugees will require high-level international involvement. The positions of the protagonists are too entrenched to trust any agreement that does not have international guarantors. Indeed, there has already been a long period of quite intensive international involvement on the official level that can be utilized. The Madrid Peace Conference in 1991 was sponsored by two superpowers; the "multilaterals" that flowed from it, such as the RWG, included a wide range of states. The Euro-Mediterranean Partnership set up by the EU in 1995 provides an important regional forum for coordinating development plans. In addition, the role played by the EU's Special Envoy to the Middle East Peace Process Ambassador Miguel Moratinos in the Taba Peace Talks in 2001 and the role played by the Swiss government in drawing up the unofficial Geneva Accord in 2003 are measures of close European interest and support for the peace process. Finally, the "Quartet," comprising the UN, United States, Russia, and the EU, is attempting to follow on the failed Oslo process with a three-stage "road map," thus encouraging negotiations over the refugees issue. In this context, while it is significant that in both the Taba Talks and the Geneva Accord there was no reference to the experience of UNHCR or to a regional framework that includes the neighboring and host countries, to some extent the issue of international involvement has been accepted in the clauses referring to an International Commission to implement any agreement.

The Beirut Declaration of 2002, mentioned in Chapter 2, seems to provide a basis for the participation of host countries in these discussions, but the lack of clarity of what actual durable solutions were envisaged has stymied efforts in that direction. However, where these discussions in the Middle East peace process have coincided with international practice there has been a consensus for the need for international funding for both compensation and repatriation. Both the target locations for repatriation—Israel and the new Palestinian state—will require assistance to absorb refugees. All parties recognize that a Palestinian state in the West Bank and Gaza Strip will not be able to generate sufficient internal revenues to simultaneously construct a new state, provide services for a growing population, and fund a large-scale repatriation program. External financial support for a repatriation program, whether in the form of individual or collective payments, will be essential.

The second prerequisite identified from similar situations has been the importance of refugee choice and participation in planning repatriation activities. Past international experience suggests that a return to the status quo ante is rarely possible and is often undesirable. The critical issue is that the options available should be transparent. They may be contained in an overall package that in totality can be deemed a just one and therefore one that is acceptable. The package may include actual but limited return, symbolic acts of return and restitution, or a mix of return compensation and resettlement to the new Palestinian state. What is unlikely to be acceptable is the absence of any formal recognition of the right of return.

Another area in which lessons can be learned from international experience is in the creation of a sense of ownership of the decisionmaking process. In the Palestinian case, this has been difficult to achieve due to the dispersal of Palestinian refugee communities, factional divisions, and the monitoring of political activity by the host countries and Israel. Nevertheless, the attempts to sideline the right of return have produced a popular reaction. Rumors that a deal was impending at the Camp David summit in 2000 in which the Palestinian side would renounce their right of return in exchange for Israeli recognition of East Jerusalem as the capital of the new Palestinian state precipitated demonstrations in many refugee camps and the launching of coalitions of groups to mobilize against this possibility. There were similar reactions to both the Geneva Accord and the Ayalon-Nusseibeh Plan where repatriation was discussed largely, although not wholly, in terms of a return to the new state of Palestine in the West Bank and Gaza Strip. It is clear that to avoid such hostile responses, new channels for refugee participation need to be created. The representation of refugee concerns since the establishment of the PNA has been problematic. The PLO has been weakened, and while it still retains a legitimacy as the formal representative body, its scope of activities has been challenged by other groups (International Crisis Group, 2004: 14). At the same time, radical Islamic groups and the various right of return committees that have been set up in the host countries and the OPTs are not consulted by the leadership. In the Palestinian context, UNRWA can be considered as a possible vehicle for such representation, fulfilling the functions normally taken up by UNHCR in this regard.

The third prerequisite concerned local and regional development. As discussed earlier, in exile, refugees had to become economic actors in a broader regional market. There is much evidence that this has also occurred in the Palestinian case with its transnational networks and the integration of refugees into the local economies of the OPTs, Jordan, and Syria (Hanafi, 1996). In addition, all the major Palestinian refugee camps are very close to either Israel or the OPTs. Thus, family, business, and political networks that have developed in exile are likely to encourage Palestinian returned refugees to remain part of the regional labor market. A Palestinian repatriation program needs to be flexible enough to build on these networks as a developmental and integrative asset. This suggests that any agreement to a transitional period should specify which refugees are permitted to retain residency status in the host country for a number of years in order that employment and accommodation in the place of destination can be explored. The Arab League could even be asked to consider temporarily suspending clauses in its charter prohibiting dual citizenship.

The issue of exilic bias needs to be considered in this context. Some have argued that the OPTs and Israel are too small for huge regional disparities to develop (Brynen, 2003). In addition, family networks remain strong and cut across the refugee-nonrefugee divide. Thus, in a kind of ripple effect, the wider Palestinian community will receive benefits from a repatriation program. However, recent research seems to conclusively show that the strong bonds developed during the period of exile are intensified during the reintegration phase (Rodicio, 2006: 226). In these circumstances, tensions between the returned Palestinian refugees and the host community must be considered as likely. This has been seen during the brief period of time when access to the West Bank from the Gaza Strip was eased in the late 1990s and refugees from Gaza were blamed for a dramatic rise in crime in the West Bank. A holistic approach to refugee absorption is thus very relevant in the Palestinian case. Finally, as we observed earlier, repatriation often places a disproportionate burden on local and municipal structures. In the Palestinian case, some authorities may not have sufficient resources to assist in the reintegration program, or the trained personnel to deal with specific refugee requirements such as information about entitlements (World Bank, 2003b). In any case, it is likely that external donors will require a high degree of transparency in procedures and accountability. Thus, a program of human resource development and capacity building at the lower levels of government will need to be prioritized.

Repatriation to Israel

Although repatriation to Israel proper is clearly a problematic option, it has had some serious consideration in the past. The basis on which any repatriation program could be constructed was Resolution 194 (III), which declared that "the refugees wishing to return to their homes and live at peace with their neighbours should be permitted to do so at the earliest practicable date."

Following their displacement in 1948, Palestinians expected to be allowed to return and to receive compensation for any damage to their property. However, for Israelis, the operable clause was "live at peace with their neighbours," which was interpreted as the need for refugees to accept the Jewishness of the State of Israel. Refugees would not be allowed to return unless Arab leaders accepted the reality of the State of Israel and made peace with it. Nonetheless, recognizing the international concern provoked by the creation of a huge refugee problem, Israel did offer to accept the return of refugees on a limited basis. At the Lausanne Conference in 1949, Israel offered to repatriate initially 200,000 but then reduced it to 100,000 refugees, some 10 percent of the total, as part of a family reunification program and only on condition that the remainder of the refugees were absorbed into the surrounding region (Peretz, 2000: 193; Takkenberg, 1998: 263). In this context, Israel would offer compensation instead of the restitution of refugee property (Fischbach, 2003: 92). Administratively it also set up a "Custodian" first of Abandoned Property and then of Absentee Property, ostensibly to safeguard the property pending a negotiated agreement over its future. Peretz estimates that 40,000 of the 100,000 permits for family reunification were issued before 1967. Unfortunately, and surprisingly, very little is known about the details of this program. It would make a useful and perhaps important contribution to policy discussions if we knew how Palestinian families and individuals were selected, what their experience on return was like, and what impact their return had on their family and the wider Palestinian and Jewish community in Israel.

After the Israeli occupation of the West Bank and Gaza Strip in 1967, Israel again refused to accept the return of Palestinians displaced by the conflict variously estimated as being between 500,000 and 1 million (Exeter Refugee Study Team, 2001: 13). Instead it agreed to a "family reunion programme" (popularly known as *lamm al-shaml*), which was facilitated by UNRWA. According to a leading Israeli adviser on the refugee issue, Shlomo Gazit, over 70,000 Palestinians have been repatriated, since 1967, while Peretz puts the figure at 93,000 permits issued since 1967 (Peretz, 1993: 192; Takkenberg, 1998: 339). The ICRC reported that between 1967 and 1987, 140,000 families applied for reunification; of these, 19,000 were accepted by Israel. However, as time progressed, the criteria were tightened up until eventually family reunification was restricted only to husbands (Takkenberg, 1998: 264). What is clear is that only a little more than 10 percent of the estimated totals have been repatriated.

Following the Madrid Peace Conference in 1991 and the setting up of the Multilateral Working Group on Refugees, Israel agreed to raise the annual limit for family reunification from 1,000 to 5,000 persons, although there has been no verification of this (Peters, 1996: 33). The most recent concrete discussions on repatriation took place after the Oslo Accord and Israeli-Jordanian peace agreement in 1994. A Quadripartite Committee comprising the PLO, Israel, Egypt, and Jordan was set up to discuss the "modalities of admission of persons displaced from the West Bank and Gaza in 1967." Unfortunately, despite a number of meetings, the Quadripartite Committee failed to agree on a definition of "displaced persons," and no new scheme was put into place. Also in 1995, the Oslo II agreement, which provided the framework for a transfer of some powers from Israel to the PNA, empowered the PNA to grant work, study, and visitor permits and to extend and upgrade these permits to residency status. Nevertheless, those provisions pertaining to family reunification were still dependent on prior clearance with the Israeli government.

In Camp David II, Israel is said to have discussed the possibility of accepting the return to Israel of 100,000 refugees on "humanitarian" grounds (MidEastWeb, 2000a: 2). At Taba, there was discussion over repatriation to Israel. Significantly, this was in addition to any family reunification program, and discussions centered around a three-track, fifteen-year absorption program. The first track referred to the absorption of 25,000 to 40,000 refugees into Israel proper, while the other two tracks referred to repatriation to areas of Israel transferred to the new state of Palestine in any land swaps and to a family reunification scheme. There is some evidence to suggest that a higher figure would be contemplated by Israel. The detailed clauses discussed include the absorption of 25,000 refugees over three years in a fifteen-year program, which would amount to 125,000 (Eldar, 2002: 3.2). However, no agreement was reached and, more importantly, it was never clear to what extent the Israeli negotiators under Yossi Beilin were being backed up by their prime minister. In the Geneva Accord, no figures were given, but it was stated that "as a basis, Israel will consider the average of the total numbers submitted by the different third countries to the International commission" (Geneva Accord, 2003: 7.v.c). Thus, an Israeli figure would depend upon the extent of resettlement in third countries.

Since 1948, therefore, the Israeli approach to the issue of repatriation has been on the one hand to emphatically reject it, but on the other hand to consider some limited returns on an ad hoc basis and strictly under the rubric of family reunification. This approach emphasized return as a humanitarian gesture and specified that no legal precedent for repatriation was being set. Indeed, even after the signing of the Israeli-Jordanian peace treaty in 1994, in which Palestinians with Jordanian citizenship would no longer be classed as enemies, the Israeli government quickly passed a law declaring that Palestinian absentees classified as such prior to the peace treaty would remain classified as absentees (Fischbach, 2003: 332). To my knowledge, there has been no contingency planning for repatriation as such at any time since 1948.

As was shown in Chapter 1 and will be shown in Chapter 5 and the Appendix, many Palestinians have carried out research documenting the loss of Palestinian land and collecting photographic and oral histories of the villages and towns that were abandoned in their flight. The most authoritative of these is the comprehensive work undertaken by Walid Khalidi and his team at the Institute of Palestine Studies (Khalidi, 1992). Important as these are in establishing a documentary archive, they remain historical works without a policy orientation. The only detailed work carried out on the possibility of actual repatriation has been by Salman Abu Sitta, director of the Palestine Land Society, who puts forward the thesis that a full repatriation of all Palestinian refugees to their homes in Israel is "sacred, legal and feasible." While brushing aside the enormous political obstacles in the way of his proposals, they do have the merit of highlighting the technical feasibility of repatriation. Abu Sitta's method is to disaggregate the refugees' places of origin and identify the large number of sites, particularly of villages, that are either still in existence or, although destroyed, not built over. In this way a significant number of Palestinians could return without any dramatic displacement of the Israeli Jewish population. For example, he refers to the refugees from Syria and Lebanon, who are

> the registered villagers from the districts of Haifa, Acre, Tibrias, Safad and Nazareth—excluding cities. All these refugees can return safely to their vacant village sites. There are only few affected villages, where their village sites have been partially or fully built-over. . . . In general, these refugees will return to a friendly environment. They will be reunited with their long-separated kith and kin in Galilee which is still largely Palestinian today. (Abu Sitta, 2001: 24–25)

Political feasibility aside, there are two main weaknesses in his proposals. First, insufficient consideration is given to the issue of secondary occupation by Israeli Jewish residents, which, as we have seen in the case of Bosnia, can present serious problems to both repatriation and restitution. International practice has shown the importance of taking into account the effects of reintegration on the absorbing community for the durability of a repatriation program. Second, it is highly unlikely that original villages and urban areas would be able to sustain the quadrupling of the refugee population that has occurred since 1948, and the multiple divisions of property, land, and other fixed assets that would have to take place in light of this demographic growth would create uneconomic agricultural and commercial units. In addition to these main weaknesses, it is still not clear how Abu Sitta arrived at the total cost of repatriation of US$45 billion. Despite these problems, Abu Sitta's work does throw into sharp relief the fact that repatriation is prevented not because it is impossible to implement but because of political reasons alone. However, what is required to give his argument further depth and credibility is a study that takes on board the experience of the international community with regard to repatriation and the issues of reintegration, rehabilitation, and reconciliation as we have been discussing. In addition, it would need to take advantage of the Israeli experience of absorbing new Jewish immigrants. As a study for the World Bank concluded:

> The Israeli experience with immigrant absorption, especially in the area of housing policy, has been very successful in international comparative terms. . . . [D]espite the fact that Israel's economy started off similar to

Palestine's, and the degree of overcrowding was 58% in the 1950's, it has declined to only 8% today. . . . [O]ne can support the conclusion that Israel's housing policy offers important lessons for other countries. (Alterman, 2003)

Such a study combined with polling data on the likely numbers of Palestinian refugees wishing to participate in such a program would also serve to remove the deep emotional and political fears that Israelis face when they consider the prospect of Palestinian repatriation to their state. While recent events and those of the past few decades give little encouragement for Israelis to consider this as an option, one should not entirely rule out the possibility that in a changed political climate, a phased, well-organized, and well-funded program that was sensitively implemented may be an option around which Israeli leaders would be prepared to negotiate. We will return to this issue in the concluding chapter.

Repatriation to the New State of Palestine

The prevailing orthodoxy since Oslo has been that the most likely destination of refugees who do not wish to take up the options of local integration or third country resettlement would be to a new Palestinian state in the OPTs. This is technically not a repatriation, nor a return to their homes, but a move to a new state. As Fagen has pointed out, international practice has recognized the variety of returns available. Thus, the UNHCR has introduced a more flexible definition of *repatriation* to include that of return to one's "homeland":

> The "right to return to one's homeland" in [former UNHCR High Commissioner Sadoka] Ogata's formulation and in practice has been interpreted as the right to return to the country of origin, but not as a firm right to return to the actual place of origin. This has potentially an important bearing on the Palestinian case where, as [of] this writing, the homeland has yet to be defined. (Fagen, 2006: 46)

It must, however, be remember that the Gaza Strip is already the most densely populated part of the globe, and is unlikely to be able to absorb more than a few thousand refugees.

Repatriation to the OPTs has already taken place on two occasions. The first was after the Gulf War in 1990 and the expulsion of 350,000 Palestinians from Kuwait and nearby Gulf countries. Some 37,000 were able to return to the OPTs (Hanafi, 1996). The second period was after the Oslo Accords when a quota of PLO members was agreed upon between Israel and the PNA. According to the 1997 census by the Palestinian Central Bureau of Statistics (PCBS), they totaled 267,355, constituting 10.5 percent of the total population, most of whom may have returned in the course of the Oslo process (Hanafi, 1996). According to a Shaml (Palestine Diaspora and Refugee Centre) survey, however, about 25 percent of returnees lacked the proper papers and were staying on illegally. It is also important to note that these were unplanned returns and no large-scale housing provision or integration program was established to facilitate their absorbtion.

The prospect of an organized mass repatriation to the OPTs became a reality after the Oslo Accords. Despite the great sensitivity of not appearing to preempt any final status agreement on refugees and their right of return to their homes, the World Bank and the Palestinian Ministry of Planning and International Coordination[1] (MOPIC) conducted a number of studies. Discussions ranged from a highly interventionist state-centered approach, with the construction of new towns, employment generation schemes, recycling of Israeli settlements for refugee housing, and so forth, to a more market-oriented and incrementalist approach of flexible border entry to allow for a gradual refugee-determined timetable of return and cash assistance for housing and starting up business (Brynen, 2006: 68–69; Nijem, 2003). Under this latter scenario, for example, there would be infilling and suburban development rather than the construction of new towns of refugees (Exeter Refugee Study Team, 2001: 78–80).

Subsequent discussions focused more on the question of costs and tailoring a program to both the regional and local economies, on institutional capacities, and the financial regulatory mechanism. As both academic and consultant to the World Bank, Rex Brynen has offered a detailed critique of some of the more ambitious plans and drawn up twelve so-called lessons. Many of the lessons have been considered above, such as the importance of refugee choice and holistic development. More specifically, with regard to the new Palestinian state, Brynen also argues that there is no such thing as the "absorptive capacity" of the OPTs to act as a brake on repatriation, but that returnees should be assisted in voluntarily relocating in a way that minimizes bureaucratic intervention. He highlights housing finance initiatives as a critical element of any refugee absorption strategy and argues that in this connection, the Palestinian state ought not to construct housing for returnees or relocate refugees to evacuated Israeli settlements or attempt to remove the existing refugee camps (Brynen, 2003; Brynen, 2006: 72, 79).

Further World Bank studies have outlined possible housing and infrastructural requirements for the phased repatriation of refugees to the OPTs. These include a relocation package, grants to municipalities, housing support for low-income returning refugees, transitional budget support for health and education costs, and modest improvements in the infrastructure of the camps. It is estimated that if this package was made available to 500,000 returned Palestinian refugees and to the 650,000 camp residents in the OPTs, it would cost around US$613 million per annum or $6.1 billion over a ten-year period (Brynen, 2003: 15–16; World Bank, 2003b). As Brynen cautions, this is an amount that is likely to exceed somewhat the capacity or willingness of international donors.

How are these studies integrated into the peace process and the negotiations we have discussed? The answer is hardly much at all. There are close similarities between the Taba Talks and the Geneva Accord over the question of management of repatriation. As pointed out above, the new state of Palestine in the OPTs is one of the five options for permanent residence. Both Taba and Geneva called for a specific committee to determine repatriation procedures and to ensure that all repatriation was voluntary; this is more fully developed in the Geneva Accord, which states that a PPR Committee will determine the permanent place of residence of the refugee, all refugees must apply for an option within two years, and all return, repatriation, or resettlement is to be achieved within five years. While such an approach may appear similar to some of the mass repatriations organized by UNHCR in Southeast Asia, Mozambique, and Guatemala, in the Palestinian case this strikes one as overorganized. Most Palestinian refugees are no more than a two-hour drive away from the OPTs and have the assets to organize their own mode of repatriation, provided the borders are open. As Brynen has observed:

> For a variety of reasons (more settled refugees, physical proximity, higher per capita incomes, higher education levels, and extensive Palestinian experience with economic migration) the physical and logistical aspects of repatriation may be very different than in Cambodia, Mozambique, East Timor or Afghanistan. . . . [A] large proportion of Palestinian refugees have secure residency/citizenship in their present host countries. Roughly 40% of all UNRWA registered refugees, and around two-thirds of all UNRWA refugees outside the [OPTs], are full citizens of Jordan. A large proportion of refugees or, perhaps, internally displaced are already living in their homeland, and are fully integrated in the [OPTs]. (Brynen, 2006: 80)

Apart from the refugees from Lebanon, where the incentives to relocate are much stronger, it is unlikely there will be a precipitous rush to move to the OPTs because the economic "pull" factors of the OPTs are weak. The advantage of this weak pull factor is that it will allow for a more measured and phased series of repatriations and a more stable reintegration process. Clearly, these assumptions would need to be reconsidered if the economic balances in the region substantially change.

Conclusion

Over the past two or three decades, we have seen shifts in the way the international community has dealt with refugee crises. Of the three durable solutions employed by humanitarian agencies, there has been a growing emphasis on the option of repatriation. A number of factors have produced this change: an insistence on burden sharing by the southern states, the collapse of the northern states' asylum regime following the opening of the Communist bloc, and renewed security concerns following the September 11 attacks on the United States and the possible threat of terrorist infiltration. Support and cooperation for the options of local integration and resettlement have declined. To some extent, this trend converges with the situation in Palestine where local integration and resettlement has been resisted by both the Palestinian refugees and the host countries. Therefore, the shift in international practice places additional pressure on Israel and its allies to consider repatriation as a possible option.

The negotiations hitherto point to repatriation to the "homeland" in the OPTs as having increasing support in Israel. However, this recognition of Palestinian rights comes at a time when Palestinian attitudes have changed. In the face of persistent Israeli land acquisitions in the OPTs and intrusive security operations, a reassertion of and mobilization around the right of return can be seen. The upshot of these trends is in all likelihood a further impasse as Israel cannot be persuaded to accept the right of return; neither can it be coerced to do so. In these circumstances, however, there is still much that can be carried out in preparation and planning for the eventuality of an agreement over the future relocation of the refugees. One of the core issues that needs to be debated is what institutional arrangements will be acceptable to the different parties in organizing a durable solution. To this end, we now turn to the role of humanitarian agencies in refugee crises and specifically to the role of lead agencies with a view to consider whether the existing structures, such as UNRWA, are appropriate vehicles for the future.

Note

1. In 2004, the functions of MOPIC were redistributed to other ministries and a Ministry of Planning was given the responsibility for refugee repatriation.

5

THE ROLE OF UNRWA

In describing methods used by the international community in tackling refugee crises, reference has already been made to the importance of "lead agencies." The role of a lead agency has been variously defined, and its function per se has been subject to much criticism. Nevertheless, its continuing prevalence in international humanitarian assistance efforts demands some further consideration in the context of the Arab-Israeli conflict and those parts of the peace process dealing with the refugee issue. Should policymakers involved in negotiations consider allocating this role to a specialized agency? If so, what can be learned from other international cases? Are there particular factors in the Arab-Israeli case that obviate the necessity of a lead agency? If not, what are the alternatives?

In this chapter, I consider the issues arising from such an examination. The first section examines the role of lead agencies as it has evolved over the past two decades in the international humanitarian response to refugee crises. In the second section, reference will be made to the work of UNHCR only briefly since its overall role in such crises has been dealt with in the previous chapter. The third section examines the work of UNRWA, in particular its activities with Palestinian refugees. In the fourth section, I endeavor to relate the first two sections to each other to see if there is any overlap with the international experience of lead agencies and the particular case of UNRWA. I consider whether UNRWA has the capacity and the political support to undertake a lead agency role prior to and following any peace agreement between Israelis and Palestinians. In the fifth section, the alternatives to utilizing UNRWA are reviewed and the pros and cons of the alternatives are examined.

Lead Agencies in Refugee Crises

Lead agencies are those humanitarian agencies that seek to achieve operational and field coordination among the bodies working on the site of a natural disaster or man-made crisis. They can also be responsible for the delivery of medical aid and for development projects and can have an important role in the protection of a vulnerable population. According to a protocol compiled by the International Red Cross and Red Crescent organizations, also known as the Seville Agreement,

> the lead agency concept is an organizational tool for managing international operational activities. In a given situation, one organization is entrusted with the function of lead agency. That organization carries out the general direction and coordination of the international operational activities. (International Red Cross and Red Crescent Movement, 1997: Article 4.3)

The responsibilities of a lead agency can be divided into two levels: (1) strategic and (2) operational or field tasks. On the strategic level, the lead agency initiates policymaking, planning, and information sharing. It acts as the main point of contact, allocating tasks and coordinating funding efforts. In some instances, experience has shown the benefits of appointing a senior official to represent the lead agency in the country of intervention, who can respond immediately to any political or military events that affect the delivery of the humanitarian assistance. For example, UNHCR found the appointment of a special envoy in the FRY to be a useful management formula (UNHCR, 2005: 4). An essential responsibility of a lead agency is to agree with other international agencies on a financial plan, work out a coordinated budget, and assemble resources in advance. As discussed in Chapter 3, the lead agency should also ensure that repatriation assistance programs are linked to broader economic revitalization of the countries concerned. Finally, in some cases the lead agency will have to separate its coordination role from its own role as an organization for the delivery of humanitarian assistance.

On the operational or field level, the lead agency is responsible for providing guidance, policy advice, and information; for coordinating field activities to avoid duplications; and for providing administrative and logistic support to the range of actors involved (Cunliffe and Pugh, 1996: 9). One of its most important tasks is coordinating the involvement of NGOs at all stages of the program, given that "they have the grassroots knowledge and field experience that the big aid agencies often lack." In some stages, local NGOs should be closely consulted, because they are "the most dynamic entities in a recovering society." (Rosenblatt and Thompson, 1999: 2). The lead agency also needs to have credibility in the eyes of refugees to ensure that their voice is heard in the delivery of programs.

However, these essential functions of a lead agency turn out to be quite limited. Some critics have argued that insofar as their broader political or representational responsibilities are curtailed, they will have limited effectiveness. As Susan Martin notes,

> Assigning a lead agency increases the likelihood that assistance will be forthcoming to all forced migrants within certain geographic areas. It reduces institutional overlaps and failures in coordination that occur when multiple agencies take responsibility for the same populations. However, if the lead agency does not have an explicit protection mandate, it may not have the expertise or authority to address serious protection problems facing its charges. (Martin, 2000: 26)

In this way, Martin identifies a key issue: Can operational coordination be simply an ad hoc arrangement, or does it require some reference to the political context? What is the legal and political basis on and in which a lead agency operates?

It is important to note that the UN system itself is in considerable disarray and is trying to improve international coordination for humanitarian assistance, which has prevented it from being able to take the lead. As a result of the Gulf War crisis in 1991, the UN reviewed its coordination of relief efforts, and in December of the same year the General Assembly appointed an Emergency Relief Coordinator to act as the chairperson and bring "together all of the disparate parts of the system," such as the UN agencies, the Red Cross, and other NGOs (Cohen and Kunder, 2001: 5). However, this new coordinator wasn't equipped with the power to direct agencies and institutions. While "it has been instrumental in improving information management," it has "lacked the authority to impose coordination on competing UN agencies" (Cunliffe and Pugh, 1996: 3). In addition, the involvement of humanitarian bodies in peace processes and being part of implementation has led to the proliferation of task forces, working groups, and subcommittees within the aid system in an attempt to coordinate the efforts of this system. As a consequence, critical analysis of international humanitarian activity and the role of lead agencies has been lacking. The lead agency designation emerged as an attempt to seek solutions for what has often been perceived as the overall ineffectiveness of the global humanitarian response system.

To some extent US ambassador to the UN Richard Holbrooke took up this challenge when he called upon the members in the UN system to consider defining much more clearly the responsibilities of lead agency responsibilities (Holbrooke, 2000). The same argument has been adopted by other refugee studies experts. Michael Pugh and Alex Cunliffe argue that "the concept of a lead agency for complex emergencies has not been satisfactorily formulated either within the UN system or outside it by regional organizations or states" (Pugh and Cunliffe, 1997). Similarly, a UNHCR evaluation of its operations in the Balkans, following the flight of Kosovars to Macedonia and Albania in 1999, concluded by saying that "the exact role of the lead agency is poorly defined, leading to variable expectations [and] interpretations. In a massive emergency, the model demanded an additional, human resource capacity dedicated to coordination" (cited in Martin, 2000: 27).

With respect to the more specific issue of refugee crises, the role of a lead agency is much broader but also lacks clarity. Its role is to guide a process that leads from repatriation to reintegration as well as in some circumstances resettlement and integration into the host country. As the number of refugee crises has increased, this lack of clarity over the role, function, and capacity of various bodies to act as a lead agency has also increased. Several international organizations have acted as a lead agency in many parts of the world. For example, the IOM and the German NGO Gesellschaft für Technische Zusammenarbeit (GTZ) have been active in the logistical tasks of transporting refugees to their places of origin. UNDP and the recently created UN Office for the Coordination of Humanitarian Assistance (OCHA) have both taken the lead in a number of postcrisis development projects. The WFP was designated lead agency during the refugee crisis in Angola, while UNICEF has taken the de facto lead in Sudan and Cambodia. At the same time, as we saw in Chapter 3, UNHCR has been the lead humanitarian agency during the conflicts in Cyprus, the Horn of Africa, the Balkans, Kosovo, and East Timor (UN, 2004).

Roberta Cohen and James Kunder sum up the situation of overlapping boundaries:

> UNHCR generally limits its interventions to refugees and to certain categories of IDPs. UNICEF does not become involved with all categories of affected children. The World Food Programme and the UNDP rarely tackle protection issues directly. ICRC becomes involved only when the Geneva Conventions apply and where it is allowed entry. (Cohen and Kunder, 2001: 5)

The international system's response to humanitarian crises is clearly largely ad hoc and limited both by mandate and the commitment of resources.

In many refugee repatriation programs, there has been an acknowledgment on the part of the main humanitarian players of the fragmented nature of relief provision. Better institutional coordination has been crucial for improving the effectiveness of the humanitarian regime. Poor coordination causes duplication of efforts and it also "presents a poor image to the international community sometimes resulting in a failure to attract international donations" (McDowell and Van Hear, 2006). Furthermore, others believe that the

> ad hoc evolution of the lead agency concept has been closely related to the problems encountered in field operations and to various pressures for structural reform within the UN reflecting the political and operational pressures arising from humanitarian interventions, rather than reflecting legal and normative standards. (Cunliffe and Pugh, 1996: 2)

They also argue rather devastatingly that it "came about not only as an answer to the problem of coordinating the UN's humanitarian missions but also became, in Former Yugoslavia at least, a substitute for effective international political management of the crisis" (Cunliffe and Pugh, 1996: 1). Thus, a lead agency structure was adopted to fill the vacuum in coordinating humanitarian efforts, particularly the UN's, in the absence of a strong political mechanism. It was, in effect, a response to perceived incoherence in coordination and the lack of effectiveness among the humanitarian agencies.

There is a need for greater clarity in the role of UNHCR itself. The fact that in some cases UNHCR has been mandated by the General Assembly to be a lead agency in a refugee crisis and not in others adds to the confusion. Some experts believe that in order to overcome this lack of clarity and coordination, UNHCR should be given greater prominence. For example, Phyllis E. Oakley, assistant secretary for population, refugees, and migration at the US State Department, contends that UNHCR is the most effective candidate for the role of lead agency. With its long experience with refugees, the international community is repeatedly turning to the agency for advice and guidance.

> It usually works best when UNHCR is declared the lead agency, and it works out with the World Food Program—WFP—and UNICEF, through existing memoranda of understanding, the modalities of who does what. This was particularly so in Bosnia—from 1991 to 1996—and in eastern Zaire from 1994 to 1996. (Oakley, 1997: 2)

Others, like Holbrooke, go further and suggest that UNHCR ought to be the lead agency not only for refugees but also for the internally displaced. He argues that "dispersal of responsibility was a major weakness of the present regime." He forcefully advocated in favor of UNHCR assuming the lead role (OCHA, 2002: 1). However, there are those who believe that allocating UNHCR to such a comprehensive role will distract the body from its protection mandate and weaken its capacity to act effectively (OCHA, 2002: 2). In addition, others argue that instead of the lead agency concept, the international community should establish a coordination regime with appropriate rules and procedures. Raimo Vayrynen argues that the difficulty of obtaining funding from a single source makes it impossible to coordinate humanitarian assistance and guide relief actions. "The lead agency," he writes, "can try to facilitate cooperation, but it cannot dictate the funding and implementation of relief projects" (Vayrynen, 2001: 5). Yet, Vayrynen's coordination regime would itself have something of a lead agency role.

Nevertheless, this strong push toward the lead agency approach has not completely persuaded all parties involved, not least because of a reluctance by UNHCR to water down its protection mandate (Castels and Van Hear, 2005: 75–76). In order to understand more clearly how these debates and responsibilities were played out, we turn to some short case studies.

Case Studies: Guatemala, East Timor, and Cambodia

Guatemala

In the 1970s, Guatemala was convulsed in an internal conflict stemming from inequalities in the land-ownership system and access to political power. Seventy-two percent of the arable land was owned by 2.1 percent of landowners, mostly from a nonindigenous minority. Power was concentrated in the hands of the conservative military and private sector interests, leading to widespread armed resistance. At their behest, the military regimes between 1978 and 1985 conducted a series of counterinsurgency campaigns, which resulted in the displacement of over 1 million people or some 20 percent of the country's total population. Between 150,000 and 200,000 people were forced into exile, and by 1981 46,000 had entered Mexico, mostly to the impoverished provincial state of Chiapas.

Following elections in 1985 for the first civilian president since 1969 and the introduction of a revised constitution, some initial efforts to repatriate refugees were made. In 1987, UNHCR was party to a Tripartite Agreement between UNHCR and the governments of Guatemala and Mexico. This established structures and operating guidelines for UNHCR in its task of enabling the voluntary repatriation of refugees. Nevertheless, while political conditions in Guatemala had changed, the refugees showed a deep mistrust of the government and its governance in the areas to which they were returning (Riess, 2000: 13). The refugees created a group known as the Permanent Commissions (Comisiones Permantes de Representantes de los Refugiados Guatemaltecos en Mexico) to negotiate the terms of their repatriation directly with their own government. In 1989, UNHCR gave them logistical and other support, and in October 1992, an agreement made a formal return program possible. UNHCR established four field offices in Guatemala in order to prepare for the return of 30,000 refugees over a two-year period. By 1996, 22,000 refugees had returned. One should note that UNHCR has a responsibility to ensure that a repatriation process is conducted in a "safe" environment and in a "dignified" manner; it is obliged to establish minimal norms for returning refugees that the parties in conflict will agree to respect. In the case of Guatemala, the return of displaced persons took place during a time of continued conflict and a heavy military presence. However, by the time the final peace agreement was signed, 78 percent of potential returnees in Mexico had already returned and this stimulated the demilitarization of those areas to which they returned and preceded the formal cease-fire that followed.

In the Guatemalan case, UNHCR adopted a two-track approach: to ensure the safe repatriation of refugees who wanted to return to their homes and to facilitate the integration of those not returning into their host communities. UNHCR assistance comprised: (a) immediate humanitarian relief, including one-off cash assistance packages; (b) the introduction of Quick Impact Projects (QIPs) contracted out to organizations with greater experience with project design and implementation (thus seeming to recognize that UNHCR was too large an organization to provide the quick response required in this kind of work); (c) a strategy of linkage with local NGOs and of planning for eventual handover; and (d) mediation between refugee groups and the government. Due to the long distances and the remoteness of most of the returnee homes, transportation was a major operation. UNHCR set up reception centers to receive new arrivals, where their various documentations, health, and other needs could be assessed. The assistance packages given to returnees consisted of cash grants, food aid, agricultural tools, and housing materials. Cash grants for those under fourteen years of age were handed over to the mother while other entitlements went to both members of each couple. In this way, female returnees played an increasingly active part in decisions about the use of these funds. An important objective was to allow returnees to exercise their civil and political rights, and all returnees were provided with the same identity documents as other Guatemalan nationals.

The Guatemala case is also characterized by a high degree of involvement of returnees in the peace process (UNHCR, 2000: 137). This process was started in the camps, and programs were established to train leaders who would be able to help and represent the community in this process. In the same way, teachers and other professionals were trained to provide the education and leadership that would be needed after return. The creation of women's networks was particularly encouraged, and UNHCR staffs were provided with training on gender awareness and how to incorporate gender issues into the planning of the repatriation program. The networks also helped to increase the confidence of female refugees, who developed skills to publicly articulate their needs and aspirations. It is important to note the extensive involvement of the international community in this whole process. One such forum was CIREFCA. This was a conference initiated by the UN General Assembly in 1989 that led to a follow-up committee representing regional governments and international organizations. Supported jointly by UNHCR and UNDP, it was designed to be an evolving mechanism for coordination (Loescher, 1993: 26–27). Another forum was the Mediation Group set up in 1990, which invited the participation of UNHCR, the Catholic Church through its standing Bishop's Conference, the newly created Human

Rights Ombudsman, and a human rights organization set up by Guatemalans in exile. In addition, an international support group known as GRICAR (Grupo Internacional de Consulta y Apoyo para el Retorno) was set up to assist with the negotiating process between returnees and the Guatemalan government. It was made up of embassy representatives from Sweden, Canada, Mexico, and France, as well as the International Council for Voluntary Agencies (ICVA) and the World Council of Churches. The involvement of these groups was seen as a key component in advancing the repatriation or resettlement of refugees.

Following a peace agreement with the rebel movement there were further returns in 1997. Some 27,000 refugees remained in Mexico, most of whom were offered the option of integration and a secure legal status (UNHCR, 2000: 95). While it is clear that refugees were closely involved in the preparation and planning elements of the repatriation process, there is also some research that shows that the concept of voluntary repatriation was applied too broadly and loosely. In many cases, the lack of suitable alternatives obliged the refugees to cooperate in their repatriation (Riess, 2000: 9). Indeed, some refugees have returned to Mexico as migrants (Flynn, 2002: 6).

Despite the caveats regarding the operation in Guatemala, the overall consensus is that the work of UNHCR provided a useful template for addressing other refugee situations. A balance was achieved in terms of international involvement, refugee participation, repatriation, and integration into the host communities. UNHCR's contribution to the resolution of the refugee issue helped cement a peace process between the government and the insurgents.

East Timor

The second case study, East Timor, also shows how the role of UNHCR has been constrained by broader political considerations leading to some unhappy results. The humanitarian crisis in East Timor (1999–2002) led to almost two-thirds of the territory's population of 750,000 people being displaced. This followed a wave of violence led by pro-Indonesian militias as a result of an overwhelming vote for independence in a referendum in 1999. It can also be seen as a model of how *not* to organize a refugee repatriation operation. There was generous humanitarian support for the repatriation efforts to East Timor from 1999 to 2000, with aid disbursements of approximately $235 per person per year for two years in East Timor, compared to $215 per person per year in Bosnia over a five-year period (World Bank, 2003b: 4, note 5). Nevertheless, the repatriation process was characterized by poor coordination between the agencies involved.

Much of the lack of coordination was attributed to the agenda being driven by foreign policy concerns of the regional powers—Indonesia,

Australia, and the United States—rather then the needs of refugees. In October 1999, the Security Council established the UN Transitional Administration in East Timor (UNTAET) to oversee the transition to independence; this functioned as a quasi-state administration. However, it was given neither the resources nor the administrative capacity, nor the time to fulfill these functions. This impacted on refugee repatriation in complex ways. Lack of security was particularly important. Returnees were the most vulnerable segment of the population, and the mechanisms necessary to monitor and act on potential problems regarding their protection were not in place. The monitoring was very limited in scope, and no arrangements were made for UNHCR to hand over returnee protection monitoring to the new Ministry of Justice.

Indeed, the murder of three UNHCR workers attested to the climate of insecurity in East Timor (Helton, 2002: 109–113). In addition, a review of the international humanitarian response revealed a serious failure in the shelter program and shortfalls in the provision of replacement housing (McDowell and Ariyaratne, 2001). The budget shifted from immediate relief to medium-term development before emergency requirements were met. The lack of preparedness also had an impact upon the health of returnees and the communities that absorbed them. In 2001, there were a number of cases where returnees with serious health problems, such as tuberculosis, were being sent to places that had no health-care facilities, and children suffering from malnutrition were sent to areas where food productivity was still recovering. The East Timor case, then, is an example of where the political will to resolve the transition from Indonesian occupation to independence exceeded the willingness to endow UNHCR and other UN agencies with the capacity to cope with the fallout from that transition. The result was fear, violence, and inappropriate assistance for many of the refugees.

Cambodia

The third case, that of Cambodia, reveals a more mixed picture. The Cambodian refugee crisis commenced in 1975 after the Khmer Rouge took over the country and thousands of refugees crossed the border into Thailand to escape starvation and death. In 1991, the Paris Peace Agreement established the UN Transitional Authority in Cambodia (UNTAC), and a repatriation unit was incorporated into the UNTAC structure under the direction of UNHCR. Its director reported both to the UN Secretary-General and to the High Commissioner for Refugees. The repatriation program assisted some 370,000 refugees and 150,000 internally displaced persons and took place under particularly difficult circumstances (UNHCR, 2000: 145). The Cambodian infrastructure had been devastated by twenty-two years of war, and the situation in the country as a whole was far from secure. Responsibilities were divided, with UNHCR taking on the task to look after the immediate needs of returned refugees in cooperation with the WFP, and UNDP focusing on longer-term reintegration projects. Less than two months after the repatriation process began, and in order to speed up the process, UNHCR started to diversify the options available to returnees. For example, while continuing to offer them arable land, it provided additional options, such as a house but with less land or cash grants (UNHCR, 1993: 1–2). In addition, UNHCR had committed millions to QIPs.

While the program achieved the objective of facilitating the large-scale return of most of the refugees in Thailand and Laos and was effectively managed, there have been longer-term problems with the integration of returned refugees (Rodicio, 2006; Ballard, 2002). The most important issue was the timing factor. As the return of Cambodian refugees was an intrinsic part of the Paris Agreement, the timing of repatriation was dictated by the elections set for May 1993. The timeframe set for this operation was too short and determined by political and logistical objectives rather than in accordance with its protection mandate. As a UNHCR evaluation team concluded, the

> UNHCR should give closer consideration to its participation in repatriation operations which are tied and dictated by a political process. In Cambodia, UNHCR was party to an agreement which effectively required the border population to return to their country of origin within a specified timeframe. . . . As a result of the Paris accords, UNHCR was also placed in a position where it could not slow down or suspend its humanitarian activities without effectively blocking the whole UN-sponsored peace settlement. . . . The Cambodian experience suggests that UNHCR should seek to avoid an involvement in operations where the organisation will feel compelled to place a higher priority on its logistical objectives than on its fundamental protection principles. (Crisp and Mayne, 1993: 10)

A second factor was the lack of a comprehensive plan. The returnees needed food, shelter, roads without landmines, basic infrastructure, health and sanitation systems, and international monitoring. But none of this existed when the refugees returned home. It was stated that more than half of Cambodian refugees did not have enough food to eat in 1993 (Rodicio, 2006: 222). It became clear that the Repatriation Unit of UNTAC and UNHCR did not have the resources or capability to respond to the large numbers of returned refugees, and a gap appeared between relief and development components of humanitarian assistance (Helton, 2002: 82–83).

What these three case studies show is that a clear legal and political mandate with sufficient resources is essential in addressing refugee crises. Even when a lead agency is appointed and coordinating structures are in place, as they were in all three of these cases, two major obstacles can still jeopardize the safe and dignified treatment of refugees. First, their needs might be subordinated to the overall political agreement sought by the political elites of the protagonists and the key regional powers. In both the East Timor and Cambodian cases, we can see how the political timetable overrode proper planning and capacity building. Second, the resources to achieve either repatriation and reintegration of returned refugees, or integration into the host community and resettlement, are not forthcoming. The result is poor coordination, disaffection among the refugees, and a possible resurfacing of tensions and communal conflict. With these considerations in mind, we can now turn to the Arab-Israeli conflict and examine what structures are in place and what role, if any, they will have in a postagreement refugee program. The most important institution to examine is clearly UNRWA.

UNRWA and the Palestinian Refugee Issue

Before I discuss the future role of UNRWA, I will briefly trace its evolution from the 1950s to the present day. In the analysis of Palestinian refugee life in Chapter 2, some of the activities of UNRWA in the camps were discussed. This section begins with an overview of its mandate and functions. It will then focus on the political and institutional challenges it faced, including the prolonged crisis in Lebanon, difficulties with providing services under the Israeli occupation of the West Bank and Gaza Strip, and the new situation brought about by the establishment of the PNA. The section closes with an overview of the budget.

UNRWA was established by the UN General Assembly in 1949 and entrusted with the temporary task of providing relief services to Palestinian refugees in the aftermath of the 1948 war. The legal basis for the creation of a specialized UN agency for Palestinians lay in UN General Assembly Resolution 302 (IV) with two main purposes:

> to carry out in collaboration with local governments the direct relief and works programmes as recommended by the Economic Survey Mission [and] to consult with the inserted Near Eastern Governments concerning measures to be taken by them preparatory to the time when international assistance for relief and works projects is no longer available. (Takkenberg, 1998: 29)

It was also asked to undertake works projects that would improve the refugees' economic conditions until a peace settlement would resolve their status. UNRWA started to operate in 1950. It was established on a temporary basis to deal with the immediate refugee crisis, but as the conflict had been a protracted one, the refugees have remained and so has the agency. After more than fifty years of existence the agency is still operating and embodies, in the words of Schiff, "a unique international commitment: no other group has an international organisation dedicated purely to its welfare" (Schiff,

1995: 4). Nevertheless, the mandate continues to be a short-term one. Given the inability of the UN to implement Resolution 194, which calls for return and compensation for the Palestinian refugees, it has been renewed on an annual basis until recently. In 2001, however, the mandate of UNRWA was renewed for an extended period until June 2005; it has been renewed again until 30 June 2008.

Today, UNRWA is the largest agency of the UN system. Currently, it administers services in fifty-nine refugee camps and employs 24,000 people, the majority of whom are Palestinian refugees. UNRWA does not run the camps itself but provides services to them. The actual administration and policing of camps are the responsibility of the host authorities. In the OPTs, due to the lack of clear lines of authority as a result of the Israeli occupation, as well as to UNRWA services, camp residents run their own activities, and camp committees have acquired the status of official bodies representing camp populations (UNRWA, 2005b: 2). UNRWA provides basic health, education, and social services for 4 million Palestinian refugees, or about three-quarters of the entire Palestinian refugee population, residing in the five areas of its operation: the Gaza Strip, West Bank, Jordan, Lebanon, and Syria. In addition to its emergency relief, the agency programs have focused on human resource development through work programs and on improvement of the social infrastructure.

Due to the longevity of its existence UNRWA has had to adapt to a changing and often violent political environment. This has included the wars of 1956, 1967, 1973, the Israeli invasion of Lebanon in 1982, the first Palestinian intifada in 1987–1982, the second intifada in 2000 and ongoing, and the Israeli military activities in the West Bank a year later. In addition, it has had to face challenges from different state policies, changing donor funding priorities, and to respond to the changing demands of the peace process. These all made new demands on UNRWA in terms of increased expenditure, new programs, as well as subjecting its personnel to danger or harassment. In addition, such challenges all took place within the wider context of an ever-increasing Palestinian refugee population. As was noted in Chapter 2, the registered refugee population increased from a little less than 1 million in 1953 to over 4 million in 2004 (Parvathaneni, 2003: 2). Thus, as an agency it has been constantly in a state of transition and crisis over the period under review. UNRWA has altered the nature of its work according to the political environment.

When it became clear that there was not to be a quick resolution of the Arab-Israeli conflict or that the refugees would be allowed to return to their homes, UNRWA was asked to implement a program of integration into the economies of the host countries. The principal donor to UNRWA, the United States, asked UN Secretary-General Dag Hammarskjöld to examine the question of whether a program with capital investment to create jobs in the host countries could make UNRWA's services unnecessary. The Secretary-General reported optimistically, and in 1952 UNRWA was authorized to spend US$200 million over three years to integrate the Palestinian refugees into host countries. Earlier, in June 1951, UNRWA had also set up an experimental migration policy in which refugees were given the opportunity to be resettled outside the host countries. However, both proposals were met with resistance from the refugees themselves and the Arab states. There were widespread demonstrations and passive noncooperation, and as a result, the integration and resettlement programs were abandoned. As Lex Takkenberg has concluded: "Although officially committed to Resolution 194, UNRWA's initial attempts towards initiating massive public works projects were tantamount to advocating local integration as an alternative solution to the refugee problem" (Takkenberg, 1998: 280).

As a result, during the 1960s and 1970s, UNRWA restricted itself to providing basic services in education, health, and welfare to refugees both in and outside the camps. Indeed, as one can see in Table 5.1, over time the budget allocated to education exceeded that of emergency relief, a situation that has continued until the current period.

It is important to note that in 1967, UNRWA took on the responsibility of providing services to Palestinians displaced as a result of the Israeli occupation of the West Bank and Gaza Strip, even though they strictly fell outside the mandate of UNRWA as defined by UNGAR 194, which referred only to those displaced in 1948.

During the 1980s, UNRWA faced new challenges in Lebanon and in the OPTs. In addition to consolidating its position as a key service provider for the Palestinian refugees, it also attempted to develop a protection mandate for refugees. We should recall that UNRWA, unlike UNHCR, has given no protection mandate in Resolution 302(iv), since this role was to be carried out by UNCCP. However, as a result of the invasion of Lebanon and

Table 5.1 UNRWA Expenditures by Program, 1950–2001 (thousands of dollars)

Year	Health	Education	Relief	Other (Emergencies, Headquarters, etc.)	Total
1950	245	207	18,768	n/a	19,220
1960	5,299	8,016	21,386	n/a	34,701
1970	6,078	20,602	18,416	2,842	47,938
1980	30,953	100,065	44,116	8,543	183,677
1990	60,576	159,303	33,727	38,933	292,545
2001	50,600	164,400	29,100	33,800	277,800

Sources: B. Schiff, *Refugees unto the Third Generation: UN Aid to the Palestinians* (Syracuse, NY: Syracuse University Press, 1995), p. 51; Report of the Commissioner-General of UNRWA, 1 July 2001–30 June 2002, Supplement No. 14 (A/4861), Annexes, table 9.

Note: n/a is not available.

the first intifada, UNRWA's protection mandate grew incrementally. Between 1982 and 1993, the General Assembly affirmed in resolutions with the title "Protection of Palestinian Refugees" a role for UNRWA in upholding "the safety and the legal human rights of the Palestinian refugees" in all the territories under the Israeli occupation and thereafter. Under this rubric, UNRWA established the Refugee Affairs Officer program, which introduced an enhanced international presence with monitoring responsibilities (Helton, 2003: 4). Israel, however, considered this initiative a unilateral extension of the agency's mandate and sought to curtail the activities of the officers, but the General Assembly recognized the importance of their role in reporting violations of human rights. In 2001, it passed a resolution that referred to the "valuable work done by the refugee affairs officers in providing protection to the Palestinian refugees" (UN, 2001: 2).

The Madrid Conference in 1991 and the Oslo Accords in 1993 (see Chapter 1) brought the prospect of a Palestinian state a little closer. The peace process raised new questions about the future of UNRWA. If there were a Palestinian state in the OPTs, how and when should UNRWA begin to hand over its responsibilities for education, health, welfare, and relief to Palestinian ministries? If the Palestinian leadership accepted that refugees should not return to their homes in Israel despite the fact that this was not accepted by the refugees themselves, how would UNRWA continue to interpret its mandate under UNGAR 194? In addition, two fora were set up as a result of the Madrid Conference: the RWG and the Continuing Committee, also known as the Quadripartite Committee. (The Continuing Committee was set up under the terms of the Egyptian-Israeli Peace Agreement in 1979, but it never met. Nevertheless, it was reactivated in this context because Israel had already agreed to its existence with Egypt.)

Despite the fact that UN resolutions form the basis of the negotiations, neither the UN nor UNRWA was included in these from the outset. UNRWA eventually succeeded in being allowed to attend RWG meetings and was able to play an increasingly active role in the multilateral track of the peace process. For example, in December 1994, the Commissioner General of UNRWA headed the UN delegation to the RWG meeting in Turkey. It continued to be excluded from the Continuing Committee.

Nevertheless, as a response to the peace process, UNRWA launched the Peace Implementation Programme, which comprised projects that would improve both services and infrastructure for refugees (Takkenberg, 1998: 31). At the same time, it tried to continue with its role as service provider. However, it faced deep budgetary cuts as donors switched their funding to the PNA in an attempt to bolster the peace process. These cuts had a serious impact on the agency's services and projects.

With the breakdown of peace negotiations in 2000 and renewed low-level conflict between Israelis and Palestinians in the OPTs, UNRWA became the main provider of humanitarian assistance to refugees. Close to a million Palestinian refugees have been saved from hunger as a result of emergency food aid (UNRWA, 2004a: 3). This phase also saw a number of new initiatives as UNRWA simultaneously sought to respond to the increased hardships experienced by the refugees and the protracted nature of the exile. On the one hand, it recruited international Operations Support Officers to facilitate the movement and delivery of humanitarian assistance to refugees and nonrefugees in the OPTs in an attempt to bypass Israeli restrictions on local UNRWA personnel. On the other hand, it also committed significant resources to new housing projects for refugees to replace those destroyed by Israeli incursions, such as projects in Jenin, Khan Younis, and Rafah, as well as those requiring renewal such as the al-Neirab project in Syria.

The financing of UNRWA has been multifaceted and beset with recurrent crises and deficits. Unlike the UN as a whole, UNRWA has no system of what is known as assessed contributions—a sort of quota from the contributions of UN member states, which provide continuity to all its UN agencies. UNRWA's budget is almost entirely funded by voluntary cash and in-kind contributions, both to the regular budget and for new initiatives and special projects. In the first two decades of UNRWA's existence, more than two-thirds of its budget was provided by the United States ("Abolish UNRWA," 2002). However, since 1988, UNRWA became less an Anglo-American operation and more one in which Europe started to play a larger role. Today, the United States finances approximately one-third of its budget, with the countries of the European Union and the European Commission combined being the largest single donor (Bekar, 2002; UNRWA, 2006). During the course of UNRWA's existence, the annual general budget increased from $43 million in 1950 to $470.90 million in 2006 (al-Husseini, 2003: 1; UNRWA, 2007). However, following the Oslo Accords there has been a sharp decline in income as donors redirected their funds away from UNRWA to the PNA (Parvathaneni, 2005: 90–98). Since 1993, the gap between budgeted and actual expenditure has reached as much as $50–70 million per year (UNRWA, 1999: 7; Shiblak, 1997: 272). Indeed, in 1997, UNRWA's budget was the lowest in per capita terms since 1991, while the refugee population was growing by 3.6 percent. Between 1992 and 1996, there was a drop of 29 percent in the average expenditure per refugee in the four years, from $100.40 to $78.20 (Badran, 2001: 257). Table 5.2 gives an indication of the declining per capita expenditure since the start of the peace process.

Ironically, it is in times of emergency and increased hardship that UNRWA's finances improve. For example, following the outbreak of the second intifada in October 2000, although UNRWA continued to face funding shortfalls in the regular budget, they were of a much smaller scale. In

Table 5.2 UNRWA Expenditures (Regular Services) per Refugee (1994–2001)

Year	Total Expenditure (Regular Activities, January–December) (Millions of $US)	Registered Population (Estimates as of June of Each Year)	Expenditure per Capita (in $US)
1994	295.3	3,006,787	98.21
1995	251.3	3,172,641	79.21
1996	258.7	3,308,133	78.20
1997	270.7	3,417,688	79.21
1998	265.2	3,521,130	75.32
1999	273.2	3,625,592	75.35
2000	280.6	3,737,494	75.08
2001	277.8	3,874,738	71.70

Sources: Annual Reports of the Commissioner-General of UNRWA, 1995–2002; cited in J. al-Husseini, "The Future of UNRWA and the Refugee Camps," paper presented for the Palestinian Center for Policy and Survey Research, Institut Français du Proche-Orient (Amman: IFPO, 2003), p. 41.

2004, actual expenditure was around US$346.2 million, while income was US$338.1 million (UNRWA, 2005a).

In order to stabilize its revenue and expenditure flows in light of the ongoing population growth and increase of emergencies and hardship cases as a result of the conflict, and in order to prepare for the transition to a Palestinian state, a Medium Term Plan was drawn up. It was submitted to the donor community in 2004 at a major conference held in Geneva to examine the future of humanitarian assistance to the Palestinian refugees. In addition, and more relevant to our discussion in the next section, the Medium Term Plan was also designed to build up capacity with UNRWA itself to deal with the challenges of the future. One result of this strategy can be seen in the aftermath of the elections in 2006 of the radical Islamist party HAMAS to power in the PNA. As a means of avoiding the transfer of funds to the HAMAS-led PNA, donors have debated the possibility of UNRWA extending its humanitarian role to nonrefugees in the OPTs. We can now turn to our discussion of the possible future role of UNRWA in a postagreement refugee resettlement and repatriation program.

Possible Role of UNRWA in Repatriation and Resettlement

This section brings together the previous two sections and identifies possible ways that UNRWA can be reconfigured to meet international norms regarding the role of lead agencies in refugee crises. In reality, there has been little detailed public debate concerning the future role of UNRWA, partly due to the political sensitivity of the topic presaging as it does assumptions about the fate of refugees and partly due to the fact that key players both in UNRWA and in the policy and donor communities have had more urgent matters to consider. What material there is on this topic is fairly general and is derived from the summaries of Track Two negotiations, some policy and academic discussions known as the Minster Lovell seminars, the Taba Talks, and the Geneva Accord. This section will delineate a number of views and explore perspectives on the future of UNRWA held by key actors in the peace process—the United States, the EU, Israel, and the PNA.

Reviewing the studies that have been carried out and the workshops held to discuss this subject, one can discern a range of views. There appear to be two main schools of thought, identified by the Exeter Refugee Study Team as "UNRWA plus" and "UNRWA minus," with a number of views positioned along a continuum between them (Exeter Refugee Study Team, 2001: 84–85). The first school considers that UNRWA should play a role in any return program, because it has already shown itself to be flexible in adapting its mandate to different circumstances, and by taking advantage of its accumulated experience, institutional memory, and credibility both locally and internationally. This view contends that UNRWA has a major role to play in the organization of a return program by taking the logistical functions carried out by agencies such as UNHCR and the GTZ in other return programs. The second school is more skeptical about UNRWA's ability to handle such a task, which it sees as outside its present mandate and areas of expertise. This school argues that a successor body or bodies to replace UNRWA would tackle the challenges of reintegration, resettlement, and repatriation more effectively. It also argues that any return program should be implemented by a PA Ministry of Immigration and Absorption, which would contract out different aspects of the return program between several agencies, of which UNRWA would be one. What needs to be emphasized, however, is that both schools agree that there has to be a transformation of UNRWA in one direction or the other. There cannot be a simple transfer of lead agency functions to UNRWA without substantial reconfiguration or a complete phasing out of UNRWA prior to sufficient institutional capacity in the PNA. We take each school of thought in turn.

Within the first school, there are some nuanced differences. Some scholars and analysts are in favor of the maximum involvement of the agency. Campaigner and scholar Abu Sitta, for example, views UNRWA as a grassroots organization ideal for implementing a durable solution to the refugee issue, pointing out that "UNRWA has a wealth of experience in this regard," and "is run by a Palestinian staff of 21,000" (Abu Sitta, 2001: 8). He continues:

> UNRWA has a lot of work to do. With its 21,000 staff and its tremendous experience of providing uninterrupted service to the refugees, through 4 wars and innumerable raids and attacks, for the last 50 years, it has a unique standing. UNRWA should be expected to take care of all operations of rehabilitation. It should turn itself into a sort of UNDP, not only to build the infrastructure but also to create economy-building projects. Its mandate will last for 10 years from the first date of return, then tails off for another 10 years. (Abu Sitta, 2001: 36)

Similarly, Takkenberg proposes the following:

> In view of its forty-five years experience in providing assistance to Palestinian refugees, UNRWA is in a unique position to act as a lead agency for the first three to five years of this endeavour. While this would imply the Agency's involvement in coordinating and, probably, also partially implementing, massive programmes for the absorption, rehousing and rehabilitation of the refugees, at the same time UNRWA's traditional, semi-governmental, services should be gradually taken over by the governments concerned. (Takkenberg, 1998: 344)

He goes on to recommend that once the emphasis is transformed from a refugee issue to that of longer-term development, UNDP should be mandated to take over those remaining functions of UNRWA.

Still, within the "UNRWA-plus" school, some scholars have argued for a continued but more focused role for UNRWA. International lawyer Susan Akram has suggested that UNRWA's role should be expanded to include certain aspects of international refugee protection, such as acting as a representative of the refugees' interests in international negotiations. However, she admits that the agency cannot replace UNHCR's role in international refugee protection. Consequently, she recommends that UNHCR should assume protection functions over the Palestinian refugees and that UNRWA should continue its role in humanitarian assistance. She writes:

> In light of the long years of experience of both UNHCR and UNRWA, it would seem most appropriate to bring Palestinian refugees under the protection mandate of UNHCR but continue UNRWA as the assistance agency. This is consistent with the special regime in providing one agency for protection of Palestinian rights and another for providing material assistance. (Akram, 2002: 47)

The complementary argument has been developed further by Schiff, who has suggested that UNRWA should cooperate with UNHCR on matters of the status of refugees and documentation in any return program. However, he goes on to propose that UNRWA should shift from its current work in assistance to that of provider of technical services and administration for governments of the host countries. Nevertheless, he admits that the agency needs to make major changes to maximize its ability to carry out these different tasks (Schiff, 2000).

A study undertaken by the Exeter Refugee Study Team, referred to above, delineated the advantages of the UNRWA-plus school: UNRWA is trusted by the refugee community, has staff with the experience of humanitarian assistance and microenterprise development projects, possesses a collective and institutional memory that contributes to the sensitivity required in organizing a return program, provides international legitimacy and hence offers a measure of protection, possesses fruitful and ongoing relations with the international donor community, has operational credibility and flexibility to manage variations in different contexts, and has experience with host governments (Exeter Refugee Study Team, 2001: 84). Nevertheless, the study also highlighted the fact that the UNRWA-minus approach delineates with greater clarity which party is responsible for which aspect of a return program. This approach also has the advantage of rectifying the anomaly of the Palestinian refugees being the sole refugee community not covered by UNHCR's protection and status in the international refugee regime. Ultimately, the Exeter Study Team opted for the UNRWA-plus approach, but it cautioned that both options involved the transfer of functions to the PNA and that this will have a considerable impact upon the PNA's finances. For example, in 1999 UNRWA expenditure in the OPTs was equivalent to one-seventh of the total recurrent spending of the PNA, and UNRWA employees were the equivalent of one-sixth of the PNA's civil-service employment. In addition, UNRWA's services represent approximately 3 percent of the Palestinian gross domestic product (GDP) (World Bank, 2000: 95). Thus, neither of the approaches would be feasible without significant support for the PNA from the donor community. A similar view was taken by a workshop on the future of UNRWA held in Minster Lovell, UK.

> [I]n the Palestinian territories, there is absolutely no prospect at all that the Palestinian budget could suddenly absorb the costs of providing former UNRWA health, education, and other social services in the immediate future. Indeed, if one presumes to the repatriation of a significant number of Palestinians to the West Bank and Gaza, one estimate presented at the workshop suggested that service costs could rise to 4.4% of GDP before stabilizing. Sustained economic growth, at higher than present levels, would be needed before this level of expenditure would become fiscally sustainable. (Minster Lovell, 2000: 5)

A leading analyst on Palestinian refugee studies, Rex Brynen, has been more skeptical concerning the contribution of UN agencies to the refugee question and his views can be seen as straddling the two approaches. Highlighting the reluctance of the US and Israeli governments to include UNRWA or any other UN agency in any plan for final agreement, and the problems of interagency rivalry, bureaucratization, and the limits of effective coordination among the UN agencies, he is ultimately in favor of a slow wind-down of UNRWA (Brynen, 2000). In this his views concur with a number of draft proposals in the negotiations, such as the Abu Mazen–Beilin Plan, the Taba Talks, and the Geneva Accord. In the first, a new international agency was proposed. At Taba, both sides appeared to agree that UNRWA would be phased out over five years, and at Geneva, more specific institutions were delineated to replace the functions of UNRWA. Another influential scholar, Donna Arzt, has argued that while not advocating "an abrupt shutdown of UNRWA," she recommends "the slow phase out in which more of the long term work of administrating services is transferred to the PA, while the temporary job of helping with repatriation and resettlement is handled by UNHCR specialists" (Arzt, 2001: endnote 137). She concludes that

> even if it is not politically feasible for UNHCR to completely replace UNRWA in the role of administering services to Palestinian refugees during the post agreement transition process, it would be useful if key, experienced UNHCR personal could be available on loan or consultations. (Arzt, 2001: 130)

The UNRWA-minus approach is the preferred option of Gazit, the leading Israeli scholar on the subject. Gazit argued for the dismantling of UNRWA and abolishing the special status of refugees. He called for "an unequivocal announcement on the cessation of UNRWA's activities" as part of the final status solution (cited in Arzt, 2001: 129). He goes even further to advise the Palestinian leaders to approach the UN Secretary-General and "ask him to dissolve UNRWA" (Gazit, 2001: 241). Similarly, another influential Israeli academic, Moshe Ma'oz, believes that "arrangements and institutions associated with refugee problems—such as camps, refugees' legal-political status, refugee ID cards, and the United Nations Relief and Work Agency (UNRWA)—must cease to exist as part of implementation of a peace agreement" (Ma'oz, 2001: 111).

In turning to the more official perspectives on the future of UNRWA, we find that these are also varied. For Israel, UNRWA has always been a dilemma. It freed it from the responsibility of provision, yet, *faute de mieux,* UNRWA played a key role in perpetuating a Palestinian national identity. Following the occupation of the West Bank and Gaza Strip in 1967, Israel tried to coexist with UNRWA, and an exchange of letters known as the Comay-Michelmore Agreement was signed, which detailed the operational arrangements between them (Takkenberg, 1998: 32). Nevertheless, for Israel, UNRWA represented a threat to the legality and morality of its right to exist. A Palestinian UNRWA employee summed up the Israeli perspective succinctly: "[The agency] is an embarrassment to Israelis. They hate the word refugee because people ask, a refugee from where? They also hate seeing the UNRWA report being discussed in the UN. And UNRWA's mandate being extended year by year" (cited in Talhami, 2001: 145).

Milton Viorst, a leading US commentator, similarly describes the Israeli perception of UNRWA as a hindrance to a solution.

> More damning in Israel's eyes, is its charge that UNRWA is a barrier to history. UNRWA, Israelis argue, perpetuates the anomaly of refugee status instead of working to have its clients, like every other body of refugees in the world, integrated into the societies where they have sought refuge. ... Israel contends that the United Nations should have cut off UNRWA's funds a long time ago. (cited in Talhami, 2001: 146)

Israel has traditionally favored a rapid termination of the agency as a way of marking the symbolic termination of the refugee issue. In addition, it has accused the agency of perpetuating inaccurate myths about Israel in its educational material and of assisting terrorist groups such as HAMAS and Islamic Jihad, and more recently it has accused its former commissioner-general, Peter Hansen, of being "a hater of Israel" and successfully blocked his reappointment in 2005 (O'Sullivan and Mizroch, 2004). However, UNRWA's importance in serving refugee needs—and the possible political consequence of a sudden disappearance of the agency—has led Israel to consider a longer transitional period (Brynen, 2000). Following the disengagement from Gaza in 2005, there were discussions as to whether Israel should increase pressure to dismantle UNRWA, at least in the Gaza Strip, but since the election of HAMAS to the interim government of the PNA in 2006, there has been reconsideration. There is a renewed interest in the agency as an alternative vehicle to the HAMAS-led PNA to ensure the provision of humanitarian assistance in the OPTs (*Ha'aretz,* 2006).

With respect to the relations between UNRWA and the Palestinians, these have also been complex. Ironically, it was not until 1994 that there was a formal agreement between the UN agency and any Palestinian institutions. With the absence of any recognized state functions, agreements were made with host country governments. However, with the establishment of the PNA following the Oslo Accords, a provisional agreement in the form of an exchange of letters was signed between UNRWA and the PLO in June 1994 and then again when UNRWA headquarters were relocated from Vienna to Gaza City in 1996 (Takkenberg, 1998: 32). In this sense the PNA is regarded by the agency as another host country government. The formal position of the PLO/PNA with regard to the future of UNRWA has evolved and has been subject to internal debate. One strand of thinking can be discerned from the position proposed in the Taba Talks. This was that UNRWA should be continued until its services are no longer needed and that the range of services should change appropriately as any agreement is implemented. Indeed some planners and proponents of a centralized state went even further and came close to the US and Israeli positions, albeit for different reasons, in supporting the rapid phasing out of UNRWA and the transfer of functions to PNA ministries.

These official Palestinian positions have come under considerable popular criticism. A survey conducted in the West Bank in 1998 showed that 83 percent of the refugees were not satisfied by how the refugee issue was handled politically (cited in al-Husseini, 2003: 119). It is also interesting to know that a survey carried out by the Palestinian Centre for Policy and Survey Research, 2002, shows that a majority of refugees, 54.8 percent, favors the preservation of UNRWA subsequent to the creation of a Palestinian state (cited in al-Husseini, 2003: 21). More recently, planners and legal advisers have realized the complexity of what is entailed by repatriation, the lack of capacity in Palestinian institutions, and the additional function of UNRWA as a conduit of international funds, and as a result, a consensus around the gradual transfer of functions has emerged.

We should also note that the views of the host countries—Lebanon, Syria, and Jordan—over the future of UNRWA are broadly similar but with some small differences. The main concern is that of burden sharing. Jordan in particular, with the greater proportion of refugees on its territory, has expressed great concern over being left with the cost of either integration or resettlements (Talhami, 2001: 89). Indeed the lack of any mention of UNRWA in the Jordanian-Israeli Peace Agreement is an indication of the lack of agreement between Jordan and Israel on the future role of UNRWA. Syria has developed a cooperative working relationship with UNRWA and has similar concerns to Jordan. However, since the proportion of refugees is small in relation to the total population of the country, it does not have the same anxieties with regard to local integration. Some have cited the flagship rehabilitation project at al-Neirab camp as an example of Syria's more relaxed approach to this issue. Lebanon, however, has a more determined policy against the resettlement of refugees on its soil. Nevertheless, at the same time as holding UNRWA accountable for the provision of services, any improvement to the infrastructure of camps that UNRWA attempted to undertake has often been prevented, as we saw in the previous chapter, on the grounds that it could be considered a prelude to integration.

International actors will also play a key role in determining the future of UNRWA, largely as a result of their financial input. The most important are the United States and the EU, both separately and as part of the peace process coordinating body known as the Quartet that emerged in 2002, which also includes the UN and Russia. As one of the largest contributors to UNRWA over the past five decades, US influence over UNRWA policy and hence its future direction is considerable. Its overall view has been to support the agency in the provision of humanitarian assistance but to limit its role in the political sphere. UNRWA has an unsympathetic press in the United States with persistent attempts by Congress to restrict and interfere with its activities (Talhami, 2001: 146). Using its leverage, Congress has obliged the US government to fund a refugee coordinator, based in Amman, and other staff whose main duties are to monitor UNRWA, including its educational materials and the use of its facilities. Since 1999, the United States has also made it a condition of its financial support that no part of the US contribution to UNRWA be used to furnish assistance to any refugee who is receiving military training or who has engaged in any act of terrorism. For example in 2003, "Operations Support Officers" supported by the US made random and unannounced inspections of 76 percent of UNRWA's West Bank facilities and 85 percent of UNRWA's Gaza Strip facilities. They reported that no use of the facilities for terrorist purposes had been detected (US General Accounting Office, 2003: 12). With regard to the future, to a large extent, the US government supports the Israeli position of seeking a rapid phasing out of UNRWA, but it is also aware of the social and political upheaval this could cause without suitable replacement structures.

The other key actor in the debate about the future of UNRWA is the EU. Over 25 percent of UNRWA's funding comes from the European Commission and bilateral aid from individual European countries increases the overall European commitment considerably. The EU position on the peace process is grounded in the Madrid principles, Oslo principles, UN Security Council Resolutions 242 and 338, and other articles of international law regarding military occupation (namely, the Geneva Convention). This position was affirmed in the Berlin Declaration of 1999 in which support for the creation of a Palestinian state was clearly stated. As a result, the EU has provided substantial aid (over US$6 billion) in addition to an equivalent amount in loans from the European Investment Bank, with the purpose of laying the infrastructure for such an entity. Despite the extent of EU activity in supporting a future Palestinian state and its reiterations on a number of occasions of its belief in the importance of making progress on the refugee issue, there is no explicit support for the Palestinian refugees' rights of return or compensation. Rather, the EU contribution to the refugee issue has been based largely on a humanitarian perspective—providing aid to Palestinian refugees via the European Commission Humanitarian Office (ECHO) and UNRWA (Dumper, 2006d). The EU's position on the refugees is reflected in its allocation of aid and loans to the Palestinians (see Table 5.3), with the lion's share going to institution and infrastructure building (including education, health, and budget support) in the West Bank and Gaza as the location of a future Palestinian state (563 million ECUs [European Currency Unit]). Only 270 million ECUs were allocated to Palestinian refugees during the same period through UNRWA, plus 47 million ECUs to refugees in the West Bank and Gaza through ECHO.

Table 5.3 EU Aid to Palestinians, 1993–1999

Sector	Amount (millions ECU)
Education	52
Health	33
Institution building	88
Infrastructure	103
Agriculture	5
Private sector	23
Budget support	138
Humanitarian assistance (ECHO)	47[a]
Human rights, democracy, support to civil society	25
European Investment Bank investment loans to West Bank and Gaza[b]	
Infrastructure	149
Private sector	31
Global loan	26
UNRWA	270[c]

Source: Exeter Refugee Study Team, *Study of Policy and Financial Instruments for the Return and Integration of Palestinian Displaced Persons in the West Bank and Gaza Strip,* unpublished study prepared for the EU Refugee Task Force, 2001, p. 46.
Notes: a. Figures for West Bank and Gaza only.
b. Total of 206 loans + 14.75 interest rate subsidies.
c. Given at 45 ECU per annum times six years.

From this range of views both across the policy spectrum and from the debates among academics we can see that determining the future role of UNRWA is a complex and highly nuanced question, contingent both on the political developments in the region and the continued support of the donor community. Perhaps the strongest argument for some form of continued role for UNRWA is the inability of the PNA to cope with any additional demands upon it. We noted above the impact upon GDP if the PNA was obliged to take on UNRWA services and absorb a limited amount of refugees. Since those figures were compiled, the situation has deteriorated. A UN report in 2004 underscored the scale of the problem:

> Both refugees and non refugees were totally dependent on UNRWA's services. In figures we speak about the following: "poverty affected 22% of the population on the eve of the Intifada. In 2004, 47% of Palestinians lived in poverty on less than US$2.10 per day, according to the World Bank. 16% of the population and a quarter of Gazans lived in deep poverty, and were unable to feed themselves adequately, even with food aid." (OCHA, 2004: 5)

According to the Palestinian authority on refugees Elia Zureik, "to expect the PA to carry out the task of nation building alone, with its limited resources, and without UNRWA, was to expect the impossible" (Zureik, 1996: 55). In these circumstances, which are likely to continue for the foreseeable future, UNRWA's function as a conduit for funds from the international community to the Palestinians (and a "safe pair of hands") should not be overlooked.

Alternatives to UNRWA

In the previous section, some indication was given of the range of views being expressed by different parties with regard to the future of UNRWA. In this section, we turn briefly to the alternatives to UNRWA. Given Israeli and US opposition to UNRWA, it is quite possible that no role, or a very limited one, will be given to the agency in a postagreement program dealing with refugees. If UNRWA was phased out, what structure or structures would need to be created to implement a durable solution? The purpose of this exercise is to "think backwards," that is, to envisage an arrived-at situation and then to work backwards detailing the various steps taken in order to get there. In this way, one can see more clearly what is required to move from one situation to another. This discussion of the alternatives to UNRWA focuses on two main areas: (1) the proposals put forward in the various peace proposals and Track Two initiatives concerning mechanisms to deal with the refugee issue in the postagreement phase, and (2) to draw out those proposals put forward by other academics and specialists in which UNRWA has only a limited or residual role.

As was noted in Chapter 3, although there are frequent references to UNRWA in both the Taba Talks and the Geneva Accord, both these prototype agreements and the Track Two discussions that led to them agreed that UNRWA should be phased out over a period of five years, after which it would cease to exist. In its place there would be two institutions: an International Commission and an International Fund. The latter would be specifically assigned the role of dealing with compensation in all its aspects. The Geneva Accord fleshes out the role of the International Commission in more detail. In many respects, it would function as a lead agency coordinating the contributions of the UN, UNRWA, and the World Bank, as well as key countries involved, such as the United States, the Arab host countries, the EU, Switzerland, Canada, Norway, Japan, the Russian Federation, and others. Its work would be carried out by subcommittees taking on specific tasks within the range of options that would be made available to the refugees. These include a Technical Committee, a Status-Determination Committee, a Host State Remuneration Committee, a Compensation Committee, a PPR Committee, a Refugeehood Fund Committee, and a Rehabilitation and Development Committee.

It is interesting to recall that some of these ideas had appeared in the Ottawa process, one of the more sustained and continuous Track Two discussions, whose ideas presaged many of the discussions in Taba and in the Geneva Accord. However, the ideas for an international commission, which found its way into the Taba negotiations, were treated cautiously in the Ottawa process because of the complexity involved (Brynen, with Alma et al., 2003). In addition, as was also noted in Chapter 3, the aggregation of these roles recreate, in effect, the functions of UNHCR as a lead agency in its repatriation, resettlement, and integration roles without calling upon UNHCR itself to provide these functions. Its involvement is therefore dispensed with altogether, and, more importantly, its refugee protection mandate is conveniently sidestepped.

The second group of discussions around the alternatives to UNRWA follow from the debates described in the previous section in which UNRWA has a more limited or complementary role to other agencies. Some of these have focused on the issue of the protection gap and, in contrast to the Taba and Geneva proposals, the importance of including UNHCR. Terrence Rempel, for example, suggests transferring the role of protection "to an existing or new international agency." This is further developed in a paper with Akram. They argue that UNHCR is essential to the Palestinian case because, besides its experience in repatriation programs, it has the protection mandate that UNRWA lacks, and thus the two agencies should work together in a highly coordinated fashion: "UNHCR/UNRWA would monitor refugee choice, and once returns have been secured, states will open other slots, based on Temporary Protection priorities, to accept refugees not wishing to return for resettlement" (Akram and Rempel, 2003).

Similarly, Schiff argues that UNRWA should coordinate closely with UNHCR (Schiff, 2000). Finally, in a memorandum submitted to UNHCR, the refugee campaigning group, BADIL, suggested:

> UNHCR should continue efforts to enhance legal protection available to Palestinian refugees, including further clarification on the issue of "returnability"; UNHCR, UNRWA and other UN agencies, as well as NGOs and refugee community organizations, should continue with a sense of urgency the constructive debate about principles and mechanisms, which could enhance the scope and quality of international protection for Palestinian refugees. (BADIL, 2004)

Thus on the protection issue, which involves registration and monitoring, there is a growing consensus that the involvement of UNHCR is vital.

At the Minster Lovell workshop, some participants were doubtful about UNRWA's ability to take on tasks outside its mandate. There was a suggestion to "designate lead agencies in different areas—UNRWA, for example, in some areas, and perhaps UNHCR or UNDP in others—which would then provide direction to broader UN or international task forces" or alternatively, "an overall coordinator might be designated, such as UNSCO or the World Bank. While UNSCO has the advantage of operating from within the UN family, the World Bank has greater experience with multi-donor coordinator and multilateral program design" (Minster Lovell, 2000).

Brynen contends that while UNHCR involvement would be essential, nevertheless, UNRWA could be replaced, for example, by "a new transitional arrangement, akin to the World Bank managed Holst Fund" to act as a credible intermediary between donors and host countries (Brynen, 2000: 5).

From this exposition of some of the differing views, it is clear that there is no consensus over an alternative to UNRWA. However, there are two trends that seem to have emerged. The first is derived from a rights-based approach, which seeks to ensure that refugee needs are protected. In this approach, a dismantling of UNRWA and a handing over of service provision to other agencies or government ministries in a postconflict agreement would need to go hand in hand with the introduction of a UNHCR mandate over Palestinian refugees. The second approach is more managerial and seeks a minimum of bureaucracy and oversight from UN-based bodies. To some extent, this approach takes into consideration the Israeli reluctance to cooperate with the UN, with which it has had a poor experience. At the same time, such an approach may reflect the lack of awareness of the expertise of the international community in postconflict refugee management.

Conclusion

Due to the great number of actors and parties involved in the Middle East peace process, the case of a lead agency to have an overall coordinating role appears to be conclusive. To construct a series of new institutions to deal with the ranges of issues that need to be addressed would be time-wasting, costly, and an inefficient use of personnel resources. As Peter Marsden has pointed out in his studies of the role of aid agencies in Afghanistan, new agencies spend much time, effort, and funds setting themselves up, recruiting, and establishing procedures (Marsden, 1999; Marsden, 2006: 249). Much of the Israeli antipathy toward UNRWA taking this role is due to Israel's pre-Oslo policy of denying the possibility of Palestinian statehood. UNRWA was seen as an institutional underpinning to Palestinian resistance to integration and resettlement as well as maintaining a strong sense of Palestinian national identity. In the twenty-first century, now that a Palestinian state has been accepted and seen to be a desirable outcome by both the United States and Israel, continued opposition to UNRWA having a central role is backward looking, unstatesmanlike, and a poor use of resources. There are some signs that these entrenched positions have begun to change. As we noted earlier, since the election of a radical Islamist party, HAMAS, to power in the PNA, the Israeli government has supported moves to allow UNRWA to expand its humanitarian programs to include nonrefugee Palestinians in the OPTs as a way of redirecting funds to the Palestinians in ways that do not require the PNA to handle them (*Ha'aretz,* 2006).

UNRWA plays a unique role in the Arab-Israeli conflict and in the lives of Palestinian refugees. Its expertise and assets can be used as a basis for delivering certain functions. For example, it can assist the PA and the host governments in upgrading the quality of their own services delivery and act as a service consultant, particularly in the fields of health, education, and social welfare. More specifically, it can play a role in refugee housing rehabilitation, particularly in the refugee camps, and to implement large-scale programs for the absorption and rehousing of refugees. UNRWA could cooperate with UNDP and other actors for planning and putting forward strategies for the future needs of refugee camps and ways to develop them. It already has experience in this area through working with host governments, and through the Peace Implementation Plan (PIP). In the broader context of national development, one of the crucial needs to address is that of Palestinian demographic change, particularly with regard to the number of refugees. UNRWA is the sole source of information, and its data needs to be upgraded and made more accessible in order to be of use for planning. By expanding the Palestine Refugee Records project with refugee registration records, it could make them more relevant for policymakers and planners. More controversially, UNRWA could play an important role in the representation of refugee interests in the Permanent Status negotiations and in program planning. In light of the fact that the agency is de facto an expert in its areas of operation, UNRWA could be either a facilitator or the lead agency to coordinate the work of the donor community, host governments, and NGOs. At this point, one should recall that UNCCP was given the role of both protecting refugee rights and bringing about conciliation between Israel and the Arab states and signally failed, largely due to the lack of international support. Thus, if UNRWA is accorded an important role in a postconflict agreement regarding Palestinian refugees, two things should be factored in and avoided: first, the experience of UNCCP, and, second, the lack of clarity about both the concept and functions of a coordinating role of a lead agency as reflected in the international debate described in this chapter. When determining what body will supervise Palestinian refugee resettlement and repatriation, a clear mandate that has international backing and that incorporates both protection responsibilities and a service function is essential.

6

THE ISSUE OF REPARATIONS

The issue of reparations at this time in postconflict settlement is vast, extremely complex, and undergoing a process of change and reformulation. The twentieth century saw a shift in beliefs from what has been called "the politics of vindictiveness," as demonstrated by the punitive Versailles Peace Treaty in 1919, to a new moral framework that draws in issues of reparation and reconciliation. From German reparations to Israel for the Nazi Holocaust, the restitution of looted art treasures in World War II, the discussion over the West's culpability in the slave trade, through to the Truth and Justice Commission set up in postapartheid South Africa, the International Criminal Tribunals for Yugoslavia, and the International Criminal Tribunal for Rwanda, the discussions in international law and practice all attest to a frame of reference in which the international community privileges the narratives of the victim rather than of the perpetrators (Barkan, 2003: 91–95). Nevertheless, this shift has not necessarily been accompanied by action on the part of all governments concerned or even consensus among the victims. A great deal is still hotly debated. As Roy Brooks has written, "There is perhaps no more contentious an issue in international human rights today than the question of reparations" (Brooks, 2003: 103).

In this context, it is not surprising that the issue of reparations for the Palestinian refugees is equally contentious. To what extent is Israel culpable for the exile of Palestinians, and, if so, to what extent should it be obliged to shoulder the responsibility of reparation? Here, in this fundamental and first question alone, we can see how the controversy between the conflicting Palestinian and Israeli narratives of the cause of the refugee problem takes on contemporary and material significance and is not merely an argument by historians over sources and their authenticity. If Israel did deliberately evict the Palestinians from their homes, as Palestinians claim, then the issue of moral and material responsibility is clear. While there may still be a question over legal responsibility, the political argument will center more on the financial amounts and the modalities of reparation rather than on the agent. However, if the Palestinians left as a result of persuasion by their leadership, as is the conventional Israeli claim, or because of the "fog of war" as some revisionist Israeli historians claim, then the issue is less clear, and who is morally and financially responsible, less easy to decide. Nevertheless, the controversy over who caused the refugees to leave should not obscure the fact that Israel took a formal decision not to allow them to return home (Fischbach, 2003: 70). Thus, the issue of reparations for the flight of Palestinian refugees should be distinguished from that of being prevented to return to their properties.

In this chapter I contextualize the issue of reparations in the Arab-Israeli conflict and consider ways in which international practice can inform the debate in the peace negotiations around attribution of responsibility and reparation modalities. For the purposes of this chapter, the term *reparation* is subdivided to encompass two further terms, *restitution* and *compensation;* the main focus here is to examine the practice of the international community in implementing these terms. It is divided into four main sections. The first section presents an outline of the main legal and political issues encountered by the international community in addressing reparations. In the second section, international practice is considered and the Cyprus and Bosnian cases are examined as examples of the difficulties involved in implementing accepted principles. The third section analyzes the evolution of the reparations question in the Middle East peace negotiations. To some extent, it follows the same path as the negotiating milestones identified in Chapter 3, but the focus is on reparations. The final section examines existing formulas by drawing on international experience to suggest the broad contours of a reparations model for the Palestinian case.

Reparations in International Law and Practice

The term *reparation,* in its broad sense, is equivalent to a remedy addressing violations of international law. In a famous judgment in 1928, concerned with the acquisition of German property by the Polish state and known as the Chozrow Factory case, the Permanent Court of International Justice ruled that "'reparation must, so far as possible, wipe out all the consequences of the illegal act and re-establish the situation that would, in all probability, have existed if that act had not been committed'" (Bradley, 2005: 9). However, as has already been suggested, the term *reparation* also encompasses in a legal framework a subset of terms or remedies: *restitution, compensation,* and *satisfaction.* The first remedy, restitution, is conceptually straightforward in that a specific property or asset is restored to the original owner (Maier, 2003: 296). According to the International Law

Commission (ILC, the UN body devoted to the codification and development of international law), restitution means "to re-establish the situation which existed before the wrongful act was committed, provided and to the extent that restitution: (a) is not materially impossible; (b) does not involve a burden out of all proportion to the benefit deriving from restitution instead of compensation" (cited in el-Malak, 2004: 6).

The important point to note is that restitution in kind does not exclude any of the other forms of reparation, such as the second remedy, compensation. In the context of Palestinian refugees, compensation has often been presented as an alternative to restitution or the right of return. In this view, Palestinians who accept compensation forfeit restitution, that is, their right to return to their homes. In fact, neither customary international law nor General Assembly Resolution 194(III) view the two rights (that of restitution and that of compensation) as being mutually exclusive (el-Malak, 2004: 7; al-Husseini, 1999). A consensus exists, however, that when it is impossible to restore the conditions that existed prior to the violations, compensation, which involves monetary payment for material and moral injury, should be provided. The third remedy, that of satisfaction, addresses nonmaterial injuries and takes various forms: an acknowledgment of the violation, an expression of regret, or a formal apology (el-Malak, 2004: 6–7).

In addition to these remedies, international law also attempts to pinpoint responsibility. Until recently, the main task has been to identify which state is responsible on the premise that claims for relief under international law always begin with the law of state responsibility (Arzt, 1999). The ILC Articles on State Responsibility affirm this traditional state-centric definition of state responsibility and set out restitution, compensation, satisfaction, and guarantees of nonrepetition as the basic legal tools possessed by states to remedy injuries (Bradley, 2005: 3–4).

The principle of state responsibility defined as such results in the omission of the duties owed to individuals and, in the context of this book, those owed to refugees. However, more recent developments in international law mean that many states have now taken on new legal obligations that concern duties owed by states to individuals. This has been translated into the incorporation of human rights into international law. Thus, there is a general agreement that an "international wrongful act" for which a state is held internationally responsible includes, specifically, action that is a violation of human rights (Lee, 1999).

For the purposes of this chapter, it should be noted that the principle that refugees in particular are entitled to compensation for their lost property is gaining increasing recognition in international law. This principle now applies not only to the property of nonnationals, but also to citizens fleeing from their own state. For example, the Cairo Declaration of Principles of

International Law on Compensation to Refugees declares that "[a] State is obligated to compensate its own nationals forced to leave their homes to the same extent as it is obligated by international law to compensate an alien" (Principle 4 cited in Benvenisti, 1999). Nevertheless the absence of enforcement mechanisms—only partially rectified by the establishment of the International Criminal Court, which has jurisdiction only over individuals and not states—means that states can often evade their duties with regard to individual victims of violations.

As a result, there have been two main approaches to reparation. The first, known as the "full restitution" approach, or *restitutio in integrum,* acknowledges that the restitution process must address both material and moral damages in order to re-establish the situation before the wrongful act was committed. This approach also accepts that restitution is not always sufficient to return to the status quo ante. Property restitution and compensation may repair material harms, but moral damage and trauma are better addressed through public apologies, trials of key individuals, and truth commissions designed to uphold the responsibility of the perpetrator and state accountability.

This approach has been reiterated and developed in a number of global fora. For example, although largely concerned with reparations regarding slavery, the Durban Declaration issued by the World Conference Against Racism embraced this approach to restitution and expanded upon it to include a vision of development. The conference concluded that reparation should be used not only to redress historical injustices, but also to address the legacies of those injustices. Thus, where violations such as dispossession and exile have spanned generations, compensation should be used as "a vehicle for rectifying the social and economic problems that underpin today's victims' continuing marginalization" (Bradley, 2005: 15). Indeed, recent arbitral practice reveals increasing acceptance of the principle that "full compensation" is indeed often required, especially where lump-sum settlements are agreed upon (Goodwin-Gill, 2000: 49).

At the same time, the difficulty of enforcing the full restitution approach and of taking into account changing circumstances in protracted conflicts has led to the evolution of the notion of "adequate compensation." In 1981, the General Assembly discussed this notion, and it was subsequently elaborated upon by Eyal Benvenisti of Tel Aviv University and a committee of experts known as the UN Group of Governmental Experts on International Cooperation to Avert New Flows of Refugees. The adequate compensation approach is derived from the perspective that full restitution is not pragmatic when dealing with large refugee communities or long-standing refugee situations. It calls for an ad hoc appraisal of the interests and constraints involved. At times, this principle could mean more than the historical value (plus interest) of the assets concerned but less than the full current market value; at other times, the rehabilitation of refugees may require more funds than the value of their abandoned property, and thus "adequate" or "just" compensation might mean more than the full value of the property.

Remedial action therefore focuses much more on compensation in lieu of repossession of property rather than restitution. In addition, the notion of adequate compensation takes into account the interests of both parties and other constraints without necessarily attributing greater culpability to the perpetrators. Compensation schemes constructed under this rubric have more limited mandates, are "context dependent," and are concerned with distributive justice rather than a more wide-ranging rights-based approach aimed at effecting corrective justice (Goodwin-Gill, 2000: 48; Benvenisti, 1999). This view can be seen in a number of recent peace proposals. The 1995 Dayton Accords provide a general framework for compensating refugees who would prefer such compensation to repossession, while the UN initiatives to resolve the Greek Cypriot refugee issues emphasize compensation as the preferred alternative and offer a procedure for processing claims. With regard to the Palestinian-Israeli issue, calculations of adequate compensation would take into account a number of factors: Israel's financial limitations, the time elapsed since the Palestinians were displaced, refugees' ability to prove property ownership, and the massive and growing number of Palestinian claimants.

While the full restitution approach has been criticized for its unrealistic comprehensiveness, the adequate compensation approach can be seen as overly restrictive in bowing to realpolitik considerations and failing to address the core issues that continue a conflict. It can equally be argued that for reparations to be effective and to tackle the underlying sense of grievance, they should involve not only compensation for seized assets, but also the return of those assets and acceptance of accountability for the human rights violations that led to displacement. In addition, straight compensation without the remedies of restitution or satisfaction may be seen as a means of legitimizing human rights violations, particularly ethnic cleansing, and lead to the tacit acceptance that money can replace the protection of human rights. Finally, the adequate compensation approach can also have the effect of releasing the perpetrating state from any further obligations toward refugees, without necessarily admitting responsibility for any wrongdoing (Bradley, 2005: 14).

In the Palestinian-Israeli case, there is a further consideration. Leading legal experts hold that there is a link between the issue of compensation with the right of return and that of self-determination. Here the principle of return to land and property is complemented by the right to compensation for damage and loss, which should be seen as complementary not exclusive (Goodwin-Gill, 2000: 42). The international expert on refugee law, Guy Goodwin-Gill of Oxford University, has highlighted the right of return of those Palestinians displaced and dispossessed by the events of 1948 and thereafter and the relation of such right to the payment of compensation according to General Assembly Resolution 194. His view is that so far as return is integrally linked to territory, national identity, and self-determination, it follows that the objective of restitution may not be met by offers of equivalent land or monetary compensation. Indeed the failure to adequately link return and property rights to the wider issue of self-determination may undermine the prospects for political settlement (Goodwin-Gill, 2000: 40–41). The drawback to this approach seems to be that the restitution issue is thus available as a vehicle to reverse the political change that took place in 1948 (i.e., the establishment of the State of Israel on refugee land) and therefore is subject to political considerations. To put it bluntly, if restitution in the Palestinian case did not also involve what would in effect be the dismantling of Israel as a state, there would be a stronger political case to implement restitution as a remedy enshrined in international law. What has not been discussed in these debates is that restitution need not imply habitation, that is, refugees can be restituted for their property without a return. As we shall see, this is to some extent envisaged in the Annan Plan for Cyprus and is what in many cases took place in Bosnia.

In 2005, there was a major advance in clarifying the role of restitution and compensation in remedying displacement and refugeedom. Guidelines developed by the UN Sub-Commission on the Promotion and Protection of Human Rights, known as the "Pinheiro Principles," offer practical advice to states, UN agencies, or other international NGOs on how to address the legal and technical issues surrounding housing, land, and property restitution. As Scott Leckie, the director of the Centre on Housing Rights and Evictions (COHRE), has written: the Pinheiro Principles "augment the international normative framework in the area of housing and property restitution rights and are grounded firmly within existing international human rights and humanitarian law" (COHRE, 2005: 4). The Pinheiro Principles are far-reaching and provide a serious basis for launching claims for restitution. For example, Principle 2 states:

> 1. All refugees and displaced persons have the right to have restored to them any housing, land and/or property of which they were arbitrarily or unlawfully deprived, or to be compensated for any housing, land and/or property that is factually impossible to restore as determined by an independent impartial tribunal.
>
> 2. States shall demonstrably prioritize the right to restitution as the preferred remedy for displacement and as a key element of restorative justice. The right to restitution exists as a distinct right, and is prejudiced neither by the actual return or non-return of refugees and displaced persons entitled to housing, land and property restitution. (COHRE, 2005: 9)

While it is clear that these principles will be contested by many UN member states as unworkable, this gathering together of various strands of international law that these principles constitute has already begun the process of setting new international benchmarks on what is accepted as good practice. Their impact on the Middle East peace process is to further consolidate the case for restitution in addition to, but as distinct from, the right of return. This is an issue that we shall return to in the following sections.

Restitution and Compensation in Practice

In this section, we turn to a brief examination of how reparations were applied in practice with a view to deriving some lessons that might be learned. There is no shortage of earlier disputes that we can turn to in order to gain insights and construct a possible model for reparations in the Middle East conflict. In the past, these encompassed the German Forced Labour Compensation Programme with respect to the wrongdoing of Nazi Germany, the establishment of Indian and Pakistani Custodians of Abandoned Property following the partition of India, and the Iran–United States Claims Tribunal following the revolution in Iran in 1979. More recently, there have been a large number of relevant cases as the international community sought to stem the flow of refugees. Since the 1990s, there has been the UN Compensation Commission set up after the Iraqi invasion of Kuwait in 1990, the Cambodian Agreements on a Comprehensive Political Settlement in 1991, the Guatemalan Agreement on Resettlement of the Population Groups Uprooted by the Armed Conflict in 1994, protocols concerning the Return of Mozambican Refugees and Displaced Persons and Their Social Reintegration in 1992, the Addis Ababa Agreement on the Restoration of Property and Settlement of Disputes for Somali refugees in 1993, the Commission on Restitution of Land Rights set up by the first postapartheid government in South Africa in 1995, the Protocol on the Repatriation of Refugees included in the Arusha Accords between the Rwandan government and the Rwanda Patriotic Army, and the Commission of Real Property Claims set up after the war in Bosnia-Herzegovina, to name but a few. What is clear from a reading of the supporting documents to these agreements and to the institutions that implemented them is that they are tailored to address the specific needs of refugees and displaced persons in a given conflict and are therefore specific to time, place, and the constellation of political and military forces party to the conflict. In this sense, there is no model or formula that can be taken off the peg and applied to the Palestinian case. Nevertheless, it is instructive to see both what choices were made in dealing with reparation issues and why particular combinations of mechanisms and processes were adopted.

Restitution

In reviewing postconflict agreements, it is noteworthy, despite the difficulties involved, the extent to which the preferred option of international law—restitution—is employed. This is in contrast to the claims advanced by Benvenisti and Eyal Zamir who have argued that "history shows that in no case of massive relocation—either in accordance with an agreed plan or as a result of the horrors of war—have the refugees regained the property they left behind" (Benvenisti and Zamir, 1995: 234). Restitution has taken place, only in part due to the difficulties of resettling secondary occupiers or those who have been allocated sequestered property by the state. In South Africa, for example, the first democratically elected parliament passed the Restitution of Land Rights Act in 1994. It was designed to implement a policy to

> restore land and to provide other restitutionary remedies to people dispossessed by racially discriminatory legislation and practice, in such a way as to provide support to the vital process of reconciliation, reconstruction and development. (cited in du Plessis, 2003: 3)

In practice, the policy has run into grave difficulties largely due to the adoption of a judicial approach in which many claims were disputed and an appeal process where there were delays. The lesson that may be drawn from this experience seems to be that, in circumstances of high political tension, an administrative approach is quicker, less costly, more efficient, and politically advantageous, and is clearly better than not to have any restitution at all (Hall, 2003; Roodt, 2003; du Plessis, 2003). Similarly, the Arusha Accords, which were designed to bring the decades-long conflict in Rwanda to an end, involved at least on paper a commitment to restitution of property to the refugees of the minority Tutsi tribe. Although the accords were superseded by events leading up to the Rwandan holocaust, it is significant that the Hutu-led government agreed to these clauses concerning restitution within the accords. In both these cases, it should be noted that while restitution was agreed upon, it was subject to a number of restrictions. In South Africa, property acquired before 1913 was not subject to restitution, while in Rwanda, a "ten-year rule" was applied (du Plessis, 2003: 4; Jones, 2003: 10).

Two cases more closely related to the Palestinian situation are the Bosnia-Herzegovina (BiH) case and the Cyprus case. A key element in the Dayton Peace Agreement in 1995 was the inclusion in Annex 7 of clauses relating to the restitution of property, which set up the Commission for Real Property Claims of Refugees and Displaced Persons. Annex 7 was a conscious policy by the international community to reverse the ethnic cleansing of the previous years and to make sure the violators of civil rights were not rewarded. For example, Article XII (2) of Annex 7 provides that "any person requesting the return of property who is found by the Commission to be the lawful owner of that property shall be awarded its return." Such a person is also offered the option of leasing the property or being awarded compensation. By May 2004, despite some concerns about the accuracy of the figures available, the UNHCR estimated that approximately one million refugees and displaced persons returned to their prewar homes—a considerable achievement in itself (cited in Prettitore, 2006: 198). However, as a former legal adviser to the Organization for Security and Cooperation in Europe (OSCE) and also to the Office of the High Representative in BiH, Paul Prettitore, points out:

> Return numbers are not the only measure of success in BiH. Probably far too much emphasis has been placed on numbers, primarily for political reasons. . . . Regardless of whether refugees or displaced persons actually did return in the end, an extremely important factor in the post-conflict reconciliation in BiH is that they had the right to chose whether or not to return and repossess property. The fact that this right became enforceable through legal mechanisms and political pressure played a serious role in reducing tension in BiH, especially in light of the fact such a large percentage of the population was displaced. Access to prewar properties was particularly important in regards to durable solutions since such properties may have been one of the few tangible assets from which refugees and displaced persons could derive some economic benefit. (Prettitore, 2006: 199)

Thus, not only was there restitution on a significant scale, thereby addressing the needs of the individuals themselves, but it also contributed to the process of rebuilding the shattered society.

The final example is that of Cyprus. Reference to this case is somewhat premature because the agreement (known as the UN Peace Plan, or the "Annan Plan") has not been accepted by both parties, having been turned down in a referendum by Greek Cypriots in 2004. Nevertheless, it demands examination in the context of the Middle East peace process because, like the Palestinian case, the Cyprus issue is one of the longest running disputes based on displacement, property loss, and national identity. In addition, it is striking that despite the fact that more than four decades have passed since the Turkish invasion of the north of the island, the issue of restitution should have been given the prominence it has. The UN plan bases itself on the principle that the property rights of lawful owners be recognized and respected and where possible such properties be restituted if the owners were unlawfully dispossessed. The interesting element to the plan is both the graduated nature of implementation and the restrictions placed on restitution. In the former, the plan also offers sale, exchange, and long lease as alternatives to full restitution, which provides considerable latitude and choice in the manner of implementation. For the latter, the plan specifies types of property not eligible for restitution and utilizes the notion of "public interest" to ensure that the principle of restitution does not jeopardize the agreement as a whole. As Madeline Garlick, a legal adviser to the UN on the Cyprus issue, puts it:

> This public interest lies in ensuring the stability and sustainability of a political settlement, based on the agreed principle of bizonality; and in regulating the flow of return movements so that sudden and massive new displacements do not occur—with the associated violence, public disorder and social breakdown that would accompany them. This idea that the exercise of rights, including property rights, can be restricted in the public interest is well established in the jurisprudence of the European Court. (Garlick, 2003: 7)

In this way, the plan appears to straddle both the notion that refugees have a right to return to their homes and the idea that this right is circumscribed by political and public order exigencies. Nevertheless, as we shall see in the next section, the plan differs from the rhetorical gestures toward the right of return as appear to be the case in both the Taba Talks and the Geneva Accord, in that it strives to offer both meaningful alternatives to full restitution and law-based criteria for deciding which properties are not eligible (Garlick, 2003: 7). Such a flexible response suggests a way forward in the Palestinian situation, too.

Compensation

In turning to compensation, there are a similar number of case studies from which lessons can be drawn. Many postconflict agreements have compensation packages that often include incentives to encourage refugees to choose this option as opposed to restitution. The restrictions involving length of time and type of property mentioned above are examples of this kind of incentive. It is important to distinguish between those packages that deal with interstate disputes and those that deal with conflicts that have led to forced mass migration. Prior to the 1990s, tribunals and lump-sum agreements were popular ways in which compensation claims were dealt with. After the 1979 Iranian revolution, the Iran–United States Claims Tribunal was established to deal with the crisis in the relations between the two countries brought about by the occupation of the US embassy in Tehran and the freezing of Iranian assets in the United States. Over 4,000 claims were filed, and by the end of 1994, most of the larger commercial disputes were resolved. However, the tribunal failed to settle most of the private claims, and in 1990 the two governments concluded a lump-sum agreement (Benvenisti, 2003; Patel, 2003). With regard to lump-sum settlements, an authoritative study by two international law scholars, Richard Lillich and Burns

Weston, concluded that lump-sum payments have become, "without doubt, the paramount vehicle for settling international claims" (Lillich and Weston, 1988: 70). The popularity of this form of compensation package is that there are clear advantages for the states concerned. They receive the compensation funds and are then delegated to filter them through to the refugees according to an internally agreed formula. Some of the funds can be directed for collective and community purposes such as infrastructure for rehabilitation. It is quick, relatively easy to administer, and allows the states to move forward from the conflict that divided them. It is, however, not always in the interests of refugees, as they are dependent upon the state to disburse the funds equitably and efficiently.

In response to these concerns, a number of alternative mechanisms were established to deal with the mass claims that followed displacement in the 1990s. One such is UNCC, set up in 1991 to process claims and pay compensation for losses resulting from Iraq's occupation of Kuwait. Regarded as "the epitome of a mass claims exercise" (Helton, 2003: 14), UNCC combined elements from both international claims commissions and national commissions that were set up under lump-sum agreements (Benvenisti, 2003: 12). Claims were made to the commission through national governments, who were also entrusted with the funds to disburse to claimants, although this process was overseen by the commission to ensure compliance. Over 2.6 million claims in a range of categories from individuals to corporate bodies to governments were submitted, and by the end of 2004, over 90 percent had been resolved. Priority was given to individual claimants in both the processing and the payment of claims. By May 2006, all remaining claims were processed and attention was redirected to completing the actual payments (UNCC, 2006). Similar mass claims facilities have been set up to compensate individuals for Nazi abuses, such as the German Foundation for Remembrance, Responsibility, and the Future, of which the IOM-administered German Forced Labour Compensation Programme is a part, and the Swiss Banks Settlement Agreement (Helton, 2003: 15).

Two further examples will prove instructive for the Palestinian case. The first is the compensation element of the reparations provisions in Annex 7 in the Dayton Peace Agreement that deals with compensation as opposed to restitution. As already mentioned, Bosnia's Commission for Real Property Claims of Refugees and Displaced Persons (CRPC) has a mandate to receive and decide

> any claims for real property in Bosnia and Herzegovina, where the property has not voluntarily been sold or otherwise transferred since April 1, 1992, and where the claimant does not now enjoy possession of that property. Claims may be for return of the property or for just compensation in lieu of return. (Article XI)

Claimants can also receive compensation in the form of monetary grants or bonds for the future purchase of property. Annex 7 also provided for the establishment of a Refugees and Displaced Persons Fund to be administered by the CRPC. However, the package did not work. The Bosnian government did not have the funds to provide compensation and the donor community, largely the EU, was not interested in targeting individuals in this way and was also under pressure to push through restitution as a way of reversing refugee flows into the EU. As Prettitore notes:

> While both the right to, and a mechanism for, compensation were established under the DPA [Dayton Peace Agreement], in practice compensation did not materialize as envisioned. The Fund was never established because no resources were made available. CRPC never undertook any activities regarding purchase, sale, lease and mortgage of property. Instead it focused its activities on issuing decisions on claims for repossession of properties—even in cases where applicants had stated a preference for compensation. In addition, no part of the BiH government made any resources available. International donors were more interested in funding reconstruction of housing and infrastructure than compensation. (Prettitore, 2003: 14)

It is important to note that while a range of measures were taken by the Office of the High Representative to enforce restitution in Bosnia, the same political will was not evident for compensation.

A final example is the UN Peace Plan for Cyprus mentioned above, which was based like Dayton on a mixture of restitution and compensation with strong international involvement. Compensation would be paid in the form of bonds drawn from a compensation fund to cover both the value of the property at the time of dispossession and appreciation since. Benvenisti argues that the Cyprus plan differed from the Dayton model in that it "envisioned only limited return and repossession. As a result, much more emphasis was devoted to the issue of compensation" (Benvenisti, 2003: 17). However, a closer reading of the plan suggests that he is overstating this emphasis. It is true that all institutions, widely defined, would receive compensation in lieu of restitution, that current users would receive a degree of protection, and that restitution would be applied in a graduated and restricted manner. However, the plan accords priority to individuals for restitution and permits reinstatement in all cases for religious sites. As Garlick explains:

> The rationale underlying this provision is that for corporate entities, property in general does not have an emotional significance. For a company, a property right is an asset—and rights to that asset can be enjoyed equally well through financial compensation. For individuals, in contrast, property may have an emotional significance which is not so easily calculated in monetary terms. Thus it is more difficult to argue for non-reinstatement as

a necessary and proportionate limitation on an individual's property rights, than on the rights of a company. (Garlick, 2003: 9)

While the Cyprus Plan clearly acknowledges the impossibility of full restitution, its formulations are designed to find ways in which this can be achieved as far as possible without causing new problems and public disorder.

What these case studies suggest is that there is no overall formula for the provision of reparations. Practice by the international community has shifted away from judicial approaches such as tribunals, which impede progress on a political and intercommunal level. Greater consideration has been given to lump-sum agreements, although the recognition of individual refugee rights has tempered its use in more recent cases where refugee constituencies are involved. Here, various mechanisms, involving to greater or lesser degree international actors, strive to strike a balance between those refugee rights and political constraints. Indeed, the case for reparations based upon international law is broadly accepted, but it is the degree to which they should be molded to fit the political circumstances that is of importance. From the case studies it is also revealing that the passing of time need not be a key factor in determining the nature of the reparation package. Nazi war crimes are still being repaired, and the UN Peace Plan for Cyprus (although in the end, it failed at the final hurdle) points to the general direction of international thinking and practice on this issue. Part of the impetus for more generous reparations is the awareness that rebuilding war-torn societies is contingent on reconciliation between the warring parties, and reconciliation can only be meaningful if restitution and compensation packages are deemed acceptable. In fact, the package should not be taken in isolation but as part of a raft of measures including restorative justice and reconciliation. These will be discussed in greater detail in Chapter 7. One should also note that there is a growing awareness in UN and NGO circles of the importance of gender bias in reparations and that none of the case studies have addressed this lacuna. A male dominance in the conduct of conflict and a male dominance in the postconflict negotiations are part of a pattern that leads to inadequately addressing the effect of conflict on women and hence specific issues such as compensation and assistance for widowhood (Bell, 2004; Goldstein, 2001).

Reparations in the Middle East Peace Process

This section focuses on the debate concerning reparations in the Middle East peace process itself. It examines the evolution of the issue from 1948 and the establishment of UNCCP with a specific mandate "to facilitate the repatriation, resettlement and economic and social rehabilitation of the refugees *and the payment of compensation*" (emphasis added). It then examines further developments following the Madrid Conference in 1991, including the Oslo Accords in 1993 and the Camp David summit in 2000. Finally, it contrasts two proposals that contain significant details of what a reparation agreement would constitute, namely, the Taba Talks (2001) and the Geneva Initiative (2004).

As was outlined in Chapter 2, in the wake of the 1948 War and the Armistice agreements negotiated in 1949, there was an expectation that the Palestinian refugees would be allowed to return to their homes. However, with the refusal of the Arab states to recognize the State of Israel, and in the absence of any peace agreements between the protagonists, Israel refused to allow the refugees to return. In this context, discussion over various options for refugees, including compensation, began.

It was notably first raised by the UN-appointed mediator Count Folke Bernadotte in his September 1948 recommendations to the UN. He proposed "payment of adequate compensation for the property of those [refugees] choosing not to return [to their homes in Israel]" (cited in Peretz, 1995: 2). His proposals, including those relating to payment of compensation, were incorporated with slight modifications into UN Resolution 194, the fundamental legal instrument concerning Palestinian refugees.

It is worth at this point looking a little more closely at General Assembly Resolution 194 because, as Michael Lynk has pointed out, it has not only formed the basis of Palestinian claims but has also provided a framework for discussion on compensation in international law:

> United National General Assembly Resolution 194, which established the availability of return, compensation, and restitution for the Palestinian refugees, was the world community's first affirmation of these principles in the context of a displaced population. Resolution 194 is commonly cited by refugee law scholars as a primary international law source for the right of refugees and displaced persons anywhere in the world to compensation and restitution. (Lynk, 2003: 100)

Resolution 194 stated that those refugees willing to live at peace with their neighbors were entitled to the restitution of their homes at the earliest practicable time. Furthermore, those refugees not returning home should be entitled to compensation for their lost property, and those refugees who were to return and find their property damaged or destroyed should be compensated for their losses (Lynk, 2003: 98). What is significant about Resolution 194 is that it has been repeatedly affirmed by the UN General Assembly—no fewer than 140 times. Some international law scholars have gone further to contend that Resolution 194 provides an appropriate standard of law to be used in regard to repatriation and compensation of Palestinian refugees. They argue that in the first place it reflects customary international law, and in the second place, Resolution 242, which was passed in 1967 and is now the legal bedrock of all negotiations between Israelis and Palestinians, in effect incorporated Resolution 194 by calling for a "just settlement of the refugee question" (Quigley, 1999; Boling, 2001: 49).

However, some scholars have argued that the right to compensation does not apply to persons displaced by war. Only individuals that are persecuted and can thus be classified as refugees in international law are entitled to payment. As Peretz has argued, compensation is an obligation that rests "upon countries that directly or indirectly force their own citizens to flee and/or remain abroad as refugees" (Peretz, 1995: 1). In this view, international law regarding compensation does not apply to Palestinian refugees. Palestinians fleeing Israel as a result of war were not persecuted as individuals in their countries of origin. Furthermore, even if they had stayed, international law could not prevent the expropriation of property of citizens in their own state. In this way, while a case for the right of Palestinian refugees to compensation can be derived from General Assembly resolutions, international law comprises more than just UN resolutions and thus the case is not conclusive. In contradiction to the views expressed by John Quigley above, Peretz and Benvenisti argue that even though Resolution 194 was never rescinded by the UN, it was superseded by Resolution 242, which since then has become the basis for peace efforts (Peretz, 1995: 2; Benvenisti, 2003: 4). From this position flows the argument that the resolution of the compensation issue will ultimately depend on agreements voluntarily entered into by Israel and the Arab states to a peace settlement.

Despite these different interpretations of Resolution 194, one result was, as we have seen, the creation of UNCCP with its main task of facilitating a peaceful settlement. UNCCP was a crucially important body whose work was much undervalued during the period of its active existence but which since the start of peace negotiations in 1991 has once again come to the fore. With a management structure comprising three member states—the United States, France, and Turkey—and accountable to the General Assembly, it was instructed to mediate between the conflicting parties over the refugee questions. One major criticism leveled at its operation was that UNCCP failed to act as an independent UN agency but tended to serve the interests of the national governments overseeing its work—a fact that needs emphasizing in understanding the constraints upon UNCCP's activities (Fischbach, 2003: 84). The question of compensation was central during the first decade of efforts to resolve the conflict. During the 1950s, UNCCP argued that if the Palestine refugees could be resettled and/or repatriated, the major obstacle to a general peace settlement between Israel and the Arab states would be removed. Payment of compensation along the lines suggested by Resolution 194 was an integral part of solving the refugee dilemma, and proposals swung to and fro from repatriation to Israel to integration in the surrounding Arab countries accompanied by compensation (Peretz, 1995: 2; Takkenberg, 1998: 25). However, in a recent study, Fischbach has shown how UNCCP personnel interpreted Resolution 194 as referring to compensation for those who chose *not to return* and not for loss of property through compensation or war damage (Fischbach, 2006: 75–78). It is this restricted view of the issue of compensation that largely accounts for the suspicion in which it was held by the Palestinians and the Arab states.

UNCCP made little or no progress on these repatriation or integration options, and in the absence of any movement in its mediation efforts, UNCCP embarked upon an incrementalist strategy based on the approach that an agreement on the compensation issue would open the door to general peace talks. Ultimately, it also failed to effect any substantial agreement on the payment of compensation (Takkenberg, 1998: 27). Israel, for its part, insisted that discussion be limited to the technical aspects of evaluation (Peretz, 1995: 13). In a series of mediation conferences organized between 1949 and 1952 by UNCCP, Israel laid down a number of preconditions. First, it argued that compensation should be part of a general peace settlement, and it rejected the UNCCP strategy of incremental steps. There would be no restitution of property, and it refused to accept any moral or political responsibility for the creation of the refugee problem. However, it would be prepared to accept up to 100,000 refugees. Second, compensation would be paid into a collective fund that would be utilized for the resettlement of the remainder of the refugees elsewhere, and Israel's contributions to this fund would be limited by its ability to pay. There would be no individualized payments. Finally, Israel would maintain the right to raise its own claims for property damages and losses, and compensation for abandoned Jewish property claims in Iraq and other Arab countries (Fischbach, 2003: 86–87; Lynk, 2003: 109–138; Peretz, 2001: 88).

For their part, the Arab states, primarily Egypt, Jordan, Syria, Lebanon, Iraq, and Saudi Arabia, argued that Palestinian refugees had to be given free choice about returning to their homes, and only then should compensation be determined according to those returning and those resettling elsewhere. They argued that the refugees must be represented at the different stages of the negotiations to ensure their views were heard. In addition, they held that compensation was to be paid to individual claimants and should reflect the true value of the property. In terms of contributions, they held that Israel bore the principal responsibility for paying the compensation to the refugees, and if Israel was unable to pay the full amount, the UN also bore responsibility because of its role in the 1948 partition. Both these approaches to refugee reparation placed obstacles in the path of UNCCP strategy, and the question of compensation was constantly linked to progress on an overall agreement. As Fischbach, the foremost chronicler of the work of UNCCP, has written, "both Israel and the Arabs had extracted the refugee property question from any humanitarian setting or UNCCP attempt to isolate it and had intertwined it instead with the overall international political dimensions of the Arab-Israeli conflict" (Fischbach, 2003: 95).

As a result of the impasse of the Lausanne and Geneva conferences in 1949 and 1950, respectively, UNCCP turned to more secondary issues on which it hoped to make more progress. This suited the interests of the United States and Israel, and their approach was implicitly accepted in the passing of General Assembly Resolution 512 in 1952. This recognized that "the governments concerned have the primary responsibility for reaching a settlement of their outstanding differences in conformity with the resolutions of the General Assembly on Palestine" (cited in Fischbach, 2003: 134). Thus, in the absence of progress, UNCCP was asked to provide the tools that would assist the main parties in their negotiations and to desist in its role as mediator.

Nevertheless, the work of UNCCP was not without some significance. Its principal accomplishments were related to technical matters of identification and evaluation of Arab property in Israel and in obtaining the release of some 6,000 Arab refugee accounts blocked in Israeli banks worth approximately 4 million Palestinian pounds (Peretz, 1995: 2; Takkenberg, 1998: 27–28). By 1961, about 450,000 record forms of properties owned by Arab individuals had been prepared. The identification of refugee property was completed in 1964, and lists of such property are still maintained by the commission (Takkenberg, 1998: 28). However, as Fischbach notes, in the light of the lack of agreement on the political level, the question of reparation was never resolved, and by 1966, UNCCP was largely moribund (Fischbach, 2003: 307). Indeed, the whole issue of reparation was swept away by the tension in the region and the whirlwind of 1967, which created a new set of political and military conditions that the international community was obliged to attend to. In this new context, restitution and compensation were subsumed into the wider struggle for Palestinian national self-determination and the trade-off between land for peace.

Although the political developments in the region created new obstacles for the resolution of the refugee issue, some useful work was conducted by Palestinian and Arab researchers to supplement and consolidate the work of UNCCP. The economist Yusif Sayigh refined UNCCP's figures to include "potentially arable" land, public institutions and commercial properties, and to provide a more comprehensive estimate of the Palestinian losses. His work was extended by Sami Hadawi, a former senior administrator in the Mandate administration, and his collaborator, Atif Kubursi. Their research allowed them to estimate the total proportion of Israel that comprised Arab-owned and refugee property and to estimate its value (Hadawi, 1988; Kubursi, 2000; Fischbach, 2003: 320–325). This work did not advance the resolution of the refugee issue, but it contributed toward a discussion based on serious work as opposed to rhetoric when the breakthrough in the impasse came in 1991 with the holding of the Madrid Peace Conference and the Oslo Accords in 1993.

The context of the Madrid Peace Conference and the Oslo Accords were described in in Chapter 2. This chapter focuses on how the issue of reparation was dealt with in those meetings. In these terms, the main contribution of the Madrid Conference was the establishment of the RWG, chaired by Canada. No breakthrough was achieved on the issue of restitution or compensation, but there was some progress in framing an agenda for debate. Indeed, as Arzt has pointed out, "this was, in and of itself, a significant development, as it meant that Arab states and Palestinians had accepted the principle—which they had previously opposed for 45 years—that the refugees could improve their quality of life without prejudicing their future rights and status as either refugees or returnees" (Arzt, 1997: 26).

For example, the Israeli proposal that Palestinian refugee property claims be dealt with in the context of exchange with Jewish refugee property claims in Arab countries was flatly rejected by the Palestinians (Tamari, 2003: 1). They appeared to have won the argument that this was a bilateral issue that Israel had to take up with the states concerned, as this position was accepted in the Camp David summit in 2000 and in the Taba Talks in 2001. Similarly, as a result of the RWG discussion, Israel agreed that as a confidence-building measure it would increase from 1,000 to 2,000 its annual ceiling of accepting returned Palestinian refugees under its family reunification scheme; that 5,000 temporary residents of the OPTs would be given permanent residence; and 80,000 permanent residents outside the OPTs would be allowed to return. Finally, there is evidence to suggest that the special treatment given to refugees created by the 1967 War (some refugees for the second time), known as the 1967 Displaced Persons in both the Oslo Accords and the Israeli-Jordanian Peace Treaty, evolved from discussions within the RWG meetings, although, as already noted in Chapter 5, the continuing committee dealing with this issue had in principle been set up after the Egyptian-Israeli Peace Agreement in 1979. An indication of the Israeli reluctance to countenance any restitution is the way, as noted earlier, it dealt with Jordanian overtures over confiscated property. The Jordanian government argued that following the peace agreement between the two countries, its citizens should no longer be viewed as enemies and therefore entitled to the restitution of their property. The Israeli government quickly passed a law declaring that those defined as "absentees" prior to the peace agreement would remain so defined. Attempts by the Jordanian government to challenge this law for contradicting specific provisions in the treaty evoked no response (Fischbach, 2003: 332–334). As many of the Jordanian citizens entitled to restitution would also be Palestinians, it is likely that the Israeli government did not wish to set any precedents that would weaken its position over this issue vis-à-vis the PLO.

By 1995, it was clear that the refugee issue was being held hostage to the deterioration of relations between the PLO, the PNA, and Israel as a result of the unraveling of the Oslo framework. Nevertheless, the role of Canada was important in that it provided continuity and funding for a number of spin-off discussions concerning compensation. The first of these was held in Ottawa in 1997 and was followed by another in 1999 (Rempel, 1999: 36–37; International Development Research Centre, 1999). Since then, the IDRC has funded a series of studies on compensation issues, some of which were presented to the Stocktaking II Conference held in Ottawa in 2003. These ranged from the comparison of mass claims mechanisms to the potential use of the Custodian of Absentee Property archives as a database for compensation claims (Patel, 2003; Nathanson, 2003). Currently, it is funding an IOM comparative study of compensation models that could be adapted to the Palestinian case (personal communication with IDRC program officer, February 2005).

As was outlined in Chapter 2, the crucial feature of the Oslo Accords as it affects reparations is that it divided negotiations over the conflict into an interim and permanent status phase. A core issue such as that of refugees was postponed until five years after the establishment of the PNA. This had the effect of redirecting the focus of the protagonists on to the interim phase at the expense of the refugees and sidelining multilateral efforts at making progress on this issue. As Arzt writes:

> A side effect of the direct bilateral process (the Oslo framework) is that it upstaged the work of the refugee and other multilateral working groups and, more significantly, obscured the issue of the refugees both by postponing the topic and by re-directing the attention of Yasser Arafat and his deputies away from the Palestinian diaspora. . . . In other words, Palestinian refugees, most of whom live outside these territories, have been lost in the shuffle of state-building. (Arzt, 1997: 29)

Perhaps as important, while the issue of refugees was placed on the negotiating table of the permanent status negotiations, the Oslo framework did not make the direct link with UNGA Resolution 194 and the right of return, basing itself instead on UN Security Council Resolutions 242 and 338. Thus, the cornerstone of the Palestinian position was no longer at the heart of the process (Masalha, 2003: 226). One should, however, recognize that the Palestinian negotiators of Oslo and their leader, Arafat, saw some advantages in postponing the refugee issue to the end of a confidence-building period, gambling that they would perhaps get more concessions at a later date than in 1993 when the Israelis were unprepared to even commit themselves to statehood.

The next milestone in the peace process was the Camp David Summit of 2000. During the course of the discussions, Israel refused to recognize General Assembly Resolution 194 or to accept responsibility for the creation of the 1948 Palestinian refugee problem. At most, it was prepared to express its regret for the sufferings of the Palestinians during and after the 1948 war and offered to take part in an international effort to provide the refugees with financial compensation, but in a framework that would also compensate Jews displaced from the Arab countries (Masalha, 2003: 236; Klein, 2005). The Palestinians refused to budge on the right of return, but agreed to the setting up of an international fund for compensation. Although the summit ended in failure, it nevertheless brought the refugee issue to the fore and placed it firmly in center stage. In retrospect and in this sense, Camp David could even be called a "success" in one sense of the word: it clarified and reduced the main points of contention between the two sides. It brought to the fore the two core issues—refugees and Jerusalem. This was in complete contrast to the Oslo Accords, which had obscured them.

Following the collapse of the talks, President Clinton made one last effort before he left office to push the peace process forward. In addition to the reference to right of return, there was a direct reference to compensation and resettlement.

> All refugees should receive compensation from the international community for their losses, and assistance in building new lives. . . . But I have made it very clear that the refugees will be a high priority, and that the United States will take a lead in raising the money necessary to relocate them in the most appropriate manner. (Clinton, 2000)

Despite Clinton offering up to US$10 billion toward a compensation fund, both Israeli and Palestinian negotiators balked at accepting such a bald formulation and strove to obtain some amendments (Shamir and Maddy-Weitzman, 2005: 240). Ultimately, however, both sides equivocated and their agreement to the Clinton parameters was conditioned on a number of reservations. Although woefully lacking in crucial specifics, in the absence of any other agreed document emanating from the formal diplomatic process, the Clinton parameters has become the starting point of negotiations, and it is likely that future negotiations involving the current set of players will refer to them as a basis.

In subsequent years there have been two other major initiatives to address the issue of reparations—the Taba Talks in 2001 and the Geneva Initiative in 2003. As the two negotiations are closely related in both substance and in the involvement of many of the same players, they can be usefully contrasted to illustrate how some items have progressed while others have not. Both sets of negotiations on reparations and compensation can be divided into four main elements: restitution and compensation objectives, financing, implementation mechanisms, and moral acknowledgment.

However, one should note that the Taba Talks were not an agreement, and the summary produced by Moratinos presents not only points of agreement but also points over which there remained differences. It is also quite short. The section on refugees amounts to two sides of A4 paper, while the articles referring to compensation are just over half a page. However, one can also make the case that in comparison with other peace agreements, the clauses on refugees and compensation in Taba are quite extensive. (See Bell, 2000, and Stedman, Rothchild, and Cousens, 2002, for examples.)

Neither the Taba Talks nor the Geneva Accord include the offer of restitution. According to the Moratinos summary, the issue of restitution of property was flatly rejected by the Israeli side (Eldar, 2002: 3.6). Instead, both sets of negotiations emphasized compensation for displacement, material loss, and, in the Geneva Accords, "refugeehood" (Article 7.3.i). Compensation would be available for individuals and for communal development. The Taba Talks proposed three forms of compensation payment: a fixed per capita payment, property-based claims, as well as collective funds for communal development and infrastructural projects. Geneva dropped the fixed per capita payment but divided the property-based claims into two types, those below a certain value being "fast-tracked." Brynen is critical of the Geneva modifications, arguing that a claims-based system is contingent on agreement on property values and is therefore a slow process. As a result, it is likely to have political consequences in trying to win over the refugee community. It is also likely to reproduce social inequalities based on property-ownership divisions of the British Mandate period, thus producing fortunate winners and unfortunate losers in what should be a unifying process (Brynen, 2004).

Both Taba and Geneva agreed that the financing of the compensation would come from two main sources: Israel and the international community. At Taba, the Israeli side wanted a macroeconomic survey to determine Israel's contribution, while the Palestinian side argued that it should be based upon land values derived from UNCCP, the Israeli Custodian of Absentee Property, and other records. At Geneva, the Palestinian view was adopted with the proviso that the data would be compiled by a panel of experts. An "economic multiplier" would be agreed upon, and the total would be Israel's lump-sum contribution to an international fund. Subtracted from this amount would be the value of fixed assets (settlements, roads, and other infrastructure, etc.) Israel would leave behind in the new state of Palestine.

In turning to mechanisms for implementation, the Taba Talks and Geneva are broadly in agreement. Both proposed an International Commission to manage the compensation funds through a number of subcommittees. Geneva contained many more details as to the composition of the commission and the functions of the subcommittees. It is important to note here that unlike the lump-sum disbursements processed by UNCC, discussed in the section on restitution and compensation in practice above, the funds would not be transferred to the state of Palestine but to the International Commission, which would have "full and exclusive responsibility" for them (Geneva Accord, 2003: Art.7.11.i.a).

The final main element, that of moral acknowledgment of refugee suffering, will be dealt with in more detail in Chapter 7. However, one should note here that Taba was more forthcoming than Geneva. The Moratinos document records that the Israeli side recognized "its moral and legal responsibility for the forced displacement and dispossession of the Palestinian civilian population during the 1948 war and for preventing the refugees from returning to their homes in accordance with United Nations General Assembly Resolution 194" and that "Israel shall bear responsibility for the resolution of the refugee problem" (Eldar, 2002: Art. 2 and Art. 3). Geneva has no reference to moral responsibility but instead a series of "reconciliation programs" between the two sides were proposed.

Three other elements to do with reparations were touched upon in these talks and should be mentioned briefly. The first of these referred to reparations for Jews from Arab countries. At Taba, the Palestinian side insisted that this was for bilateral negotiations between Israel and the Arab states concerned, and this appears to have been accepted by the Geneva teams in that there was no mention of this topic. The second element is the issue of compensation to host countries for the cost of supporting Palestinian refugees. There was broad agreement at Taba for the principle with some differences over the wording, while at Geneva it was simply stated that there should be remuneration. Presumably the teams recognized the importance of having consultations with the Arab states prior to releasing any suggestions. The final element is that of "end of conflict." Both Taba and Geneva concurred that any agreement would constitute the removal of refugee status and therefore no individual claims could ensue. To a large extent, the prospect of the PLO and the PNA signing up to such a clause without the consent of the refugee community provoked much of the backlash against the peace process and Track I and II negotiations.

Although neither Taba nor Geneva led to an agreement, they can be seen as completing some of the essential groundwork. Most of the participants have expressed the view that the gap between the two sides had narrowed considerably as a result of these discussions. Broadly speaking, restitution was no longer an option and there would be a substantial Israeli contribution to a compensation program managed by the international community. However, the problem for these participants has been, crucially, the growing disconnection of their positions from what their respective constituencies were prepared to accept. The government of then Israeli prime minister Barak distanced itself from the Taba Talks and was also voted out of office just as they concluded, while the Geneva Accord led to a mobilization of opinion against the signatories on both sides.

Conclusion: Toward a Compensation Regime for Palestinian Refugees

In the light of an ongoing low-level conflict and growing polarization between the two camps, it is difficult to imagine a scenario in which a peace agreement encompassing reparations will be agreed upon. Compensation will always be a default position for refugees, and restitution not much better in that the experience of dispossession, exile, and refugeehood cannot be forgotten. Nevertheless, if there is to be an agreement, some mixture of elements along the lines discussed in Taba and Geneva is likely to be the starting point. This section brings together the principles drawn from international practice of reparations as exemplified in the case studies and applies them to the Taba and Geneva talks to see if there are ways in which practice elsewhere can inform the debate. It then outlines the political and resource constraints of the key actors: Israelis, Palestinians, and the donor community. Finally, it suggests a possible reparations regime that takes into account international practice and the specific context of the Arab-Israeli conflict. It will not suggest a model but rather indicate the elements that need to be included in order to have some likelihood of acceptance by the refugee community and to meet the criteria of durability and fairness.

The first section of this chapter showed how two schools of thought have emerged in recent decades with regards to reparation—that of full restitution and that of adequate compensation. Both schools have their weaknesses, and for the Palestinian case, there are two additional obstacles to the prospect of full restitution. The first is that a full restitution in the Palestinian-Israeli case is much more than the return of refugees to their properties. Because a very large amount of Palestinian refugee property now constitutes the Israeli state, restitution will also lead to an erosion of the Israeli state as a Jewish state and therefore of its raison d'être. This touches on the existential issue at the core of the conflict, which was outlined in Chapter 1. However, as we have discussed, restitution need not lead to rehabilitation of properties, and this option has not been fully explored in the policy debates on this issue. The second additional obstacle to full restitution is the very real realpolitik of Israel, which has the capacity to reject it out of hand, a position that is backed by the United States. Hence, the Israeli position that restitution will not be on the agenda of any future talks appears quite credible.

The compensation route, however, also has its problems. Foremost is the fact that the Palestinian refugees are unlikely to accept any compensation regime that does not involve some measure of restitution. It may be possible to finesse this position by a raft of cathartic measures and incentives: conciliatory measures involving a public apology by Israel, well-funded commemorative and reconciliation programs, in addition to a very generous compensation package and huge investment in the region. This approach would be contingent also on the support of the region and the host countries. The other problem for the compensation route is the willingness of donors to supplement the payments by Israel. As Brynen has pointed out, the amounts are likely to be high in comparison with other refugee situations, but much less than those in the region might expect (Brynen, 2006). Certainly, they will be nothing like the figures calculated by Hadawi or Kubursi (Hadawi, 1988; Kubursi, 2000).

In this sense, the Israeli-Palestinian case is unique and a reparations regime or model is unlikely to find much that is useful from international practice. Nevertheless, it is still possible to recognize and factor in the specificity of the Israeli-Palestinian case at the same time as reflecting on the lessons learned by the international community and, in this way, incorporate some elements that might help construct a model more likely to be implemented. From the BiH case we saw not only how restitution was incorporated into the provisions of the Dayton Peace Agreement, but also how its implementation was only achieved through the very strong intervention of the international community to enforce these provisions. At the same time, this was supposed to be balanced by strong incentives for compensation, the funds for which, however, never materialized. The result was a mix of property being restored to the former owners on the one hand, and property being sold or leased where refugees either found it uncomfortable to reside or difficult to find employment on the other. Thus, there was a situation of strong international support for some elements of the treaty and less support for other elements. It is clear from the Cyprus case that despite the protracted lapse of time, restitution was still considered. However, priority was given to private ownership and religious sites, and the rights of current occupants were protected to some degree.

From these examples, one can see how international practice would lead one to recommend the inclusion of the following elements: gender-neutral per capita payments to ensure that women and vulnerable members of the family also benefit; a compensation model that involves a choice for individual property owners of either restitution or compensation; special arrangements for the restitution of religious sites; collective compensation in the form of financing of infrastructural development in the new Palestinian state; prioritization of a reconciliation program; and, finally, strong international community involvement in the management and enforcement of the reparations regime.

7
TRUTH, JUSTICE, AND RECONCILIATION

When the fighting is done and the ink begins to dry on the papers of the political settlement, the task of rebuilding begins. In order for previously warring peoples to live side by side, a series of steps has to be taken: homes, schools, and markets may need rebuilding; weapons must be decommissioned; militias or armies must be reintegrated into civilian society; refugees will need assistance in their absorption into the new political and economic conditions; and compensation may have to be paid. Individuals will have ongoing memories and traumas to deal with, and community leaders, teachers, and business people will need to foster trust so that coexistence can take place and some form of normality evolve. One of the major issues that divided societies and war-torn countries have to deal with is the aftermath of human rights abuses and violent displacement of people, particularly if it is considered that state institutions have carried out these abuses (Chesterman, 2004: 154). There is an increasing recognition that these activities will not take place spontaneously and will require encouragement and support. Hence the emergence of programs and institutions that seek to promote peace and coexistence through the search for truth, justice, and reconciliation. International experience is showing that without these programs and institutions and without their encouragement, old enmities will resurface and the conflict will reignite. Indeed, it is now recognized that they need to be factored into peace agreements in a more integrated way and that they are not a sentimental add-on after the hard bargaining over land, resources, and military force is dealt with. More recent research also highlights that notions of justice and reconciliation are essential, even in the prenegotiations phase. A mutual understanding by the protagonists of what caused the dispute and what needs to be reconciled is an essential part of framing a political settlement that has enough widespread support for it to be durable.

However, there are two main problems in designing programs to encourage the search for truth, justice, and reconciliation. The first is what

Christine Bell has termed the "meta-conflict," meaning the lack of agreement over what the conflict is about in the first place (Bell, 2004: 15, 316). To some it may be, say, the lack of equity in land-ownership, for others, the violent protests of dispossessed farmers or shanty-town dwellers. In the Palestinian-Israeli case, there is clearly a dispute over whether the core of the issue is rejection by the Palestinians and the Arab leaders of a UN resolution to partition Palestine, or the prevention of refugees from returning to their homes, or recognition of Israel as a Jewish state, or over the land acquired by Israel in 1967, or particular forms of Palestinian resistance. Unless this meta-conflict is resolved, peace agreements and postconflict institutions will be offering solutions to issues that are not at the heart of the conflict. The second problem is the degree of politicization of the norms of law and justice in order to secure a peace agreement. This dilemma is sometimes referred to as "transitional justice." To what extent does one adulterate these norms so that the protagonists concerned have sufficient incentives to remain committed to an agreement (Bell, Campbell, and Ni Aolain, 2004: 306)? A more positive perspective on this dilemma has been expressed by Kader Asmal, the international human rights lawyer and former minister of interior in postapartheid South Africa who referred to this approach as a "third way" and "beyond the twin traps of naivete and *realpolitik*" (Asmal, 2000: 19).

This chapter begins by examining some key terms in this search for truth, justice, and reconciliation, notably the ideas of transitional justice, retributive justice, and restorative justice. In doing so, it will both discuss some of the main issues and review the debate in the research and policy literature. The second section explores the evolution of international practice by examining a number of case studies. South Africa, Northern Ireland, Chile, Rwanda, and Guatemala have been selected as examples that throw up issues that are relevant to the Israel-Palestine situation. The third section delineates the development of justice and reconciliation ideas in the Middle East peace process. It looks at a number of different approaches to this issue and their inclusion in the Taba Talks and the Geneva Accords. The final section considers if international experience can inform the debate around Palestinian and Israeli reconciliation and identifies a number of relevant issues and modalities.

Transitional Justice, Retributive Justice, and Restorative Justice: An Overview

Transitional Justice

The study of peace agreements has shown that in order to achieve a political settlement, the protagonists have nearly always had to make compromises that seem to contradict their sense of justice. So as to move on from the conflict and secure a cessation of hostilities, they have had to suspend some elements of the rightness of their position as they perceive it. In many cases, the very perpetrators of violence and war crimes against the other side are the cosignatories of a peace treaty. Yet, the desire for peace is so strong that certain injustices are tolerated and swallowed in view of the prospect for a greater and longer-term good. This resulting tension between peace and justice in the postagreement phase has been the focus of increasing debate, and the suspension of some norms of justice for an unspecified period has given rise to the notion of *transitional justice* in international law (Asmal, 2000; Bell, 2004; Nedelsky, 2004; Crocker, 1998; Moon, 2004; Welchman, 2003). In discussing the Northern Ireland context, some scholars have described transitional justice "as a collective title for the numerous forms of political and legal accommodation that arise in the shift from conflict and negotiation. Its concerns are with conflict-related legal legacies as well as with the myriad of internal legal quandaries that are part of the postconflict world" (Campbell, Ni Aolain, and Harvey, 2003: 317).

Transitional justice is transitional in two senses, both as a set of rules and procedures that operates for a limited period only, and in the sense that it itself is undergoing and must undergo amendment. The question that exercises the skills of legal scholars is how much justice needs to be sacrificed in order to achieve peace.

Since the early 1990s, the debate about transitional justice has focused on how to get the balance right and a number of ideas have been put forward. On one hand, the notion of transitional justice permits the parties to move on and is forward looking. On the other hand, in order to do so, historical injustices have to be addressed. Some scholars note that a failure to address the question of the past adequately may hinder prospects for a successful transition (Bell, Campbell, and Ni Aolain, 2004: 314). In the same way, in her analysis of postcommunist regimes in Eastern Europe, Nadya Nedelsky argues that struggles associated with transitional justice issues are not solely "the politics of the present" (Nedelsky, 2004: 65). Instead of "forgetting and moving on," which would constitute what is known as a "victor's justice," David Crocker argues for an alternative model for societies seeking transitional justice. This model has the following elements:

- An authoritative investigation and disclosure of the known facts with respect to human rights victims and their violations and a general picture of the violators within their institutional chain of command.
- A platform for the victims or their families to tell their stories publicly and receive public redress in the form of acknowledgement or compensation.
- The fair ascription to individuals and groups of responsibility for past violations and the enforcement of appropriate sanctions.

- Compliance with the rule of law and due process.
- Promotion and elevation of public deliberation about what happened, who was responsible, and how society should respond. All sides should be given a fair hearing rather than requiring unanimity or consensus.
- Recommendations for changes in the law and governmental institutions, including the judiciary, the police, and the military. The purpose of this is to remove the causes of past abuses and ensure that they will not be repeated.
- Good long-term changes such as further democratization and just economic development should be promoted (Crocker, 1998: 496).

As will be shown in the case studies examined in the next section, a varied body of measures have been used to deal with these dilemmas. These include amnesties, prisoner releases, limited prosecutions, restitution or compensation, new constitutions, the exploration of a common narrative of the past, and the public airing of grievances and trauma through what have become known as truth commissions (or truth and reconciliation commissions). These activities can be seen as expressing two types of justice: *retributive justice,* where prosecutions or restitutions are seen as essential for the peace process to have credibility or to consolidate such a process, and *restorative justice,* where punitive measures are not necessarily excluded, but the emphasis is on a collective endeavor to understand the reasons for the injustices of the past and to provide an opportunity for forgiveness to be sought and be given. Thus, the transitional justice discourse can provide important tools for understanding how societies emerge from violent conflict and how to confront the legal, moral, and political dilemmas that result from holding abusers of human rights accountable at the end of a conflict.

Retributive Justice

Retributive justice can be seen as comprising two polarities with a range of views in between. The first takes retributive justice to mean vengeance, although it is not synonymous with it (Crocker, 2000). The main difference is that the basic logic of retribution is one of proportionate harm (Wetzel, 2002). The mechanisms for implementing retributive justice are, for the most part, judicial. They may comprise military tribunals, such as the Nuremberg and Tokyo tribunals after World War II. Nowadays, this kind of approach is viewed as a victor's justice and is not seen as facilitating reconciliation within or between war-torn societies. Ad hoc tribunals created by the UN Security Council, such as those established for Yugoslavia and Rwanda, are also seen as a form of retributive justice but also as essential in terms of giving support to the peace agreements. There are also examples of national courts taking steps outside their sovereign territory against abusers of human rights such as those taken against General Augusto Pinochet of Chile and Prime Minister Sharon of Israel, or national courts prosecuting perpetrators within their own judicial system, and special courts that are set up as part of a peace agreement and operating under national and international law, such as in Sierra Leone. Finally, the International Court of Justice and the International Criminal Court, both in The Hague, are fora where human rights violations can be redressed (Chesterman, 2004: 155; Vicente, 2003: 9).

The second polarity suggests that justice entails an element of reintegration into the community and hence forgiveness. Clair Moon, for example, rejects the idea of retributive justice founded on vengeance and arbitrated by the state. This, she argues, reproduces the very conditions it aims to redress and threatens to further, rather than curb, the cycles of violence. In light of these considerations, she proposes including the idea of forgiveness, which breaks "the system of equivalent exchanges and the cycle of vengeance at the heart of retributive justice" (Moon, 2004: 196–197). However, adding the forgiveness component can move retributive justice toward the second element of transitional justice, restorative justice.

Restorative Justice

There is an increasing diversity of opinion on what constitutes restorative justice in theory and practice. Part of the reason for this is the way the concept is used not only in international relations but also in domestic criminal law, particularly as an alternative way of dealing with juvenile crime. As a result, an often-quoted definition is that of Tony Marshall writing in a report for the UK Home Office, which, nevertheless, provides a concise formulation: "Restorative Justice is a process whereby all the parties with a stake in a particular offence come together to resolve collectively how to deal with the aftermath of the offence and its implications for the future" (cited in Gavrielides, 2005: 84).

In the main, restorative justice can be divided into two broad categories. The first argues that it cannot be in any way punitive, while the second asserts that rather than an alternative to punishment it constitutes an "alternative punishment" (Gavrielides, 2005, 91). However, in both categories it is designed to facilitate political and social transformation. An essential ingredient to all restorative justice theories and practice is the opportunity for direct contact between the perpetrators and their victims. Various fora have been proposed for this dialogue, but it should be free of state intervention. Restorative justice occurs, therefore, in a "public space" and most frequently takes the form of a truth commission (Cohen, 2001: 212, 221). Other scholars argue that reconciliation is intrinsic to restorative justice. Some studies of the South African Truth and Reconciliation Commission suggest that arriving at truth about what happened is more important than implementing justice (Moon, 2004: 193; Cohen, 2001: 225; Crocker, 1998: 496; Asmal, 2000: 2). Indeed, Cherif Bassiouni has questioned the extent to which truth commissions can address serious human rights violations and concludes that they cannot ultimately serve justice (cited in Asmal, 2000: 10).

In turning to the issue of refugees, the reconciliation component within restorative justice entails a reintegration of returned refugees through a process of inclusion and the rebuilding of relationships within a community in the country of origin (Rodicio, 2000: 30). According to Rodicio's study of the repatriation process in Cambodia, "reconciliation aims to restore human dignity, to heal social wounds and to recover a just political culture disrupted by the conflict. Restoring the personal and social sense of trust is essential to re-start building a history together" (Rodicio, 2000: 30).

It is revealing to compare Moon's idea of reconciliation in restorative justice in South Africa with that of Rodicio's in the Cambodian case. Both regard reconciliation as intrinsic to restorative justice, yet Moon refers to the South African case in which reconciliation had more to do with gaining respect and equality of the black African community vis-à-vis the white (Afrikaner) community, both of whom are in the same country. Rodicio's concept of restorative justice is the repatriation of returnees to the country of origin from another country. In the South African case, what is emphasized is the forgiveness discourse, while in the Cambodian case what is emphasized is the reacquisition of respect and equality of the returnees from the community in the country of origin through repatriation. In other words, the political context, whether it be, for example, a colonial-settler paradigm or a noncolonial-settler paradigm, can determine the nature of the justice sought. Connected to this, one also needs to note the culture-specific nature of some of these commissions. The South African Truth and Justice Commission was guided by a discourse deeply rooted in Christian theology, and there are other indigenous discourses that can be utilized in establishing them (Moon, 2004: 185; Findlay, 2000).

Before proceeding to the next section to examine some case studies of how conflicting parties have dealt with these issues of truth, justice, and reconciliation, the extent to which the international refugee regime has been informed by them should be considered. It has been shown how there have been many attempts to infuse the transition process from conflict to peace with various judicial mechanisms. To some extent international law is lagging behind comparative research in this area, and there is a limited corpus of documents that can be used as a reference point. One example of attempts to build up an international consensus is the UN's *Draft Basic Principles and Guidelines on the Right to a Remedy and Reparation for Victims and Violations of International Human Rights and Humanitarian Law.* The document is an attempt to include both retributive and restorative approaches to justice and explicitly adopt a victim perspective. With regard to reparations, the draft argues that states "should provide victims of violations on international human rights and humanitarian law the following forms of reparation: restitution, compensation, rehabilitation, and satisfaction and guarantees of non repetition" (cited in Welchman, 2003: 12).

Since 1989, the document has undergone many redraftings and consultations and is still working its way though the UN system (Welchman, 2003: 12). In terms of operationalizing issues concerning refugees in the postagreement phases, we saw in Chapter 4 how UNHCR developed the concept of 4Rs in order to plan for the reintegration of returned refugees. This recognized that a program involving a series of phases was required in which different donors and agencies and different programs were constructed for each phase. As the Refugee Studies Centre report explains:

> The 4Rs is seen as one element of a general transition strategy for countries emerging from violent conflict. . . . The idea is to plan 4Rs as a package, so that UNHCR does not embark on repatriation (the first R) before the other parts of the package are also in place. The responsibilities of different agencies would phase in and phase out at different stages of the 4Rs process. (Refugee Studies Centre, 2005: 100)

However, while UNHCR seeks to pursue its refugee protection mandate in this way so as to ensure the return of refugees in a safe and dignified manner, it does not itself take on any of the functions of ensuring security and the rule of law. Its mandate may require it to coordinate with other UN agencies such as the UN High Commission for Human Rights (UNHCHR) and international human rights organizations (IHROs), but it does not establish courts or commissions. In this way it is dependent both on other agencies and the parties of the peace agreement to ensure that refugees can return safely and have their rights respected. Thus, the international refugee regime does not appear to incorporate any specific or preferred set of procedures during postagreement periods. Therefore, it is important to examine how these are evolving in practice and to pull together the various strands connected to this issue.

Case Studies

This section examines cases where postconflict agreements have had to address the tension between justice and peace. The cases chosen are South Africa, Northern Ireland, Chile, Rwanda, and Guatemala as providing good examples of how divided or war-torn societies have sought to heal the wounds of the past. Each case offers a slightly different approach, partly as a result of particular political factors, partly due to cultural and historical legacies. In each case, the transitional justice process shall be discussed to identify how and whether restorative justice and/or retributive justice was used. It should be remembered that it is not simply a question of a postagreement introduction of a truth commission (TC), as in the case of Northern Ireland and Chile. It was and is an evolutionary process resulting from the campaigns conducted by civil society and human rights groups. In the Rwandan and Guatemalan cases, we have examples of how refugees played a prominent part in determining the nature of the postconflict phase.

South Africa

The South African case can be seen as a classic example of a struggle between a colonial-settler group and the indigenous population, which transmuted into an ethnic conflict. This case has been selected as an example of restorative justice in practice and the conscious attempt to heal the wounds of a divided society. The apartheid system established by the settler Afrikaan community lasted until 1994 and was based on racial segregation and discrimination. Following the establishment of democracy in 1994, there was an attempt to reconstruct society and construct a new national identity to include both victim and oppressor. The main institutional framework of the transitional justice process was the Truth and Reconciliation Commission (TRC). The TRC was established to provide as complete a picture as possible of the causes, nature, and extent of gross human rights violations occurring between 1 March 1960 and 10 May 1994 (Cohen, 2001: 225). According to Asmal, the leading international lawyer and minister of interior in the postapartheid democratic regime, the TRC had a number of clear objectives. In the first place it sought to establish the illegitimacy of the apartheid system and ensure that those privileged by it were made collectively responsible for the racist system. But, at the same time, it was designed to prevent the further alienation of the right-wing apartheid elements in the South African polity. In addition, it was to identify corrective measures to undo apartheid's racially biased socioeconomic legacy, to address the issue of property rights and redistribution, and to establish equality before the law. Finally, it was a means to acknowledge regional and international claims and the norms of international law (Asmal, 2000: 11–12).

The transitional justice process adopted was an attempt to promote cooperation between people and establish harmony within the community (Asmal, 2000: 14). It provided a platform for the victims to articulate their trauma and offered a way for their reparation. Simultaneously, the TRC provided for the rehabilitation of the perpetrators of human rights abuses through an amnesty and public forgiveness that was contingent upon the full disclosure of past misdeeds (Asmal, 2000: 1, 18, 23–24; Moon, 2004: 186–187; Minow, 1998: 341). A Register of Reconciliation was set up for people to write their reactions, which in turn assisted in the creation of a shared national narrative of the apartheid period. One should also note the important role played by the media in the therapeutic and healing process. By publicizing the commission's hearings, it brought the victim's stories and suffering into the public domain (Minow, 1998: 325, 336). The TRC also had a developmental aspect and addressed systemic injustices. It proposed specific economic reparations, such as land reform and the restructuring of the medical and educational systems, in order to redress the imbalances in the country (Minow, 1998: 341).

Significantly, one should note that, in contrast with transitional justice processes in Latin America, where criminal trials were a central ingredient of justice, South Africa did not adopt criminal proceedings against perpetrators. For example, it did not ratify the 1973 Convention on the Suppression of the Crime of Apartheid, which called on subscribing states to punish acts of apartheid through their national criminal justice systems. Thus, the "desk murderers," as Asmal puts it, were not prosecuted for the everyday implementation of the apartheid laws (Asmal, 2000: 11, 18). Instead the TRC invited members of the business community, media, and legal profession to offer submissions for amnesty for their complicity with apartheid. However, almost no one responded (Minow, 1998: 336–337). In eschewing the retributive justice approach, therefore, there has been a sense in which justice was only applied partially.

There were a number of additional problems with the restorative justice approach. The TRC offered the incentive of an amnesty in return for "full confessions," which allowed the amnestied perpetrators to walk free. The victim, on the other hand, had to wait for decisions about reparations. To this day, the land redistribution program has proceeded very slowly. Furthermore, the idea of forgiveness was sullied to some extent by the state's involvement and endorsement of the forum and the fact that the perpetrator's public remorse was not necessarily an expression of internal remorse but a ticket to rehabilitation and amnesty. As it was not produced "freely," there was some skepticism as to the authenticity in some cases (Minow, 1998: 326, 342; Moon, 2004: 191).

Northern Ireland

The Northern Ireland case is somewhat unusual and anomalous in that it is also an incomplete process that has no clear direction. There are similarities with the South African case in that it is a conflict between a colonial-settler group (English and Scottish Protestants) and an indigenous population (Irish Catholics), but after eight hundred years of divisions, it has transmuted into an ethnic-religious conflict. However, the liberal-democratic character of the UK polity makes the case quite unique in that there is not a transition to democracy in the same way. The emergency and antiterror powers of the state have been promulgated by a democratic state, and thus it has been exempted from the same international pressures as other states (Campbell, Ni Aolain, and Harvey, 2003; Bell, 2004: 311–312).

Irish independence from Great Britain in 1921 did not include the province of Ulster, which had a large Protestant population. In the following years, violence erupted in the province due to discrimination against the Catholic minority and led to a partial segregation of the two communities. The irredentist Provisional Irish Republican Army (IRA) sought to drive the British out through guerrilla operations and terrorism. Their activities were countered by a heavy British presence and Protestant militias that divided the province even further. In 2003, the Belfast Agreement (also known as the Good Friday Agreement) was signed between the UK and Irish governments and representatives of the main Catholic and Protestant groupings, which sought to end conflict through the devolution of power and through democratic means. In June 2005, the Provisional IRA formally renounced the armed struggle. Nevertheless, neither prosecution of past crimes nor amnesty was addressed in the agreement (Vicente, 2003: 7).

The important aspect of the Northern Ireland case is that in contrast to the South African experience, there has not been a unitary or centralized institution for examining the conflict nor an agreement on what institution would implement such an examination (Bell, 2004: 315). A Human Rights Commission and a separate Equality Commission have been created to examine a limited range of abuses. In terms of transitional justice, these exhibit a combination of retributive and restorative components. At the same time, it is open-ended and there are no cutoff dates. The result is a sense of incompleteness to the process, a lack of closure on what is for many a deeply traumatic past. In addition, every institutional reform becomes a new political battleground and a "surrogate continuation of the conflict" (Bell, Campbell, and Ni Aolain, 2004: 316). The continuing demands of civil society and particularly of women's peace groups to hold the militia and British government accountable for the past is evidence of the unfinished nature of the peace process in Northern Ireland. On the other hand, the advantages of this piecemeal approach is that it sidesteps the difficulties of establishing an overarching explanation and understanding of the conflict and allows for engagement in the political process on specific issues.

However, the main problem of the Northern Ireland case is the continued dispute of what constitutes the core of the conflict, what are the key issues that need to be addressed, and hence what institutions or procedures to adopt. Here we see an example of the "meta-conflict" discussed earlier, which proves to be a critical stumbling block in moving on from the past (Campbell, Ni Aolain, and Harvey, 2003; Bell, 2004: 315–316, 320). One can see the similarities of this case with the Israeli-Palestinian dispute over what is the essence of their conflict. Is it the return of the refugees or the right of Israel to live in peace? Is it over 1948 or 1967?

Despite the limited progress made in the Northern Ireland case, it is relevant to our study for what has been achieved in the circumstances. As Terence McCaughey observes:

> What was achieved by the Good Friday Agreement of 10th April, 1998 was not forgiveness, much less reconciliation. What was achieved was an agreement to disagree, a *modus vivendi*. In a situation such as existed in Northern Ireland, that is an enormous step forward, however modest it may sound to outsiders. (McCaughey, 2001: 266)

Thus, while reconciliation is perhaps some distance away in Northern Ireland, some of the prerequisites, such as the cessation of hostilities and improved coexistence, are being consolidated.

Chile

The case of Chile is again quite different from the two preceding cases and is illustrative of the role of transitional justice measures in the transition from authoritarian rule to democracy. As in the cases of Brazil, Portugal, South Africa, and Uruguay, the peaceful return to democracy has been the outcome of extended negotiations that have emphasized forgiveness over justice (Lagos, Munoz, and Slaughter, 1999: 32). Chile was ruled by a military dictatorship under General Pinochet's regime between 1973 and 1990 in which 2,000–4,000 people were killed or disappeared, up to 60,000 detained and tortured, and possibly up to 200,000 forced into exile (UNHCR, 2000: 126–127). It saw a gradual increase in popular sovereignty with the elections of President Patricio Aylwin in 1990 and President Eduardo Frei in 1993. This period was characterized by extensive amnesties and exemptions from prosecution of a wide range of military leaders, including the former head of state, Pinochet. The military also retained an influential role in political life (Vicente, 2003: 5). The search for justice and reconciliation was thus intertwined with the struggle for greater democracy, and it was not until January 2006 that the last vestiges of authoritarian rule disappeared when President Michelle Bachelet was elected with a popular mandate to examine the horrors of the Pinochet era (Lagos, Munoz, and Slaughter, 1999: 3).

This period of transitional justice has been divided by Vicente into two phases: a political phase and a judicial phase. The first phase was constrained by the executive's consideration of the military's role in the constitution. A Truth and Reconciliation Commission was established in 1990, but its results were limited. After nine months of proceedings in an effort to uncover past human rights violations, a report was published and a national

Reparation and Reconciliation Corporation was established to assist relatives of the "disappeared." More far-reaching attempts to reform the system—which produced such abuses and the immunity of the perpetrators, such as those directed at the constitution, the legal system, and the military—failed. Here we have an illustration that unless TRCs have the support of the government and far-reaching powers in themselves, they are not sufficient to put the past to rest (Lean, 2003: 172).

Support for this view can be seen in the reopening of the amnesty issue in the second phase, which took place after 1993 when human rights organizations brought to the fore the atrocities committed in Chile. Civil society groups, and particularly the Roman Catholic Church's Vicaria de la Solidaridad (1976–1992), collected thousands of judicial transcripts concerning disappearances, which were invaluable to the investigations of the abuses of the Pinochet era (Crocker, 1998: 505). In 1997, the Geneva Conventions were applied for the first time since 1973, curtailing some of the amnesties that had been in place. Following the temporary detention of Pinochet in London in January 2000, there were renewed tensions with the military that drew attention to the tension between peace and justice in the country. As Alexandra Barahona de Brito noted, Chileans

> have had to wrestle with a tendency to premature "reconciliation," a euphemism for the acceptance of a limited democracy with authoritarian enclaves. They have also had to confront real obstacles in the form of a powerful military and right wing, as well as legal limitation of a kind not found in any other democratized country of the region. The law has been both an obstacle and a source of new opportunities. (Barahona de Brito, 2001: 175)

While Pinochet ultimately escaped prosecution in London and returned to Chile and subsequently was declared medically unfit to be put on trial, a taboo was broken and new inroads are being made into the impunity of the military. The case of Chile is still unfolding, and at the time of writing, the new government is putting into place new measures to reexamine the question of human rights abuses. In this sense, justice is still transitional and the prospects of reconciliation are unlikely before some kind of retributive justice has occurred. Restorative justice and reconciliation will follow only after truths are established as to the fate of the disappeared, the nature of the abuses of the victims, and the depth of culpability of the perpetrators.

Rwanda

The Rwandan case is particularly useful as it illustrates the results of a failed peace process and of a failed truth and reconciliation process. This is a case rooted in deep-seated ethnic antagonisms exacerbated by competition over land resources and state power. After the colonial period of domination by Belgium and the Tutsi tribe, a succession of Hutu governments from 1962 onward failed to either incorporate the marginalized Tutsi elite or to prevent Hutu reprisals against them (Khadiagala, 2002: 464–467). However, the mobilization of Tutsi refugees in Uganda into the armed units of the Rwanda Patriotic Front (RPF) led to a damaging civil war and paralysis in the Rwandan government. By 1993, the two parties signed the Arusha Peace Agreement, which provided for a transitional government. Part of the agreement included provisions for power-sharing, an independent judiciary, and a commission for national unity and reconciliation. As a matter of urgency, the transitional government was "to rid the administrative apparatus of all incompetent elements as well as authorities who were involved in the social strife or whose activities are an obstacle to the democratic process and to national reconciliation" (cited in Khadiagala, 2002: 478). In addition, the commission was to launch a national dialogue on unity and to prepare the population for reconciliation.

The failure of the demobilization components of the agreement and the spill-over effects of Hutu-Tutsi conflict in Burundi, however, led to the collapse of the agreement and a renewed round of Hutu attacks against Tutsi civilians culminating in the slaughter of approximately 800,000 people, mostly Tutsis. The failure of the UN to effectively intervene led to the RPF taking over the country and, in turn, to the flight of nearly 2 million Hutus to neighboring countries (UNHCR, 2000: 245).

The new government abandoned the restorative justice approach expressed by the reconciliation commission and, due to the magnitude of the crimes committed, it pursued the path of retributive justice. It sought the UN's backing for an International Criminal Tribunal for Rwanda (ICTR) and reformed its national judicial system to allow the prosecution of perpetrators of human rights violations. This was in part due to the large numbers of accused, which overburdened the Rwandan judicial and governmental system, but also because of the depth of antagonism resulting from decades of violent conflict between the two groups (Crocker, 1998: 511; Lemarchand, 1998: 3–16). As Asmal contends, the 1994 genocide in Rwanda changed the political landscape, and the restorative approach was abandoned and Rwandans turned away from facing the past. It was deemed impossible to arrive at a true national reconciliation without eradicating the culture of impunity, and prosecutions had to take place in order to restore the credibility of the rule of law. The government believed that harsh retribution was the only way to end the cycles of violence that had begun in the 1950s—only then could socioeconomic rebuilding be contemplated (Asmal, 2000: 20–21).

In many senses, post-1994 Rwanda cannot be said to be in a transitional justice phase, as the Tutsi government in Rwanda is not democratic and the retributive justice sought appears more like victor's justice. This seems confirmed in a number of ways. First, the tendency to attribute collective guilt for individual culpability in the planning and execution of the killings has resulted in distorted facts. Without more attention given to the different versions of "truth" about the genocide, coming to terms with the crisis will prove difficult (Lemarchand, 1998: 3, 11). Furthermore, unlike the TRC proceedings in South Africa, which were highly publicized, the ICTR proceedings did not involve the population in a real sense. The court was located in Tanzania, its mandate was restricted to the crimes of 1994 only, and there is a lack of involvement of the victims (Vicente, 2003: 10). Whereas the TRC in South Africa exemplified the dilemma involved in the pursuit of reconciliation without justice, the experience of Rwanda is an example of another dilemma: that of pursuing justice without reconciliation (Lemarchand, 1998: 13). One result of the abandonment of the restorative path is the continuing political marginalization of the Hutus. The power-sharing formula embedded in the so-called Government Convention of September 1994 was unsuccessful as it rendered both an electoral victory and the constitution meaningless. In this way, we can see that irrespective of how detailed they are, negotiations alone cannot replace the healing required to move on from the past.

Guatemala

The Guatemalan case is of particular relevance to this study as it involves significant refugee repatriation and is distinguished by the important role played by civil society in supporting transitional justice in the postagreement phase. In the 1970s, Guatemala was immersed in social and political upheaval with state forces reacting oppressively to any attempts at political participation. The conflict stemmed from inequalities in the land-ownership system where 72 percent of the arable land was owned by 2.1 percent of landowners, mostly from a nonindigenous minority. Power was consolidated in the hands of the conservative military and private sector interests leading to widespread armed resistance in the 1970s. As a consequence, the military regimes between 1978 and 1985 conducted a series of counterinsurgency campaigns, which led to 160,000 deaths, approximately 40,000 disappeared, and over 1 million, or some 20 percent of the country's total population, being displaced, including between 150,000 and 200,000 people forced into exile (Lean, 2003: 175). Despite holding elections in 1985, the continued influence of the military in political life prohibited any examination of the past or the possibility of redress and hence reconciliation. Nevertheless, the activities of human rights groups, women's groups, and mothers of the disappeared and the Catholic Church kept the issue alive. Particularly active was the decision of the Guatemala City Archdiocese

One of the most important and difficult challenges confronting a post-conflict society is the re-establishment of faith in the institutions of the state.... In territories where state institutions themselves have been used as a tool of oppression, building trust in the idea of the state requires a transformation in the way in which such institutions are seen. (Chesterman, 2004: 154)

We also saw in the case studies various forms in which transitional justice can be expressed, ranging from retributive justice, with tribunals and national and internationalized courts, to restorative justice, emphasizing reparation, the search for truth, giving recognition to the suffering of victims, and providing a platform for the seeking of and giving of forgiveness. We saw that a mix of measures was possible, involving some restorative and some retributive elements, such as amnesties and the barring from public office (legally known as lustrations). In this section, we turn to the Middle East peace process to see if and how these issues of truth, justice and reconciliation have been debated, and what mechanisms have been suggested to deal with them.

Before doing so, we need to clarify how the notion of transitional justice can apply to the Middle East peace process. There are two main problems with applying this term, which can be seen in the need to answer the questions what is the transition *from* and what is it *to*? First, we have to acknowledge the "meta-conflict"—the lack of agreement about what the conflict is about. To the Palestinians, the conflict began once the Zionist settlers started colonizing Palestine in large numbers in the 1920s and 1930s, culminating in the *nakba* of 1948. For the Israelis, the deal that has been struck is over the land acquired in 1967 not 1948, the recognition of Israel as a Jewish state, and the nature of the Palestinian state vis-à-vis Israeli security. We can see the mismatch very starkly when dealing with the causes of Palestinian refugeedom. While clearly this began with the creation of the Israeli state in 1948, the Oslo Accords in 1993 refer only to "persons displaced from the West Bank and Gaza Strip in 1967" (Declaration of Principles, 1993: Article XII). As Welchman observes, "the provision regarding refugees in the Israeli-Palestinian agreements so far concluded are minimal; indeed, it is part of the 'deal' so far that the refugee issue is postponed till the final status agreement" (Welchman, 2003: 14).

The second problem regards the "transition to what" part of the question. Even though during the period leading up to the Oslo Accords there was a grudging consensus on both sides that an Israeli withdrawal from the West Bank and Gaza Strip and a two-state solution would be the core of the bargain, the declaration was very unspecific and details were postponed for later negotiations. The result of this is the privileging of security issues over resolution of the conflict. As Bell concluded in her comparative study of peace agreements, the Oslo Accords and subsequent agreements demonstrate an almost complete divorce between the concept of peace and

human rights office to launch the Project for th[e]
Memory (REMHI), which subsequently undertool[
]tigation of Guatemala's past gross human rights v[
]6–7; Crocker, 1998: 504–505).

In 1994, a UN-brokered Framework Agreem[ent
]malan government and the main rebel forces of t[
]Revolutionary Union (URNG) was signed. The a[
]role of civil society, and issues such as the formatic[
]indigenous rights, and socioeconomic developme[
](Crocker, 1998: 503). As a result, the government [
]an official Commission for Historical Clarificatio[n
]debate through theater, radio, videos, and public w[
]keeping up public pressure on the commission to nar[
]1998: 507). The report *Guatemala: Memory of Si[*
]1999 and found that over 93 percent of deaths and [
]ried out at the hand of the military or police (Lean[,
]ommended compensation for victims and further [
]question of the disappeared. In this way, the appr[
]the government and civil society was that of rest[
]process is incomplete. As Vicente observes, "Altho[
]onciliation had a beginning with the truth commis[
]mechanisms, there is a lack of judicial sanctions, c[
]military and civilian elites that still remain in the c[
]any real democratic transition" (Vicente, 2003: 7). [
]malan case does illustrate how international interv[
]UN, and civil societies working in tandem can pron[
]By providing local groups with material resources,[
]legitimacy, and moral support, reluctant government[
]being more rigorous in confronting their complicit[
]abuses.

Truth, Justice, and Reconciliation in the Middle East Peace Process

From the case studies above, it has been shown ho[w
]dealt with the problem of, on one hand, securing and [
]agreement, and, on the other hand, of taking into a[
]created the conflict and the human rights abuses that [
]period of conflict. This balance between the exigen[
]ment and upholding the rule of law during the posta[
]acterized by profound social, political, and institutic[
]difficult to achieve. As Simon Chesterman writes:

the concept of justice" (Bell, 2000: 203). Consequently, the right of return of Palestinian refugees becomes subject to a bartering dynamic that overrides both UNGA resolutions and international human rights law in order to attain a "realistic peace" (Welchman, 2003: 14). In addition, there has since been an unraveling of this consensus during the interim period. Both sides have been disappointed in the Oslo framework and are hardening their positions: the Israelis over the question of their security, and the Palestinians over the questions of land and refugees (justice). Thus, there is also a meta-conflict here that will have an impact on the ultimate shape of the agreement, let alone the specifics. In these senses, the Middle East peace process is not yet in a transitional phase, and the term *transitional justice* should therefore be applied cautiously. However, the fact that some norms of justice have been traded for peace is in itself a step toward transitional justice, and references to a shared narrative and to achieving reconciliation have not been entirely absent from the discussions and negotiations. There are therefore elements of a transitional justice phase present, and it is worthwhile to attempt to draw out what there is and consider it in the light of our previous discussions.

It has to be admitted that the precedents for injecting truth and reconciliation into the peace process have not been overwhelming. The Israeli-Egyptian peace agreement in 1978 did not include a significant commitment to reconciliation between the two adversaries (Israel-Egypt Peace Treaty, 1979: Annex II, Articles 3 and 5). While there was an expectation that trade and cultural exchanges mentioned in the treaty would lead to greater interaction between the two countries, these were limited to some elite conferences and lecture tours and a one-way tourism of Israelis, including many Palestinian Israelis, to Egypt. There was no provision for any acts of atonement or forgiveness. There certainly was no attempt to construct a shared narrative of the conflict or to encourage a mutual understanding of each others' societies. The ongoing Israeli repression of the Palestinians and the 1982 invasion of Lebanon put an end to any hopes of breathing some life into the peace agreement.

The Jordanian-Israeli treaty of 1994 contains remarkably similar clauses on cultural exchanges and good neighborliness:

> The parties, wishing to remove biases developed through periods of conflict, recognize the desirability of cultural and scientific exchanges in all fields, and agree to establish normal cultural relations between them. Thus, they shall, as soon as possible and not later than 9 months from the exchange of the instruments of ratification of this Treaty, conclude the negotiations on cultural and scientific agreements. (Jordan-Israel Peace Treaty, 1994: Article 10)

Article 11 binds the parties to seek "to foster mutual understanding and tolerance based on shared historic values" and outlines specific points to address regarding inflammatory propaganda. It is quite astonishing, given the preponderance of Palestinians living in Jordan, that a more far-reaching program of reconciliation and its attendant truth and reparation activities were not envisaged. Other milestones, such as the Madrid Peace Conference in 1991 and the Oslo Accords in 1993, did not refer to reconciliation. In the former, a multilateral framework was established and included five separate working groups on regional development, water, disarmament, environment, and refugees. The framework failed to consider truth and reconciliation issues, and in the latter, a number of issues, such as settlements, water, refugees, borders, security, and Jerusalem were deferred for permanent status negotiations on a later date, but truth or reconciliation was not one of them.

One should not overlook the numerous attempts by civil society to take the initiative and design a number of collaborative ventures to promote truth, justice, and reconciliation. In this respect, the Middle East peace process shows some similarities with the cases we looked at in Chile and Guatemala, where civil society activism was crucial in pressuring the government to be more proactive on truth, justice, and reconciliation issues. Professional groups, such as the Israeli-Palestinian Physicians for Human Rights, and dialogue groups and educational projects, such as the Israeli-Palestinian Centre for Research and Information, are examples of attempts to cross the divide and establish a joint vision (Kaminer, 1996; Hurwitz, 1992). In this field, women on both sides of the divide have been particularly active (Hilterman, 1991; Sharoni, 1995). As Simon Sharoni and Muhammed Abu-Nimer conclude:

> Even if the parties to the conflict sign a peace agreement, its successful implementation depends on the support of grassroots constituencies on both sides of the political divide. In fact one of the major shortcomings of the Oslo Accords lies in the failure of both Palestinian and Israeli-Jewish officials to draw on the experience and expertise of peace and community activists on both sides of the Palestinian-Israeli divide. (Sharoni and Abu-Nimer, 2000: 192)

Louis Kreisberg has surveyed the various steps that could be said to contribute to reconciliation in the post-Oslo period. Examples include public renunciations of terrorism by the Palestinian leadership, alterations to educational textbooks on both sides, and the visit of President Arafat to the widow of the assassinated prime minister of Israel Yitzhak Rabin in 1995. Nevertheless, the overall conclusion is that "neither side's reconciliation acts were of a magnitude sufficient to influence the other camp directly and substantially" (Kriesberg, 2002: 567). Significantly, neither of the two governments extended a formal invitation to the leaders of the other side for an official state visit.

While there may have been little support at the official bilateral level for these initiatives, external encouragement has been very forthcoming, particularly from European NGOs and the EU. An example is the EU's People to People (P2P) program (1998–2001) and its successor, the Partnership for Peace (PfP) program from 2002. Emerging out of the European Mediterranean Partnership designed to increase dialogue, exchange, and cooperation, these two programs were specifically introduced as an "essential means of reinforcing dialogue and restoring mutual confidence between the parties" (Luxembourg European Council, 1997: 81). Specifically the guidelines asserted that the programs were designed to "broaden the base of support for the peace process in both Israeli and Arab societies" and "help provide a solid foundation at the civil society level for a just and lasting peace in the Middle East" (EU People to People Programme, 2000: 3). Over 22 million euros were disbursed to support projects categorized under mutual understanding, peace education, conflict resolution, capacity building, embedding justice, and peace concepts across both communities. While these programs did have the effect of empowering Israeli and Palestinian civil society and building networks that are a long-term investment for the future, the linking of the programs so directly with the flawed and failing peace process undermined the programs' effectiveness and reduced their impact.

In turning to the main negotiations under discussion in this study—the Taba Talks and the Geneva Accords—we can see how little consideration has been given to the issues of truth, justice, and reconciliation. Indeed, just prior to his departure to the Camp David Summit, which preceded the Taba Talks, the Israeli prime minister Ehud Barak declared that one of his "red lines" was "no Israeli recognition of legal or moral responsibility for creating the refugee problem" (cited in Lustick, 2005: 121). The Moratinos summary of the Taba Talks contains no reference to the need to establish mechanisms for reconciliation. Article 3.1, entitled "Narrative," indicates there was a discussion on the need to establish a joint narrative on the refugees but no agreement was reached. The background papers reveal that on one level the Israeli side responded positively to the Palestinian proposal that Israel recognize "its moral and legal responsibility for the forced displacement and dispossession of the Palestinian civilian population during the 1948 war and for preventing the refugees from returning to their homes in accordance with United Nations General Assembly Resolution 194" (Palestinian Authority/Palestine Liberation Organization, 2001: 2).

The Israeli side proposed in reply that:

> The State of Israel solemnly expresses its sorrow for the tragedy of the Palestinian refugees, their suffering and losses, and will be an active partner in ending this chapter that was opened 53 years ago, contributing its

part to the attainment of a comprehensive and fair solution to the Palestinian refugee problem. (Israeli Non-Paper, Draft 2, 2001: 2)

Nevertheless, on closer reading of this paragraph in the context of the succeeding paragraphs in which other parties are also called upon to share responsibility for the solution and where the Jewishness of the Israeli state is affirmed, the Israeli position is that of accepting only partial responsibility. Nowhere in the papers are there any discussions of reconciliation programs or any form of retributive or restorative justice.

In contrast, the Geneva Accord contains no statement of moral regret or responsibility. Instead it devotes a single paragraph, under the article on refugees, to that of reconciliation programs. Here the protagonists agree to create fora for "exchanging historical narratives and enhancing mutual understanding regarding the past" (Geneva Accord, 2003: 7.14). It specifically suggests the educational sector as the main vehicle for these exchanges and also the possibility of commemorating "those villages and communities that existed prior to 1949." It is not clear what mechanisms are envisaged to implement such an agreement, but elsewhere in the text there is provision for an Israeli-Palestinian Cooperation Committee, which presumably will be given the task of this kind of activity. However, one cannot help but conclude that issues of truth, justice, and reconciliation either did not feature strongly in the deliberations of the negotiating teams or that they were too intractable to include in any detail. When one compares what is proposed in both the Taba papers and in the Geneva Accord to the case studies in the previous section, we can see the absence of an equivalent of a truth commission to determine both what happened in 1948 and to reconcile the differing narratives, the absence of any demand for legislation that would render illegitimate certain forms of discriminatory activity or institutions, the absence of any mechanisms to address offensive literature in schools and public discourse, and the absence of any consideration of how the overall peace agreement will be linked to moving on from the past. According to Menachem Klein, concurrently a political scientist, Israeli negotiations adviser, and participant in the Geneva talks, the Geneva Accord leaves this task to the two civil societies

> on the presumption that a diplomatic accord cannot suddenly change deeply-rooted memories, nor modify national and historical myths overnight. Reconciliation and openness toward the narrative of one's fellow human being are the result of long-term processes that take place within civil society. Diplomatic mechanisms can promote reconciliation processes but not dictate them. (Klein, 2006)

It is also significant in this context that while the road map, which was agreed upon by Israel and the PNA and which has the backing of the international community, utilizes terms such as "fair," "just," and "living side-by-side," it contains no clauses that either define what such fairness and justice is in such contexts or that propose specific measures to enhance truth and reconciliation.

Conclusion

This final section will attempt to draw together some of the key factors that can be discerned from the case studies and examine the extent to which they can be applied to the Middle East peace process. In doing so, it will also take into account cultural and regional issues and the parameters set by the historical and political legacies of the Palestinian-Israeli conflict. While the uniqueness of the Palestinian-Israeli case poses some difficult challenges in this attempt, it is clear that the precedents set by international experience elsewhere offer useful pointers to the direction those concerned with this issue can take.

There are five main points that can be drawn from the case studies discussed in this chapter. First, restorative justice and truth and reconciliation commissions are insufficient on their own. They need to be part of a broader package of measures that will consolidate the peace process and convince the public that past injustices are being addressed either collectively or indirectly. For example, in the Rwanda case, the Arusha Accords included a restorative justice approach, but the breakdown of other aspects of the peace agreement swept it away. By itself, it was not strong enough to prop up the whole edifice of postconflict transition. Similarly, the South African Truth and Reconciliation Commission was embedded into a broader process of dismantling apartheid. These included the democratic transfer of power, land reforms, and the repeal of discriminatory legislation and practice. Indeed, the strongest criticism of the South African approach stems largely from the slow implementation of these supporting measures, which undermine the sense of the restorative justice process being completed.

Second, the active participation and support of civil society in the implementation of restorative justice has been essential. This is because of the dual role it plays. It acts as the audience for the cathartic effects of truth seeking and public apologies, and at the same, it can offer the forgiveness and rehabilitation into society that the process requires. Furthermore, civil society acts as a catalyst and a spur to official institutions in their tasks. As we saw in the Chilean and Guatemalan cases, it was the pressure of civil society that kept the process alive and ensured that a genuine confrontation with the past was undertaken. Connected to this is a third factor. The case studies show that restorative justice is an important vehicle for restoring a gender balance in the postconflict phase. The exclusion of women from postconflict political processes in the transitional phase, despite sometimes both having borne the brunt of the suffering and been central to dialogue activities, is a phenomenon that can be seen in many conflicts. As a study of the Northern Ireland conflict highlights:

> Peace processes are typically deeply gendered, raising awkward questions about the neutrality of the transitional project. While women have been at the forefront of peace initiatives through the conflict, peace agreements are usually negotiated predominantly, if not exclusively, by men. . . . Addressing gender is not just a question of addressing women's needs. The experience of how women work can be vital to peace-making and peace-building. In particular women are often well-positioned to further connections between civic society (where women often predominate) and political institutions (where men often predominate). (Bell, Campbell, and Ni Aolain, 2004: 320–321)

The roles of women's groups and coalitions in the cases of Chile and Guatemala also support the importance of this factor. Also connected to the role of civil society is the fourth point. The support given to civil society from international human rights organizations and other external agencies put pressure on recalcitrant governments to achieve some minimal standards and benchmarks in their dealing with past injustices. The international scrutiny of the work of tribunals, truth commissions, and amnesty commissions ensure that some internationally agreed-upon norms are maintained. While this was not so applicable in the case of Northern Ireland, where the democratic traditions of the British state appeared to have absolved it from this kind of attention, it is a pattern one can see in the other case studies examined.

Finally, the disaggregation of the process of restorative justice over time and institutionally has both its advantages and disadvantages. A decentralized and fragmented set of institutions brings with it many problems with regard to an open-ended, ongoing process, but it also has the merit of keeping the issue alive until the circumstances are more propitious to deal with it. In the Northern Ireland, Chilean, and Guatemalan cases, we can see how issues that were not dealt with at the start of the postconflict phase were tackled at a later date when the process had been consolidated and there was less risk of a reversal. Thus, while this piecemeal approach did not have the advantages of the South African case, where a national process of catharsis and healing took place within a given time span, in situations where the peace agreements are fragile it has allowed for greater flexibility and incrementalism, and hence a degree of stability.

One of the criticisms of transitional justice models is that not enough attention has been given to cultural differences and indigenous forms of conflict resolution and reconciliation. The participation of external agencies, it has been argued, has led to the marginalization of "custom-based justice" (Findlay, 2000; Andersen, 1999). This is a point taken up by George

Irani in his study of Islamic mediation and conflict resolution techniques. In a study for the US Institute for Peace, he examines the importance of conflict resolution rituals based upon family, kinship, and clientism. Identifying *wasta* (patronage-mediation), *tahkeem* (arbitration), *sulh* (settlement), and *musalaha* (reconciliation) as key procedures and rituals in Arab and Islamic society, he believes they need to be drawn into any negotiations in the Middle East.

> The problem confronting Western approaches to reconciliation, is that in Middle East societies in which the conceptual category of the individual does not have the same validity and importance as in Western cultures, . . . the individual is enmeshed within his or her own group sect, tribe or millet. Religion continues to play a crucial role [in] individual and collective lives. (Irani, 1999: 14)

He goes on to argue that without addressing age-old grievances, peace in the Middle East is unlikely, and the techniques of *sulh* and *musalaha* can be usefully employed. Nevertheless, where there have been attempts to confront the past in the Middle East, such as recent attempts at national reconciliation in Morocco, Algeria, and Tunisia, one should note that the methods employed are very much at variance with the indigenous forms described by Irani. They are also characterized by state-imposed discourse and procedures and can be seen as attempts to control grievances rather than to provide a platform for their expression and resolution (Silverstein, 2005; Slyomovics, 2001).

In turning to the Middle East peace process, we need to consider the extent to which the above discussions are relevant. In the Palestinian-Israeli case, can we talk about a transitional justice phase when the only agreements signed are interim ones that have gradually unraveled over the past decade? It appears to me that in the light of the collapse of the Camp David Summit in 2000 and the eruption of the al-Aqsa intifada in the same year, the peace process as envisaged by the Oslo Accords is over. Attempts to revive it, such as the road map of the Quartet and the Arab Initiative, have not succeeded, and the election in 2006 of a radical Islamist party in the OPTs that refuses to accept the Oslo premises and a new Israeli party that is committed to unilateral steps and not a negotiated process only suggest an interring of the Oslo framework. A new peace process will be embarked upon, but not in the short term.

What is clear is that in these circumstances a retributive justice option is not available as part of a peace settlement. This could only possibly occur if and when there was a complete defeat of one party and the defeated party agrees to the punishment of its leadership. In the Palestinian-Israeli case, we are seeing the mutual exhaustion of both parties, and the search for a formula for a settlement is driven by the fact that neither side has been able to defeat the other. In this context, there are at least two ways of characterizing the substance of the peace process. On the one hand, there is the view that what we have been witnessing since the Madrid Conference in 1991 of a gradual exploration of a peace settlement based on an asymmetry of power, with Israel being able to dictate most of the terms and the Palestinian leadership too weak to extract more concessions or to persuade their constituency to support it. On the other hand, one can argue that we are witnessing a gradual softening of Israel's former hard-line positions, which refused to countenance any notion of a Palestinian state, or the division of Jerusalem, or the evacuation of any settlements.

In which case, if an agreement is ultimately achieved, is a restorative justice approach a serious option? Is the search for truth, justice, and reconciliation relevant or feasible? It is clear that the institutions and procedures that would be adopted are contingent upon the nature of the peace settlement agreed upon by the two main parties—Israelis and Palestinians. Immediately we encounter a major problem to do with the meta-conflict. Which conflict is being resolved, and hence what are the likely remedies suggested? Are we attempting to establish a collective narrative on what happened to Palestine in 1948 and hence a basis for the solution to the refugee issue? Or are we attempting to accommodate Zionism and thus recognition of Israel as a Jewish state living alongside a Palestinian state in the West Bank and the Gaza Strip?

There are many skeptics of elements of the restorative approach. For example, Yael Tamir has argued that a truth commission in the Palestinian-Israeli conflict would not be beneficial. In a series of discussions held by the Harvard Law School Human Rights Program, she pointed out that the most severe abuses of human rights, such as the expulsion and dispossession of the Palestinians, are embedded in the Zionist ethos, which continues to have widespread Israeli support. In addition, there would be an imbalance in the focus of a truth commission since Israel would be subject to investigation of many abuses since 1948, while Palestinians would undergo investigation for atrocities committed mostly in the pre-1948 years and by nonofficial groups. Finally, she argues that due to their close identification with the army, most Israelis would be unlikely to countenance any investigation into its wrong-doings. She concludes that a truth commission would be seen as serving a partisan political goal, and its social and political benefits would be unclear to most Israelis (Harvard Law School Human Rights Program, 1997). The Palestinian-Israeli political scientist Nadim Rouhana similarly believes that reconciliation in the present circumstances is unattainable:

> Israeli society is too far from facing the truth about the establishment of Israel to discuss Israel's historical responsibility for the Palestinian catastrophe, introduce an element of justice into the framework of negotiations,

and, above all, pay the bill of reconciliation in the coin of the political restructuring that it requires. (Rouhana, 2005: 273)

Another Israeli scholar, Jessica Nevo, is similarly skeptical but at the same time draws attention to the potential role of civil society in Israel in precipitating change. She agrees with Tamir and Rouhana that a truth-seeking process that scrutinizes Zionist history in Palestine over the past century or since 1948 or 1967 may put the whole Zionist project on trial (Nevo, 2004: 5). Nevertheless, she goes on to argue that while it is unlikely that the Israeli establishment will formally engage with a "peace with justice and reconciliation" process, like in Chile and Guatemala, Israeli civil society organizations are acting autonomously to document abuses and to bring an awareness of the Palestinian dispossession to the Jewish-Israeli public. This is a graduated truth-seeking and transitional-justice process that will put pressure on the Israeli government to review its approach (Nevo, 2004: 6).

When one spells out the implications of what is meant by addressing the past, then one can see what a long way the parties have to travel, particularly the Israelis, before such a scenario is likely to come about. If the solution being suggested to the conflict is what is known as a "one-state solution," that is, a single binational state involving the return of refugees to their homes in what is now Israel, then there are a series of essential reforms to be carried out and institutions to be established. From the case studies, one can envisage that, as part of a package of restorative justice measures, there would have to be a degree of land and property restitution, compensation for destroyed or appropriated land and property, and the repeal of laws that discriminate against non-Jews on the Israeli side and non-Palestinians on the Palestinian side. Other important measures would include a formal apology from both sides to the citizens of the other side for any harm and suffering experienced during the course of the conflict. A series of commemorative activities would be necessary, such as national days of mourning and reconciliation, museums, public monuments, and the like, to mark the refugee experience, dispossession, achievements in exile, and the role of peacemakers and other leaders. A truth commission that sought to record the experience of the conflict from the viewpoints of the different actors would be an essential component to the package. It would be part of a healing dialogue and forge a new national consensus about the past that would feed into new educational curricula and cultural exchange programs and programs for reconciliation. In addition, in exchange for a full confession by those involved in terrorist activities and war crimes, the perpetrators would receive an amnesty. In the current balance of power, this scenario might seem unrealistic, but there can be no gainsaying the fact that opponents of apartheid in South Africa were also dismissed as unrealistic but had their ideals vindicated.

If the solution is based upon what is known as a "two-state solution," in which a new Palestinian state would be established in the OPTs, where it would be the main location for resettlement of refugees, then there would be many differences with the case studies. In the first place, it would be a reconciliation process between two states rather than between two peoples within a single state. As such, the process would be much more a top-down process, with the focus on more official institutions and formal programs. It would in all likelihood be a more limited process due to the physical separation of the populations. In addition, similar to the Northern Ireland case, it is unlikely that there could be a vision of the future shared by both peoples. Second, as the level of interactions between the two peoples would presumably be less, the psychological and emotional dimensions of the past conflict would not be addressed to the same extent and with the same urgency. Finally, a peace agreement that is backed by international guarantees would not engender the same international support for the activities of civil society groups within Palestine and Israel that were trying to address issues of the past independently. Therefore, there would be much less international protection for them, less room for their maneuver, and less opportunity and space for public discussion.

Despite these limitations on a restorative justice approach in a two-state solution, one would nevertheless envisage that a number of measures would need to be included in the agreement itself or in the postconflict phase. An essential first step would be an apology for the harm done and for the suffering of the other side to be complemented by an amnesty for the criminal actions of political and military leaders. We can see that the first tentative steps for this were taken in Taba, where the Israeli side suggested an expression of "its sorrow for the tragedy of the Palestinian refugees, their suffering and losses" without accepting full responsibility (Israeli Non-Paper, Draft 2, 2001: 2). An important second step would be a limited restitution and compensation package that recognized both material losses and the trauma of dispossession and exile. This was discussed more fully in Chapter 6. It would also be important to include a program of official visits for leaderships on both sides to express their remorse and commitment to coexistence at a suitable national site or monument. This would be supported by a range of measures to encourage harmonious interactions in trade, culture, and education. There would need to be a review of legislation, media policy, and curricula that promoted contentious and negative images of the other side. Connected with this would be the establishment of a truth commission to determine the events leading up to 1948 and to clarify the subsequent actions of the Israeli government and the PLO. As we have already mentioned, there may be considerable resistance to this idea, particularly from the Israeli establishment, but this should not deter Israeli and Palestinian civil society from taking the initiative with international support. As Said wrote in 1999 (emphasis added):

> Might it not make sense for a group of respected historians and intellectuals, composed equally of Palestinians and Israelis, to hold a series of meetings to try to agree on a modicum of truth about this conflict, to see whether the known sources can guide the two sides to agree on a body of facts—who took what from whom, who did what to whom, and so on—which in turn might reveal a way out of the present impasse? *It is too early, perhaps, for a Truth and Reconciliation Commission, but something like a Historical Truth and Political Justice Committee would be appropriate.* (Said, 1999)

Thus, in this second scenario of a two-state solution (in which the issue of refugee return is either sidestepped or occuring in the new state of Palestine), the role of civil society remains crucial. It is important both in terms of filling in the gaps that the leaders feel too weak to accomplish themselves and in terms of continuing to pressure the leadership to go further and be held more accountable for their previous actions.

8

Conclusions

Peace negotiations and their agreements are messy, fluid affairs with multiple variables, conflicting agendas, and key actors jockeying for advantage over each other. There is also a constant tension between the demands of realpolitik and principle. It is not surprising, then, that the attempts by international agencies and international lawyers to bring some consistency into the process encounter enormous difficulties and achieve only partial success. As a result, it is not possible to identify a discrete formula, a set of buttons to press, or an off-the-peg package for what is required to resolve conflicts. Although the Palestinian-Israeli conflict has been under way for the best part of a century, and the prospects of a resolution seem as remote as ever, the experience of the international community is that conflicts do end. This in itself provides both hope and some useful concepts and tools that can be applied to other conflicts. The argument of this book has been that the special and unique features of the Palestinian-Israeli conflict have for too long obscured the fact that there are enough features held in common with other conflicts for some lessons to be learned. This is particularly true of the refugee issue.

In some senses all refugee situations are unique in their specificities. Yet at the same time, the phases in the refugee cycle of displacement, dispossession, exile, local integration, resettlement, return, reparation, and reintegration are also features that they all share to some degree with other cases. In this way, legal frameworks, operational practices, and agreed procedures that have evolved over the past few decades become a critical reference point through which peace agreements and those clauses relating to refugees can be evaluated and assessed. Indeed, they provide a range of options that can be adapted and utilized to guide the construction of agreements and programs required to deal with a new set of conflicts. We should remind ourselves that it is not because they do not work that they are in existence, but because in most cases they have proved to be useful and in some circumstances they have even proved to work fairly well. It would be foolish to ignore this fact.

This study has had three main purposes. The first aim has been to draw upon the experience of international practice and to apply it to the refugee issue in the Palestinian-Israeli conflict. The second aim has been to compare the proposals put forward in the Middle East peace process with the accumulated experience of the international community. The third aim has sought to bridge the gap between the realist position and those positions rooted in rights-based discourse. The findings are quite startling. The degree to which there has been a disconnection between the various proposals under consideration in the peace process, not simply with international humanitarian law but also with operational practice elsewhere, has been shown clearly. For example, we saw in Chapter 3 how the various peace proposals and Track II discussions paid little attention to international experience. By contrasting the sum of that experience, as contained in the Repatriation and Resettlement Handbooks of UNHCR, with what has taken place within the major milestones of the Palestinian-Israeli negotiations, such as the Taba Talks and the Geneva Accord, reference to international norms has been revealed to be very limited. Similarly, in Chapter 4 the failure of early attempts to integrate Palestinian refugees into their host countries or to resettle them in third countries was shown. This was largely due to the refusal of Palestinian refugees to surrender their political right to self-determination and their right of return as recognized in international law and applied elsewhere. This adherence to their rights also complicated approaches to repatriation. Palestinian and Israeli proposals that have sidestepped this legal framework and that did not support the right of refugees to choose whether or not they return to their ancestral homes, have not been accepted and have led to a gradual delegitimization of the PLO leadership and the rise of HAMAS as an alternative leadership. Chapter 5 considered institutional and operational issues concerning the protection of refugees and the delivery of services in a postconflict phase. It concluded that a revised and strengthened mandate for UNRWA would be a way forward. It would also be an approach that is most consistent with international practice and that recognizes UNRWA's credibility in the eyes of most refugees because of its long experience and capacity to deliver services.

Our consideration of international practice also encompassed one of the most contentious issues in any conflict: that of reparations for loss and harm done. Chapter 6 examined Palestinian and Israeli proposals on restitution and compensation in the light of international experience and concluded that, while in this debate there has been considerable borrowing from international practice, insufficient attention has been given to property restitution and the need to include some enforcement mechanisms. The argument advanced is that dismissal of this option has less to do with the logistical impossibility than it has to do with an ideological rejection of the prospect. The penultimate chapter on truth, justice, and reconciliation acknowledged that the discussion of this topic is in its infancy but, nevertheless, highlighted its limited role in the major negotiations. International experience has shown the importance of including it as a central and critical element to any peace agreement, and while some NGOs and intellectuals on both sides have shown an awareness of this, there has been little incorporation of these ideas into official or Track II negotiations.

What is clear from these findings is the centrality of the Jewishness of the State of Israel to the question of the Palestinian refugees. Here we can return to the concentric rings that were outlined in the first section of Chapter 1. Many of the elements in the outer rings are logistical and technical ones that can be solved given time and resources. However, their resolution is also, crucially, contingent on a resolution of the core two elements—Palestinian refugee identification with the homeland and the need for Israelis to have an exclusively Jewish state on the same piece of land. There is very little prospect of the Palestinian refugee issue being resolved within a broadly human rights perspective while Israel continues to hold its current positions. As Rouhana puts it succinctly and bluntly:

> The Israelis will first have to recognise a simple historical truth: when the Zionist project started in the late nineteenth century, there was a Palestine and a people who lived in it as its indigenous population. Zionism sought to establish an exclusive Jewish state in Palestine while another group of people, a nation—or at least a nation in formation—was already living there. Thus the Zionist goal could only have been achieved by force. Establishing a Jewish state in Palestine inevitably entailed uprooting the indigenous population. (Rouhana, 2005: 266)

The question, therefore, that academics, policymakers, the donor community, and activists have to face is, how does one return (to paraphrase Douglas again) "matter out of place," that is, refugees back to their "place" without causing a secondary displacement and a further round of conflict? One view, supported by the proponents of the Oslo framework, is that you do not. A line has to be drawn between the present and the past and the land of historic Palestine shared. This is the two-state solution. Palestinian refugees would be asked to renounce the right of return to their homes as enshrined in UNGA Resolution 194 in exchange for Israeli recognition of a Palestinian state in the OPTs to which they would be allowed to relocate. As we saw in Chapter 4, in some senses this also corresponds with the new thinking in UNHCR, which is attempting to conflate "homes" and "homeland" in order to exactly get round the intractability of this kind of problem. But as we saw in Chapter 1, the problem in the Palestinian-Israeli case is that the Palestinian sense of national identity is closely tied to the notion of return to their homes and to the need to make any concessions to that right of return in a free and uncoerced manner.

It is possible that ultimately Palestinian refugees will accept this option, but not on its own or in the form that it has been presented in the peace negotiations so far. It would have to be part of a package that recognized their right to return, acknowledged that they were giving it up for peace, and which included a raft of reparations, including a modicum of property restitution and compensation, a redrawing of the borders of 1967 to ensure the viability of a Palestinian state and a degree of equity in the sharing of the land and resources, as well as an Israeli apology. Finally, it would require a genuine program of truth seeking and reconciliation as a way of healing the wounds. Only under these circumstances can this researcher envisage the two-state solution to the refugee issue (irrespective of the complexity of other issues, such as Jerusalem) being acceptable to Palestinian refugees. If this seems far-fetched, it is worth noting the observation of Ian Lustick, whose study of German-Israeli reconciliation negotiations led him to conclude:

> Given that it is virtually impossible to imagine a more horrible crime committed by one nation against another than that which Nazi Germany committed against the Jews, we may therefore infer that: if at least a workable form of reconciliation has been possible between Israel and Germany, it cannot be said to be impossible with regard to Israel and Palestine. (Lustick, 2005: 121)

The proposals in the peace negotiations hitherto have not included such a wide-ranging approach. Thus, it is hard to see, in the light of continuing Israeli security operations and fears that lead it to demand humiliating limits on Palestinian sovereignty, and in the light of continuing land acquisitions for both settlements, for the separation wall constructed through parts of the OPTs, and along the Jordan valley, how a two-state solution is a feasible option.

It is highly significant that in a top-level Israeli postmortem on the Camp David summit attended by former Israeli prime minister Barak; his chief negotiators such as Gilead Sher, Itamar Rabinovich, and former Israeli intelligence officials; and senior US participants such as Aaron Miller, Martin Indyk, and Robert Malley, one of the observations that emerged was that if the two-state solution was not a feasible option in the eyes of the Palestinians, by default they would be driven to the alternative option—the "one-state" solution. If Palestinians assessed that a Palestinian state in the OPTs was not viable, that it did not meet minimum benchmarks of sovereignty, and that the complete package would not satisfy the views of the refugees, then they had little choice but to either defer an agreement or work toward a one-state solution (Shamir and Maddy-Weitzman, 2005: 233). In essence, the one-state solution is a vision of a binational state in which Israeli Jews and Palestinian Arabs would be equal citizens in a nonsectarian democracy. Palestinian rights would be established through a campaign of democratization similar to those carried out in East Asia and Central and South America in the late 1980s and 1990s. Because it has been proposed at various times by Palestinians over a long period as a solution to both the refugee issue and their long-term relations with Israel, in the closing paragraphs of this study we should consider it a little more deeply.

In the aftermath of the collapse of the Camp David summit and the al-Aqsa intifada, Palestinian interest in this original PLO proposal of the 1960s has been rekindled. Despite the challenges it contains to their self-identity as being part of the Arab world, serious thought has been given to the idea. This is partly due to disillusionment with the Oslo process, disillusionment with international efforts to constrain Israeli settlement and military activities, disillusionment with fragmentation of the Palestinian leadership, and the failure of international law to reverse the building of the separation wall across the OPTs. A debate started by BADIL's Arabic-language magazine *Haq al-Awda* has received broad media attention and closer academic examination. Clearly, no Israeli politician would support such a move and in that sense there is no "partner" to this project.

However, there are two perspectives that give some credence to the proposals and suggest that the binational vision should not be dismissed out of hand. First, as Palestinian intellectuals and activists begin to unpack the idea and examine the details of the idea more closely, one can see that there is a continuum of options in the binationalism vision ranging from equal citizenship within a single, centralized state through to a "binational framework" comprising two entities with a phased convergence of political structures through to a higher degree of cooperation and functional interconnectedness (Ghanem, 2005: 15–18). What is interesting about this continuum is that the end of the continuum, which stresses the cooperative and functional interconnectedness, is not so distant from the more idealized vision in the two-state solution with its proposals for open borders, economic unions, and security cooperation, but it is differentiated from the two-state solution through a greater sense of equality between the two polities.

The second perspective is that of *la longue duree*. This views the Zionist project as a project in retreat, with the best guarantor of a continued Jewish homeland in its biblical homeland being an accommodation with the indigenous population. From the apogee of expansion in 1967 with the conquest of the Golan Heights, West Bank, Gaza Strip, and Sinai, the retreat has been intermittent but the overall trend of withdrawal is steady. In 1982, Israel controlled all the land from the Egyptian border up to and including Beirut. Since then, it has withdrawn in stages from south Lebanon and most of the Gaza Strip and is contemplating further withdrawals from parts of the West Bank. In its refusal to accommodate Palestinian rights or to countenance for a long time an independent Palestinian state, it has made these later withdrawals without any concession by Palestinians. Dressing the withdrawals up as an exhibition of strength and terming them "unilateralism" cannot mask strategic and intellectual confusion in these steps. An example is the separation wall. By abandoning the international borders of 1967 through the construction of the wall, it opens up the question not only of the permanence of Israel's eastern border, but also of those to the north and south of the West Bank. Unraveling what little consensus there was on the 1967 borders, Israeli political elites have raised the question of the future of Galilee and the Triangle, both predominantly Palestinian areas inside Israel and close to the West Bank. A similar confusion is apparent over Israeli positions on Jerusalem. In order to safeguard its security in the city, Israel policies result in controlling more than 200,000 Palestinians in East Jerusalem and the surrounding suburbs. One should recall that at the same time Israel opposes, on demographic grounds, significant Palestinian repatriation to their ancestral homes. On the one hand, it increases the non-Jewish population of the state, on the other, it seeks to prevent any increase by refusing the right of return of refugees.

One way of connecting this long view to the debate over the one-state solution is by reference to the literature on democratization. In a seminal article about what is known as the transitional theory of democratization, Dankwort Rustow identifies four phases through which a divided society has to pass before democracy is established. All the phases are accompanied by conflict ranging from civil strife to civil war. The first phase is that of defining the nation; it concerns the establishment of consensus over borders and which cultural or ethnic groups constitute the nation. The second phase is the phase of "historic compromise" in which the political elites of the competing groups recognize after a long struggle that neither side can achieve supremacy. They finally agree to negotiate a bargain, which constitutes the basis of the national political system. The third phase is that of "habituation" where the political elites begin to work out how the system they have constructed can be used to their advantage without jeopardizing the overall bargain, and the final phase, the "consolidation" phase, is where these systems are embedded and group competition is mediated through normal democratic processes (Rustow, 1970; Dumper, 1996). In this context, the debate over the one-state solution reflects the Palestinian-Israeli conflict as being in the first phase, that is, defining who comprises the emerging nation, but moving gradually toward the second phase of historic compromise. In this case, the historic compromise will be the Palestinians agreeing to share the land and the Israelis accepting a more inclusive vision of having a Jewish national home.

This study has confirmed the view that the refugee question remains the core issue of the Palestinian-Israeli conflict. The focus of the peace process hitherto on territorial and sovereignty questions has reversed the order of problems that have to be solved in order to attain an agreement. Refugees constitute 70 percent of the Palestinian population and are thus too large a constituency to be marginalized by the Palestinian leadership or have their concerns finessed by economic incentives and other palliatives by the international community. Palestinian nation building and the resolution of the refugee issue are two sides of the same coin. Furthermore, refugees constitute nearly 50 percent of the combined Israeli-Palestinian populations and thus remain a significant political force within and influence on the dynamics between the protagonists. This study has also led me to the view that the solution will not be a simple choice of options: on one hand, repatriation to Israel, or on the other, repatriation to a new state, or local integration, or resettlement. It will not be of Israeli dominance accompanied by Palestinian powerlessness. As the study of the other refugee situations has shown, the solution to refugee crises is usually a mix of options, not simply one alternative or the other. A broad range of alternatives for the refugees is more often than not a central part of any peace agreement, and this will, similarly, be part of the final agreement between Israelis and Palestinians. Some elements of the agreement will meet their expectations and some of them will not, but taken in total, only an agreement that appears to be fair "enough," and consists of a minimum of principles for a just solution will be acceptable and durable.

In addition, it is not as if a solution will arrive out of thin air. It will be, as Rashid Khalidi has put it, part of a "dialectical" process, with Israel offering more generous terms, which in turn will result in the softening of negative attitudes in the Arab world, thus making a comprehensive peace and Israeli security alike more achievable (Khalidi, 1999: 233). In this context, it is possible to envisage a package that could be construed as achieving the right of return without undermining Israeli concerns. The package would include the return of the original 1948 refugees and some of their descendants to their homes with a limited restitution package and extensive compensation scheme. In addition, there would be a quota system for other refugees contingent upon economic development in Israel, and there would be free access to the new Palestinian state. The land and property laws of Israel would need to be amended to allow for a more democratic access to ownership, and there would need to be constitutional amendments to ensure the equality of the Palestinian minority in Israel. The search for truth, justice, and reconciliation will remain open and subject to debate and further campaigning until a compromise over the question of responsibility is achieved. The quid pro quo for Israel would be the cessation of conflict, acceptance into the Middle East region, secure borders with its neighbors, and a framework of cooperation and mutual security with the new Palestinian state. Indeed, the Palestinians would have an investment and a sense of guardianship in such an agreement, since it would have met many of their needs and aspirations.

At the same time, Israel is militarily and economically too strong and too wedded to the fears and securities of the first two to three decades of its existence to accept such a package at this stage. In order to be accepted in the Middle East, it will have to confront the fact that it will need to find a way in which its Jewishness can be maintained and indeed celebrated without effacing the culture of the indigenous inhabitants of Palestine. This will require a great deal of internal debate and even perhaps strife, but it is possible, nevertheless, to imagine a way in which Zionism as an exclusivist ideology is either gradually softened so that non-Jews can be embraced or is retained symbolically in a state that is committed to equality, justice, and peace. Completing this study in the spring of 2006, one has to accept that these required changes both in the Palestinian and Israeli societies are only in their very early stages, but that is the challenge and that is the work that needs to be done.

APPENDIX: SOURCES OF DATA FOR POLICY FORMULATION

For much of the period under review, data on Palestinian refugees was collected on an ad hoc, fragmented, and partial basis. There was, and continues to be, no central coordinating body or archive. While UNRWA is the main depositary of data on registered Palestinian refugees, it is not the only source, and it is only recently that its archives have been organized. One should note that other sources, such as UNCCP, the International Committee of the Red Cross (ICRC), and American Friends Service Committee (AFSC), also hold information about Palestinian refugees that predates that of UNRWA (Tamari and Zureik, 2001).

Renewed interest in data collection and sources on the Palestinian refugee issue began after the establishment of the Refugee Working Group (RWG) following the Madrid Conference in 1991. Although not responsible for a database itself, the RWG was responsible for greater coordination of data collection, storage, and accessibility. The RWG allocated themes to specific countries, as can be seen in Table A.1.

This work produced some useful surveys, particularly those carried out by the Norwegian Institute for Applied Social Science (FAFO) on behalf of the Norwegian government (Tamari, 1996: 15, web version).[1] In addition, there is an increasing amount of literature being produced by Palestinian NGOs such as BADIL and Shaml that act as resource and information centers. However, there have been three fundamental gaps in the research. First, there are the problems inherent in the documentation of property claims, which include lack of longitudinal depth. More important, there have been severe restrictions on the access of researchers to the data. Second, there is little data available on Palestinian refugees living outside the mandate areas of UNRWA, thus there is little data on Palestinian refugees living in the Arab Gulf states, North Africa, and other parts of the world. Third, despite some high-profile and controversial surveys, very little is known about Palestinians' views on the future and on the question of

194 APPENDIX

Table A.1 Thematic Responsibilities of the Refugee Working Group

Responsibility (Theme)	Responsible Party (Shepherd)
Databases	Norway
Human resources development	United States
Vocational training and job creation	United States
Family reunification	France
Public health	Italy
Child welfare	Sweden
Social and economic infrastructure development	European Union

return. This appendix is intended to give an indication of the sources and their accessibility and is divided into two main categories: large institutional and state archives, and independent NGO centers and initiatives. It does not claim to be comprehensive and exhaustive, but it should give the reader a clear idea of where to go and what might be found.

Large Institutional and State Sources

The main potential source of data is UNRWA archives, which provide a unique source of data on Palestinian refugees. Since its inception in 1950, UNRWA has kept archives of data on refugees at the agency's headquarters in Amman, which contain the following data:

- The Unified Registry System (URS). This is the core of UNRWA's database detailing its services to their registered refugees. The information is updated from the field offices.
- The Demographic Database. This holds information about the status of registered refugees as well as additional information on individual refugees.
- The Socio-Economic Database. This contains information on particular hardship cases that require supplementary assistance.

UNRWA also preserves the original family files, which include historical information on refugees. Some 684,136 or so family files contain information on registration dating in many cases back to 1948 and are supported by copies of birth, marriage, and death certificates; records of property ownership or leases; taxation receipts; employment records; and passport and travel documents. In total there are an estimated 25 million critical documents, which constitute a valuable archive of the lives of a major sector of the Palestinian population at the time they became refugees. UNRWA wishes to store this information electronically in order to link it with the registration and socioeconomic databases in the URS, to make it more accessible. Some progress has been achieved toward the realization of setting up a Family Files Archiving System that could, when put together with the other URS components, constitute a future national archive for the Palestinians. In addition to this statistical-based data, UNRWA possesses audiovisual data, which consists mainly of films, slides, still pictures, and posters and provides a unique source of material on various aspects of the Palestinians' lives since 1948. However, access to the data is restricted.

In order to preserve all this data, the Institute for Jerusalem Studies has conducted an assessment and feasibility study of digitizing paper forms (Tamari and Zureik, 2001). In addition, the Palestine Refugee Records Project, a project of the UN, has embarked upon establishing a unified computerized registration system and, more significantly, to preserve the family files, which may include data about original claims, conditions of flight, and authentication (Nasser, 2003). Once implemented, this project would provide the computerized foundation for future links, providing easier access to historical data that could one day be useful in future compensation and restitution claims.

A second very important source is the archives of UNCCP, which hold extensive data on confiscated Palestinian refugee property. Among the documents are records that identify and detail almost every parcel of Arab-owned land in Israel that UNCCP compiled during the 1950s and 1960s. UNCCP's last program of research, the Technical Programme of 1952–1964, remains as the most far-reaching study ever made of the scope and value of Palestinian refugee property (Fischbach, 2003). There are several drawbacks in the use of UNCCP data, one of which is that the records do not include all types of property that was lost by the refugees in 1948. Individual land (or *waqf* land) was recorded, but land that was communally owned by a tribe or village or land that was public or state owned was omitted. In addition to this, the transliteration of Arabic names is inconsistent and can cause confusion. However, most of these records are not available to the public and remain locked up at the UN archives in New York.

A third major potential source is the Israeli Custodian of Absentee Property. After the 1948 War, Israel began expropriating refugee property through a series of legal and administrative procedures (Peretz, 1958; Jiryis, 1976; Dumper, 1994). In 1950, the Absentee Property Law delineated the responsibilities of a custodian who was to administer and preserve the property and the land of any Palestinians who fled or were forced to leave the country and were defined by this law as "absentees." Much of the property was eventually transferred to a Development Authority and the Jewish National Fund. In the course of these transfers, detailed records were kept and have recently been made accessible to selective researchers, and the results are potentially very helpful (Nathanson, 2003). An urgently required project is to reconcile this data with that held by UNCCP.

A further potential source is that of the British Mandate government tax records. Although assembled and made ready for shipment to Britain in 1948, they did not leave the country and are now held by the Israel State Archives (Fischbach, 2003: 253–255). Much of the material collected by Sami Hadawi, a former tax officer in the Mandatory government, and published in a number of books is based upon this material (Hadawi, 1990; Hadawi, 1988).

An increasingly useful source is the Palestinian Central Bureau of Statistics (PCBS) established by the PNA. Its censuses of the Palestinian population carried out in 1995 and population and housing in 1997 have provided important socioeconomic data on refugees in the OPTs, while in 2003 it conducted a survey monitoring preferences and expectations regarding the future of refugees (Abu Libdeh, 2003). Proposals are under way to coordinate the work of the PCBS with that of UNRWA and FAFO.

Due to its responsibilities as "gavel-holder" in the RWG, the Canadian government has also sought to support research on the refugee issue. This has been carried out by the Expert and Advisory Services Fund (EASF), which was set up in 1992 and managed by the International Development Research Centre (IDRC) based in Ottawa. The objective is to commission research and promote increased capacity for policy planning and coordination. The focus has been on planning for demographic change as a result of the movement of people and modalities of compensation to Palestinian refugees. The IDRC has also been responsible for two groundbreaking "Stocktaking" conferences on Palestinian refugee research that brought together researchers from a range of academic, government, and NGO sources to identify existing work and prioritize new areas of research.[2]

The final two potential sources for data on Palestinian refugees in the first category are the World Bank and UNHCR. The World Bank's involvement in the West Bank and Gaza began in 1993, when the Bank was asked by the cosponsors of the Middle East Multilateral Peace Talks to lead and support a program of economic assistance. The outcome was a report, "Developing the Occupied Territories: An Investment in Peace," which presented a definitive economic survey and analysis of the West Bank and Gaza and provided the blueprint for subsequent donor involvement in the area (World Bank, 1993). From then, the Bank's role has grown to encompass many services: provider of technical assistance and development grants, an administrator of trust funds, a primary donor coordinator, and, of primary interest to this study, preparation for a key role in any repatriation or resettlement agreement. A number of studies examined the costs of a repatriation program to the OPTs, giving a detailed breakdown of infrastructural costs under different scenarios (World Bank, 2000b; Brynen, 2006; Krafft and Elwan, 2003). In addition to the Bank's work in producing detailed studies and providing assistance, it is likely to have a key role to play in terms of financing and assisting in the implementation of an agreement. For example, the international fund to finance the activities of an international commission for Palestinian refugees proposed at Taba would be comanaged by both the UN and the World Bank. This would include compensation payments, payments to the host countries, and payments to the Palestinian state (Brynen, 2006).

UNHCR was established as a temporary agency to provide international protection and to seek durable solutions to refugee problems. This usually meant assisting governments with repatriation programs or the absorption of refugees within new communities. Despite the huge increase in responsibilities since the 1950s, its core mandate has not changed. UNHCR has experienced something of a complex relationship with the Palestinian refugees, and as we have seen, the provision of services to Palestinian refugees was given to UNRWA and therefore outside of UNHCR's framework. However, UNHCR has a great amount of information regarding its work, which is available in many different forms, mostly available to the public, regularly updated, and user friendly. Its *State of the World's Refugees* and the *RefWorld* CD-ROM provide in-depth information regarding its work and field programs. Although they do not provide data on Palestinian refugees per se, they do provide the raw material for comparative study. The experience of UNHCR can provide lessons to be learned for the Palestinian case. Through the examination of UNHCR's *Handbook for Registration* (2003), for example, guidelines and case studies can provide common features from which it is possible to extrapolate core elements of a program dealing with refugees. By studying the role of lead agencies, especially UNHCR, who carry out repatriation and resettlement programs, one can examine the procedures, standards, and management of such programs in other refugee cases.

Independent NGO Sources

In turning to research centers and NGOs dealing with Palestinian refugees, we encounter a wide variety of databases and research activities. The following are illustrative and focused on some of the better known, and as already stated, it is not an attempt to provide a comprehensive list. One of the better-known Palestinian NGOs devoted to refugee work is Shaml, the Palestine Diaspora and Refugee Centre, based in Ramallah in the Occupied Palestinian Territories. Shaml conducts primary research on the Palestinian refugee issue, including comparative research in the sociology of migration. It houses a number of online databases to serve as resources for research. Current research focuses on three areas: memories of exile, the right and sociology of return, and transnational life. In conjunction with Birzeit University, Shaml is running an Oral History Programme to record the rich historical seam of orally transmitted memories. The program is built upon work carried out in the 1980s by the Birzeit Research Centre that traced hundreds of Palestinian villages destroyed in or after the 1948 War. The current program intends to create a database of recorded personal histories of these towns and villages, although recent changes in personnel and internal difficulties have rendererd this planned work uncertain.

Another Palestinian NGO active in this field is BADIL (Resource Center for Palestinian Residency and Refugee Rights). BADIL provides resources on the question of Palestinian refugees and displaced persons. As part of its work, BADIL carries out legal research and analysis of refugee rights, particularly the right of return and restitution. Through its advocacy work and through its community-based campaign, which seeks to articulate the views of refugees, BADIL has succeeded in ensuring that Palestinian refugee rights has been placed on the domestic, regional, and international agendas. Its publications include analyses of domestic and international law related to Palestinian refugees; policy advice related to refugee rights; and reports for submission to relevant international, including UN, human rights treaty monitoring committees, in order to advance Palestinian refugee rights.

Less directly involved in the refugee issue per se are several other NGOs whose work touches on refugee issues. For example, the Palestinian Society for the Protection of Human Rights and the Environment (LAWE), dedicated to preserving human rights through legal advocacy, sees its work overlap with refugee issues through its defense of the rule of law and property restitution. It began compiling a database of Arab landownership in pre-1948 West Jerusalem in 1996. There are also a number of small Israeli NGOs concerned with the rights of IDPs that have instituted public awareness campaigns concerning Palestinian refugee rights. One of the best known is a group called Zochrot, meaning "remember." Zochrot attempts to involve the Jewish public in Israel in remembering the *nakba* of 1948 and to draw attention to Israel's moral debt to the Palestinians. It seeks to support the Palestinian right of return for Palestinian refugees through the organizing of tours to destroyed Palestinian villages as well as maintaining a Hebrew-language database of maps and information about the *nakba*.

Outside Israel and the OPTs, probably the most important research being carried out on Palestinian refugees is by FAFO. Commencing its research activities in the Middle East in the 1980s, its work includes studies on living conditions, demography, impact of structural adjustment programs, poverty, and Palestinian refugees. The bulk of FAFO work on Palestinian refugees has been directed toward gaining accurate and updated information on their living conditions in the various host countries in the region, with an aim of using such information for advocacy and for planning of humanitarian assistance. Its data on living conditions of Palestinian refugees in Jordan, Syria, and Lebanon have become the baseline for research and policy formulation in these areas. One of its best-known projects is the *Survey of Living Conditions* among Palestinians in Gaza, the West Bank, and Arab Jerusalem (Heiberg and Øvensen, 1993). FAFO has also recently completed a study of the coping strategies of Palestinian refugees and of the potential of administrative data gathered by UNRWA for research on the situation of the refugees (Hanssen-Bauer and Jacobsen, 2004). FAFO was commissioned by the Norwegian government to undertake its commitment to develop databases on this issue (see Table A.1).

A leading research institute that straddles Palestinian, Arab, and international spheres is the Institute for Palestine Studies (IPS), with research centers in Paris, Beirut, Ramallah, and Washington, DC. In addition to publishing numerous articles on refugee issues in its house journals, IPS has published a number of analyses of the refugee issue and the peace process. Its most noteworthy contribution is the authoritative and extensively researched reference work by Walid Khalidi on the destroyed villages of Palestine (Khalidi, 1992). Detailing hundreds of Palestinian villages that were destroyed or depopulated in 1948, the text comprises for each village a narrative, statistical data, and a description of the current status of the site, including post-1948 Israeli settlements established on expropriated land. The Institute for Jerusalem Studies, affiliated with the Institute for Palestine Studies, also collected and published information on Palestinian property in West Jerusalem in 1999 (Tamari, 1999).

Another important source is the Palestinian Refugee ResearchNet based in McGill University, Canada. A nonpartisan project devoted to the dissemination of ideas and scholarly information, its website fosters scholarly collaboration, policy research, and innovative thinking on the Palestinian refugee issue.

Two other international NGOs deserve mention. The first, the Palestinian Return Centre, is an independent institute founded in the UK in 1996 (www.prc.org.uk). It specializes in the research, analysis, and monitoring of issues pertaining to the dispersed Palestinians and their right to return. It also serves as an information repository on other related aspects of the Palestine question and the Arab-Israeli conflict. While primarily an activist organization and associated with an Islamist perspective, it provides a useful entry into the views and perspectives of those refugees who take a more maximalist approach to negotiations with Israel. The second, formerly Centre d'Etudes et de Recherches sur le Moyen-Orient Contemporain (CERMOC) and currently Institut Français du Proche Orient (IFPO), has moved away from its work on refugees, but in the 1990s it was responsible for a remarkable series of conferences on UNRWA that collected some excellent studies on the situation of refugees (CERMOC, 1996, 1997, and

1998). Finally, Civitas, a project directed by Karma Nabulsi of Nuffield College, Oxford University, and funded by the European Union, has produced a detailed report on refugee perceptions of their needs and aspirations. Data was collected through extensive interviews and scores of public meetings for Palestinian refugees in the Arab world, but also across the world in key locations (Nabulsi, 2006: A-2).

Sources for Further Research

Websites

UNISPAL (United Nation Information System on the Question of Palestine)
www.un.org/Depts/dpa/docs/unispal.htm

Al Mashriq (the Levant, Lebanon and the Middle East)
www.almashriq.hiof.no

Al-Nakba
www.alnakba.org

Bitter Lemons: Palestinian-Israeli Crossfire
www.bitterlemons.org

CERMOC
www.diplomatie.gouv.fr

Global IDP Project
www.idpproject.org

Foundation for Middle East Peace
www.fmep.org

Guardian
www.guardian.co.uk

Gush Shalom
www.gush-shalom.org

Institute for Jerusalem Studies
www.jqf-jerusalem.org

The Institute for Palestine Studies
www.palestine-studies.org

International Development Research Centre (IDRC)
www.idrc.ca

The Israeli Government's Official Website
www.mfa.gov.il

Middle East Research and Information Project (MERIP)
www.merip.org

Norwegian Institute for Applied Social Science (FAFO)
www.fafo.no

Palestinian Center for Policy and Survey Research (PSR)
www.pcpsr.org

Palestinian Central Bureau of Statistics (PCBS)
www.pcbs.org

Palestinian Diaspora and Refugee Centre (Shaml)
www.shaml.org

Palestinian Peace Coalition
www.geneva-initiative.net

Palestinian Refugee ResearchNet (PRRN)
www.arts.mcgill.ca/mepp/new_prrn

The Palestinian Return Centre
www.prc.org.uk

Palestinian Right to Return Coalition
www.al-awda.org.uk

Resource Centre for Palestinian Residency and Refugee Rights
www.badil.org

The World Bank Group
www.worldbank.org

UNHCR
http://unhcr.ch

United Nations
www.un.org

University of California–Santa Cruz
www.ucsc.edu

York University
www.yorku.ca

Tables and Diagrams

United Nations, An Easy Guide on Refugee Resettlement Programs 2003/2004 www.unhcr.org.uk/resettlement/resettlement_pdfs/resettlement_programs
    03-04.pdf (accessed 12 February 2006)

UNHCR, Resettlement Procedures
www.unhcr.org/cgi-bin/texis/vtx/protect/opendoc.pdf?tbl=
   PROTECTION&id=3bd58ce9a (accessed 10 February 2006)

UNRWA, Total Registered Refugees per Country and Area
www.un.org/unrwa/publications/pdf/rr_countryandarea.pdf (accessed
   8 February 2006)

Notes

1. For a detailed overview of FAFO's projects for the RWG, see Updated Activity/Project Summary on Data Bases (Norway) January 1998. Available online at www.fafo.no (accessed 21 March 2005).

2. See Stocktaking I (1997) and Stocktaking II (2003) for references to online sources for the conference proceedings.

Acronyms

4Rs	Repatriation, Reintegration, Rehabilitation, Reconstruction
AFSC	American Friends Service Committee
AHLC	Ad Hoc Liaison Committee
BADIL	Resource Centre for Palestinian Residency and Refugee Rights
BiH	Bosnia-Herzegovina
CCPP	Comisiones Permantes de Representantes de los Refugiados Guatemaltecos en Mexico
CERMOC	Centre d'Etudes et de Recherches sur le Moyen-Orient Contemporain
CHC	Commission for Historical Clarification
CIREFCA	International Conference on Central American Refugees
COHRE	Centre on Housing Rights and Evictions
CRPC	Commission for Real Property Claims of Refugees and Displaced Persons (in Bosnia)
DAR	Development Assistance for Refugees
DLI	Development through Local Integration
DPA	Dayton Peace Agreement
EASF	Expert and Advisory Services Fund
ECHO	European Commission Humanitarian Office
EU	European Union
FAFO	Norwegian Institute for Applied Social Science
al-FATAH	Harakat al-Tahrir al-Watani al-Filastini (Palestinian National Liberation Movement)
FRY	Former Republic of Yugoslavia
GAPAR	General Authority for Palestine Arab Refugee Affairs (in Syria)
GCIP	Global Consultations on International Protection
GDP	gross domestic product

ACRONYMS

GNP	gross national product
GRICAR	Grupo Internacional de Consulta y Apoyo para el Retorno
GTZ	Gesellschaft für Technische Zusammenarbeit
HAMAS	Islamic Resistance Movement
ICRC	International Committee of the Red Cross
ICTR	International Criminal Tribunal for Rwanda
ICVA	International Council for Voluntary Agencies
IDF	Israel Defence Forces
IDP	internally displaced people
IDRC	International Development Research Centre
IFOR	Implementation Forces
IFPO	Institut Français du Proche Orient
IHRO	international human rights organizations
ILC	International Law Commission
ILO	International Labour Organization
IOM	International Organization for Migration
IPS	Institute for Palestine Studies
IRA	Irish Republican Army
IUST	Iran-US Tribunal
LAWE	Palestinian Society for the Protection of Human Rights and the Environment
MDSD	Most Different Systems Design
MOPIC	Ministry of Planning and International Coordination
MSSD	Most Similar Systems Design
NATO	North Atlantic Treaty Organization
NGOs	nongovernmental organizations
OAU	Organization for African Unity
OCHA	Office for the Coordination of Humanitarian Assistance
OPTs	Occupied Palestinian Territories
OSCE	Organization for Security and Cooperation in Europe
P2P	People to People
PA	Palestinian Authority
PARI	Palestine Arab Refugee Institution
PCBS	Palestinian Central Bureau of Statistics
PfP	Partnership for Peace
PIC	Peace Implementation Council
PIP	Peace Implementation Plan
PLO	Palestine Liberation Organization
PNA	Palestinian National Authority
POP	People-Oriented Planning
PPR	Permanent Place of Residence
QIPs	Quick Impact Projects
REMHI	Project for the Recovery of Historical Memory

RH	Resettlement Handbook
RPF	Rwanda Patriotic Front
RR	registered refugees
RWG	Refugee Working Group
TC	truth commission
TRC	Truth and Reconciliation Commission
UK	United Kingdom
UN	United Nations
UNCC	United Nations Compensation Commission
UNCCP	United Nations Conciliation Commission for Palestine
UNDP	United Nations Development Programme
UNGA	United Nations General Assembly
UNGAR	United Nations General Assembly Resolution
UNHCHR	United Nations High Commission for Human Rights
UNHCR	United Nations High Commission for Refugees
UNICEF	United Nations Children's Fund
UNPROFOR	United Nations Protection Force
UNRWA	United Nations Relief and Works Agency for Palestine Refugees in the Near East
UNSC	United Nations Security Council
UNSCO	Office of the United Nations Special Coordinator
UNTAC	United Nations Transitional Authority in Cambodia
UNTAET	United Nations Transitional Administration in East Timor
URNG	Guatemalan National Revolutionary Union
URS	Unified Registry System
VRH	Voluntary Repatriation Handbook
WFP	World Food Programme

BIBLIOGRAPHY

"Abolish UNRWA" (2002) *Jerusalem Post* (15 April).
Abu Libdeh, H. (2003) "Statistical Data on Palestinian Refugees: Prospects for Contribution to Final Settlement," paper presented at the 2nd International Stocktaking Conference on Palestinian Refugee Research, International Development Research Centre, Ottawa, 17–20 June.
Abu Sitta, S. (1999) *Palestinian Right to Return: Sacred, Legal, Possible* (London: Palestinian Return Centre).
——— (2001) *From Refugees to Citizens at Home* (London: Palestine Land Society).
Adelman, H. (2002) "Refugee Repatriation," in S. J. Stedman, D. Rothchild, and E. M. Cousens, eds. (2002) *Ending Civil Wars: The Implementation of Peace Agreements* (Boulder, CO: Lynne Rienner Publishers), pp. 273–302.
Agha, H., and R. Malley (2001) *Camp David: The Tragedy of Errors,* available online at www.gush-shalom.org/archives/campdavid1.html.
Akram, S. (2002) "Palestinian Refugees and Their Legal Status: Rights, Politics, and Implications for a Just Solution," in *Journal of Palestine Studies,* Vol. 31, No. 3 (Spring), pp. 36–51.
Akram, S. and T. Rempel (2003) "Temporary Protection for Palestinian Refugees," paper presented at the 2nd International Stocktaking Conference on Palestinian Refugee Research, International Development Research Centre, Ottawa, 17–20 June.
Alterman, R. (2003) "Land Housing Strategies for Immigrant Absorption: Learning from the Israeli Experience," paper presented to the 2nd International Stocktaking Conference on Palestinian Refugee Research, International Development Research Centre, Ottawa, 17–20 June.
Andersen, C. (1999) "Governing Aboriginal Justice in Canada: Constructing Responsible Individuals and Communities Through 'Tradition,'" *Crime, Law and Social Change,* Vol. 31, pp. 303–326.
Aruri, N. (2001) *Palestinian Refugees: The Right of Return* (London: Pluto Press).
Arzt, D. (1997) *Refugees into Citizens: Palestinians and the End of the Arab-Israeli Conflict* (New York: Council on Foreign Relations).
——— (1999) "The Right to Compensation: Basic Principles Under International Law," paper delivered at the Workshop on Compensation for Palestinian Refugees, International Development Research Centre, Ottawa, 14–15 July.

—— (2001) "Actual Repatriation: A Minimal Israeli Gesture," in J. Ginat and B. Perkins (eds.) *The Palestinian Refugees: Old Problems, New Solutions* (Brighton: Sussex Academy Press).
Asmal, K. (2000) "Truth, Reconciliation and Justice: The South African Experience in Perspective," *The Modern Law Review,* Vol. 63, No. 1 (January), pp. 1–24.
Avni-Segre, D. (1969) "Israel: A Society in Transition," *World Politics,* Vol. 21, No. 3 (April), pp. 345–365.
Ayalon-Nusseibeh Plan (2004) *The People's Voice,* available online at www.mifkad.org.il/en.
BADIL (2000a) *Palestinian Refugees in Exile: Country Profiles* (Bethlehem: BADIL Resource Center for Palestinian Residency and Refugee Rights).
—— (2000b) "What Role for UNRWA: Opportunities and Constraints. A Durable Solution to the Palestinian Refugee Issue" available online at www.badil.org/Publications/Monographs/UNRWA.Refugees.pdf.
—— (2001) "The 1948 Palestinian Refugees and the Individual Right of Return: An International Law Analysis," Bethlehem, BADIL Resource Center for Palestinian Residency and Refugee Rights, January.
—— (2004) "Palestinian Refugees: Closing the Gaps: Between Protection and Durable Solutions," memorandum submitted to the UNHCR Pre-Excom NGO, Geneva, BADIL Resource Center for Palestinian Residency and Refugee Rights, September.
Badran, A. (2001) "The Role of UNRWA: Refugee Statistics and UN Resolutions," in J. Ginat, and B. Perkins (eds.) *The Palestinian Refugees: Old Problems, New Solutions* (Brighton: Sussex Academy Press).
Bagshaw, S. (1997) "Benchmarks or Deutschmarks? Determining the Criteria for the Repatriation of Refugees to Bosnia and Herzegovina," *International Journal of Refugee Law,* Vol. 9, No. 4, pp. 566–592.
Ballard, B. (2002) *Reintegration Programmes for Refugees in South-East Asia: Lessons Learned from UNHCR's Experience* (Geneva: UNHCR, Evaluation and Policy Analysis Unit and Regional Bureau for Asia and the Pacific).
Barahona de Brito, A. (2001) "Passion, Constraint, Law and Fortuna: The Human Rights Challenge to Chilean Democracy," in N. Biggar (ed.) *Burying the Past: Making Peace and Doing Justice after Civil Conflict* (Washington, DC: Georgetown University Press).
Barkan, E. (2003) "Restitution and Amending Historical Injustices in International Morality" in J. Torpey (ed.) *Politics and the Past: On Repairing Historical Injustices* (Lanham, MD: Rowman and Littlefield), pp. 91–102.
Bekar, A. (2002) "Refugees First," *Ha'aretz* (Israel), 6 June.
Bell, C. (2000) *Peace Agreements and Human Rights* (Oxford: Oxford University Press).
—— (2004) "Women and the Problem of Peace Agreements: Strategies for Change," in R. Coomeraswamy (ed.) *Women, Peace-making and Constitutions* (New Delhi: Women Unlimited).
Bell, C., C. Campbell, and F. Ni Aolain (2004) "Justice Discourses in Transition," *Social and Legal Studies,* Vol. 13, No. 3, pp. 305–328.
Benvenisti, E. (1999) "Principles and Procedures for Compensating Palestinian Refugees: International Legal Perspectives," paper delivered at the Workshop on Compensation for Palestinian Refugees, International Development Research Centre, Ottawa, 14–15 July.
—— (2003) "The Right of Return in International Law: An Israeli Perspective," paper presented at 2nd International Stocktaking Conference on Palestinian Refugee Research, Ottawa, 17–20 June.

Benvenisti, E., and E. Zamir (1995) "Private Claims to Property Rights in the Future Israeli-Palestinian Settlement," *American Journal of International Law.*

Benvenisti, E., and S. Hanafi, eds. (2006) *Israel and the Palestinian Refugee Problem* (Heidelberg: Max Plancke Institute).

Bisharat, G. (1994) "Displacement and Social Identity: Palestinian Refugees in the West Bank," in S. Shami, ed. *Population Displacement and Resettlement: Development and Conflict in the Middle East* (New York: Center for Migration Studies), pp. 212–226.

Black, R. (2006) "Return of Refugees: Retrospect and Prospect," in M. Dumper (ed.) *Palestinian Refugee Repatriation: Global Perspectives* (London: Routledge).

Black, R., and K. Koser, eds. (1999) *The End of the Refugee Cycle? Refugee Repatriation and Reconstruction* (Oxford: Berghahn).

Bokae'e, N. (2003) *Palestinian Internally Displaced Persons Inside Israel: Challenging the Solid Structures* (Bethlehem: BADIL).

Bokae'e, N., and T. Rempel, eds. (2000) *Survey of Palestinian Refugees and Internally Displaced Persons* (Bethlehem: BADIL).

Boling, G. (2001) *The 1948 Palestinian Refugees and the Individual Right of Return: An International Law Analysis* (Bethlehem: BADIL).

Bowker, R. (2003) *Palestinian Refugees: Mythology, Identity, and the Search for Peace* (Boulder, CO: Lynne Rienner Publishers).

Bradley, M. (2005) "The Conditions of Just Return: State Responsibility and Restitution for Refugees," *Refugee Studies Centre Working Paper* (21).

Brand, L. A. (1988) *Palestinians in the Arab World: Institution Building and the Search for State* (New York: Columbia University Press).

——— (1995) "Palestinians and Jordanians: A Crisis of Identity," *Journal of Palestine Studies,* Vol. 24, No. 4 (Summer), pp. 46–61.

Brooks, R. L. (2003) "Reflections on Reparations," in J. Torpey (ed.) *Politics and the Past: On Repairing Historical Injustices* (Lanham, MD: Rowman and Littlefield), pp. 103–114.

Brynen, R. (1997) "Imagining a Solution: Final Status Arrangements and Palestinian Refugees in Lebanon," *Journal of Palestine Studies,* Vol. 26, No. 2 (Winter), pp. 42–58.

——— (1999) "Financing Palestinian Refugee Compensation," presented to the Workshop on Compensation as Part of a Comprehensive Solution to the Palestinian Refugee Problem, Ottawa, July.

——— (2000) "The Future of UNRWA: An Agenda for Policy Research," Workshop on the Future of UNRWA, Minster Lovell (UK), 19–20 February, available online at www.arts.mcgill.ca/MEPP/PRRN/papers/future.html.

——— (2003) "Refugees, Repatriation, and Development: Some Lessons from Recent Work," 2nd International Stocktaking Conference on Palestinian Refugee Research, International Development Research Centre, Ottawa, 17–20 June.

——— (2004) *The Geneva Accord and the Palestinian Refugee Issue,* Department of Political Science, McGill University, February, available online at www.arts.mcgill.ca/mepp/new_prrn/research/research_papers.htm#articles.

——— (2006) "Perspectives on Palestinian Repatriation," in M. Dumper (ed.) *Palestinian Refugee Repatriation: Global Perspectives* (London: Routledge).

Brynen, R., with E. Alma et al. (2003) "The 'Ottawa Process,' An Examination of Canada's Track Two Involvement in the Palestinian Refugee Issue," paper presented at 2nd International Stocktaking Conference on Palestinian Refugee Research, International Development Research Centre, Ottawa, June.

Brynen, R., and R. el-Rifai, eds. (2006) *The Absorbtion of Palestinian Refugees* (London: I. B. Tauris).

Butenschon, N. A., U. Davis, and M. Hassassian, eds. (2000) *Citizenship and the State in the Middle East: Approaches and Applications* (Syracuse, NY: Syracuse University Press).
Campbell, C., F. Ni Aolain, and C. Harvey (2003) "The Frontiers of Legal Analysis: Reframing the Transition in Northern Ireland," *The Modern Law Review*, Vol. 66, No. 3, pp. 217–245.
Castels, S., and N. Van Hear (2005) *Developing DFID's Policy Approach to Refugees and Internally Displaced Persons* (Oxford: Refugee Studies Centre).
Cattan, H. (1982) *Solution of the Palestinian Refugee Problem* (Vienna: International Progress Organization).
Centre d'Etudes et de Recherches sur le Moyen-Orient Contemporain (CERMOC) (1996) *UNRWA: A History with History*, Proceedings of the 20–22 December 1996 Workshop, Amman, Jordan (unpublished).
——— (1997) *UNRWA: A History with History*, Proceedings of the 25–27 August 1997 Workshop, Amman, Jordan (unpublished).
——— (1998) *UNRWA: A History with History*, Proceedings of the 9–11 October 1998 Workshop, Amman, Jordan (unpublished).
Chesterman, S. (2004) *You, the People: The United Nations, Transitional Administration and State-Building* (Oxford: Oxford University Press).
Chimni, B. S. (2003) "Post-Conflict Peace-Building and the Return of Refugees: Concepts, Practices and Institutions," in E. Newman and J. van Selm (eds.) *Refugees and Forced Displacement: International Security, Human Vulnerability and the State* (Tokyo: United Nations University), pp. 195–220.
Clinton, W. (2000) "Clinton Parameters," available online at www.fmep.org/documents/clinton_parameters12-23-00.html.
Cohen. R. L. (2001) "Provocations of Restorative Justice," *Social Justice Research*, Vol. 14, No. 2 (June), pp. 209–232.
Cohen, R., and J. Kunder (2001) "Humanitarian and Human Rights Emergencies," Brookings Institute, available online at www.brookings.org/comm/policybriefs/pb83.htm.
COHRE (2005) "The Pinheiro Principles," booklet from Centre on Housing Rights and Evictions (COHRE).
Crisp, J. (2001) "Mind the Gap! UNHCR, Humanitarian Assistance, and the Development Process." New Issues in Refugee Research, Evaluation, and Policy Analysis Unit, Geneva, UNHCR.
Crisp, J., and A. Mayne (1993) *Review of the Cambodia Repatriation Programme*, UNHCR EVAL/CAM/13 September (restricted distribution) (Geneva: UNHCR).
Crocker, D. (1998) "Transitional Justice and International Civil Society: Toward a Normative Framework," *Constellations*, Vol. 4, No. 4, pp. 492–516.
——— (2000) *Retribution and Reconciliation*, available online at www.pauf.umd.edu/IPP/Winter-Spring00/retribution_and_reconciliation.htm.
Cunliffe, A., and M. Pugh (1996) "The UNHCR as Lead Agency in the Former Yugoslavia," *The Journal of Humanitarian Assistance*, available online at www.lja.ac/articles/a008.htm.
Darby, J., and R. MacGinty, eds. (2003) *Contemporary Peacemaking: Conflict, Violence and Peace Processes* (Basingstoke: Palgrave Macmillan).
"Declaration of Principles on Interim Self-Government Arrangements" (1993) Government of Israel and PLO (13 September).
Dolowitz, D. (2000) "Introduction," *Governance*, Vol. 13, No. 1, pp. 1–4.
Dolowitz, D, and D. Marsh (2000) "Learning from Abroad; The Role of Policy Transfer in Contemporary Policy-Making," *Governance*, Vol. 13, No. 1, pp. 5–24.

Dorai, M.K. (2002) "The Meaning of Homeland for the Palestinian Diaspora: Revival and Transformation," in N. Al-Ali and K. Koser (eds.) *New Approaches to Migration? Transnational Communities and the Transformation of Home* (London: Routledge Press).

Douglas, M. (1966) *Purity and Danger: An Analysis of Concepts of Pollution and Taboo* (New York: Praeger).

Dumper, M. (1994) *Islam and Israel: Muslim Religious Endowments and the Jewish State* (Washington, DC: Institute for Palestine Studies).

――― (1996) "Israel: Constraints on Consolidation," in D. Potter et al. (eds.) *Democratization* (London: Polity Press).

――― (2006a) "Comparative Perspectives on the Repatriation and Resettlement of Palestinian Refugees: The Case of Guatemala, Bosnia and Afghanistan," in E. Benvenisti and S. Hanafi (eds.) *Israel and the Palestinian Refugee Problem* (Heidelberg: Max Plancke Institute).

――― (2006b) "The Comparative Study of Refugee Repatriation Programmes and the Palestinian Case," in M. Dumper (ed.) *Palestinian Refugee Repatriation: Global Perspectives* (Routledge: London).

――― (2006c) "Palestinian Refugee Repatriation in Global Perspective," in M. Dumper (ed.) *Palestinian Refugee Repatriation: Global Perspectives* (Routledge: London).

――― (2006d) "The Return of Palestinian Refugees and Displaced Persons: The Evolution of an EU Policy on the Middle East Peace Process," in R. Brynen and R. el-Rifai (eds.) *The Absorption of Palestinian Refugees* (London: I. B. Tauris).

Dumper, M., ed. (2006) *Palestinian Refugee Repatriation: Global Perspectives* (London: Routledge).

du Plessis, J. (2003) "Notes on Restitution in South Africa," paper presented to BADIL Expert Forum for a Rights-Based Approach to the Palestinian Refugee Question, Geneva, 2–5 October. http://www.badil.org/Campaign/Expert_Forum/Geneva/paper09.html.

Eldar, A. (2002) "'The Moratinos Document'—The Peace That Nearly Was at Taba," *Ha'aretz*, 14 February.

El Khazen, F. (1997) "Permanent Settlement of Palestinians in Lebanon Recipe for Conflict," *Journal of Refugee Studies*, Vol. 10, No. 3, pp. 275, 280–281.

El-Malak, L. (2004) "Israel's State Responsibility vis-à-vis Palestinian Refugees," paper delivered at the International Symposium *A Just Solution for Palestinian Refugees?* organized by the A'idun Group in cooperation with the University of Damascus, 6–7 September.

EU People to People Programme (2000) *Guidelines for Applicants.*

Exeter Refugee Study Team (2001) *Study of Policy and Financial Instruments for the Return and Integration of Palestinian Displaced Persons in the West Bank and Gaza Strip*, unpublished study prepared for the EU Refugee Task Force.

Fagen, P. (2006) "Repatriation in UNHCR: Practices and Policies," in M. Dumper (ed.) *Palestinian Refugee Repatriation: Global Perspectives* (London: Routledge), pp. 41–62.

Findlay, M. (2000) "Decolonising Restoration and Justice: Restoration in Transitional Cultures," *The Harvard Journal*, Vol. 39, No. 4 (November), pp. 398–411.

Fischbach, M. (2000) "Land," in P. Mattar (ed.) *The Encyclopaedia of the Palestinians* (Chicago and London: Fitzroy Dearborn).

――― (2003) *Records of Dispossession: Palestinian Refugee Property and the Arab-Israeli Conflict* (New York: Columbia University Press).

——— (2006) *The Peace Process and Palestinian Refugee Claims: Addressing Claims for Property Compensation and Restitution* (Washington, DC: United States Institute of Peace Press).
Flynn, M. (2002) "Is This Peace?" *Bulletin of the Atomic Scientists*, Vol. 58, No. 6, pp. 62–70, available online at www.thebulletin.org/article.php?art_ofn=nd02 flynn_035.
Garlick, M. (2003) "The UN Peace Plan for Cyprus: Property Displacement and Proposed Solutions," paper presented to BADIL Expert Forum for a Rights Based Approach to the Palestinian Refugee Question, Geneva, 2–5 October.
Gavrielides, T. (2005) "Some Meta-Theoretical Questions for Restorative Justice," *Ratio Juris*, Vol. 18, No. 1 (March), pp. 84–106.
Gazit, S. (1995) *The Palestinian Refugee Problem*, Final Status Issues Study No. 2 (Tel Aviv: Jaffee Centre for Strategic Studies).
——— (2001) "Solving the Refugee Problem: An Israeli Point of View," in J. Ginat and B. Perkins (eds.) *The Palestinian Refugees: Old Problems, New Solutions* (Brighton: Sussex Academic Press).
Geneva Accord (2003) *The Geneva Accord: A Model Israeli-Palestinian Peace Agreement*, available online at www.geneva-accord.org/Accord.
Ghanem, A. (2005) "The Binational State Is a Desired Palestinian Project and Demand," *al-Majdal* (Quarterly Magazine of BADIL Resource Center for Palestinian Residency and Refugee Rights), No. 28 (Winter), pp. 15–18.
Ginat, J., and B. Perkins, eds. (2001) *The Palestinian Refugees: Old Problems, New Solutions* (Brighton: Sussex Academic Press).
Goldscheider, C. (2002) *Israel's Changing Society: Population, Ethnicity, and Development*, 2nd edition (Boulder, CO: Westview Press).
Goldstein, J. S. (2001) *War and Gender* (Cambridge: Cambridge University Press).
Goodwin-Gill, G. (1999) "Closing Address: Principles and Protection: Making It Work in the Modern World," UNHCR and International Protection, Refugee Studies Centre Working Paper No. 2 (June).
——— (2000) "Return and Compensation," in Palestine Liberation Organization, Department of Refugee Affairs, *The Final Status Negotiations on the Refugee Issue: Positions and Strategies* (Ramallah: PLO Department of Refugee Affairs).
Ha'aretz (Israel) (2006) "Israel Asks UNRWA to Expand Its Humanitarian Program," 1 April, available online at www.haaretz.com (accessed 1 April 2006).
Hadawi, S. (1988) *Palestinian Rights and Losses in 1948: A Comprehensive Study* (London: Saqi Books).
——— (1990) *Bitter Harvest: A Modern History of Palestine*, revised and updated edition (Brooklyn, NY: Olive Branch Press).
Hall, R. (2003) "Rural Restitution," in *Evaluating Land and Agrarian Reform in South Africa Series*, No. 2 (Cape Town: University of Western Cape, Programme for Land and Agrarian Studies).
Hammami, R., and S. Tamari (2001) "The Second Intifada: End or New Beginning," *Journal of Palestine Studies*, Vol. 30, No. 2, pp. 5–25.
Hammond, L. (1999) "Examining the Discourse of Repatriation," in R. Black and K. Koser (eds.) *The End of the Refugee Cycle? Refugee Repatriation and Reconstruction* (Oxford: Berghahn Books).
Hanafi, S. (1996) "Palestinian Sociology of Return: Social Capital, Transnational Kinship and Refugee Repatriation Process," in S. Hanafi (ed.) *The Palestinian Sociology of Return* (forthcoming).

Hanssen-Bauer, J., and L. B. Jacobsen (2004) *Living in Provisional Normality: The Living Conditions of Palestinian Refugees in the Host Countries of the Middle East* (Oslo: Norwegian Refugee Council, FAFO).

Harvard Law School Human Rights Program (1997) *Truth Commissions: A Comparative Assessment—Proceedings from an Interdisciplinary Discussion Held at Harvard Law School, May 1996* (Cambridge: Harvard Law School), available online at www.law.harvard.edu/programs/hrp/Publications/truth1.html.

Heiberg, M., and G. Øvensen (1993) *Palestinian Society in Gaza, West Bank and Arab Jerusalem: A Survey of Living Conditions*, available online at www.almashriq.hiof.no/general/300/320/327/fafo/reports/FAFO151/index.html.

Helton, A. (2002) *The Price of Indifference: Refugees and Humanitarian Action in the New Century* (Oxford: Oxford University Press).

—— (2003) "End of Exile: Practical Solutions to the Palestinian Refugee Problem," paper presented at the International Conference on Israel and the Palestinian Refugees, Max Plancke Institute, Heidelberg, 11–13 July.

Hilterman, J. (1991) *Behind the Intifada: Labor and Women's Movements in the Occupied Territories* (Princeton: Princeton University Press).

Holbrooke, R. (2000) Statement by Ambassador Richard C. Holbrooke, US Permanent Representative to the United Nations, New York, 28 March 2000, available online from www.un.int/usa/00_044.htm.

Hunter, R. (1991) *The Palestinian Uprising* (Berkeley: University of California Press).

Hurwitz, D. (ed.) (1992) *Walking the Red Line: Israelis in Search of Justice for Palestine* (Philadelphia: New Society).

al-Husseini, J. (1999) "Observations on Compensation in the Palestinian Refugees' Case," paper delivered at the Workshop on Compensation for Palestinian Refugees, International Development Research Centre, Ottawa, 14–15 July.

—— (2002) "UNRWA and the Palestinian Nation-Building Process," in *Journal of Palestine Studies*, Vol. 29, No. 2 (Winter), pp. 51–64.

—— (2003) "The Future of UNRWA and the Refugee Camps," paper prepared for the Palestinian Center for Policy and Survey Research, Institut Français du Proche-Orient (Amman: IFPO).

International Crisis Group (2004) "Palestinian Refugees and the Politics of Peacemaking," *Middle East Report*, No. 22, available online at www.crisisgroup.org/home/index.

International Development Research Centre (1999) "Final Report," Workshop on Compensation for Palestinian Refugees, International Development Research Centre, Ottawa, 14–15 July, available online at www.arts.mcgill.ca/mepp/pprrn/PRCOMP3.HTML (accessed 29 June 2005).

International Red Cross and Red Crescent Movement (1997) "The Agreement on the Organization of the International Activities on the Components of the International Red Cross and Red Crescent Movement," available online at www.cdr.dk/working_papers/wp-99-5.htm (accessed 6 June 2005).

Irani, G. E. (1999) "Islamic Mediation Techniques for Middle East Conflicts," *Middle East Review of International Affairs*, Vol. 3, No. 2 (June), pp. 1–17.

Israel-Egypt Peace Treaty (1979) Available online at www.mfa.gov.il/MFA/Peace%20Process/Guide%20to%20the%20Peace%20Process/Israel-Egypt%20Peace%20Treaty.

Israeli Ministry of Foreign Affairs (2005) *Israel's Disengagement Plan Documents*, available online atwww.mfa.gov.il/MFA/Peace+Process/Guide+to+the+Peace+Process/Israeli+Disengagement+Plan+20-Jan-2005.htm.
Israeli Non-Paper, Draft 2 (2001) *Israeli Private Response to the Palestinian Refugee Proposal of January 22nd, 2001* (23 January).
Jacobsen, K. (1996) "Factors Influencing the Policy Responses of Host Governments to Mass Refugee Influxes," *International Migration Review*, Vol. 30, No. 3 (Autumn), pp. 655–678.
Jacobsen, L. B. (2003) "Finding Means—UNRWA's Financial Situation and the Living Conditions of Palestinian Refugees," FAFO Summary Report 415 (Norway).
Jamal. A. (2005) "The Palestinian IDPs in Israel and the Predicament of Return: Between Imagining the Impossible and Enabling the Imaginative," in A. M. Lesch and I. S. Lustick (2005) (eds.) *Exile and Return: Predicaments of Palestinians and Jews* (Philadelphia: University of Pennsylvania Press).
Jiryis, S. (1976) *The Arabs in Israel* (London: Monthly Review Press).
Jones, L. (2003) "Giving and Taking Away: The Difference Between Theory and Practice Regarding Property in Rwanda," paper presented to BADIL Expert Forum for a Rights-Based Approach to the Palestinian Refugee Question, Geneva, 2–5 October, available online at www.badil.org/Campaign/Expert_Forum/Geneva/paper09.html.
Jordan-Israel Peace Treaty (1994) From 26 October, available online at www.kinghussein.gov.jo/peacetreaty.html.
Kaminer, R. (1996) *The Politics of Protest: The Israeli Peace Movement and the Intifada* (Brighton: Sussex Academic Press).
Kapeliouk, A. (1987) "New Light on the Arab-Israeli Conflict and the Refugee Problem and Its Origins," *Journal of Palestine Studies*, Vol. 16 (Spring), pp. 16–24.
Keely, C. B. (2001) "The International Refugee Regime(s): The End of the Cold War Matters," *International Migration Review*, Vol. 35, No. 1, pp. 303–314.
Kelley, N., and J. F. Durieux (2004) "UNHCR & Current Challenges in International Refugee Protection," *Refuge*, Vol. 22, No. 1 (March).
Khadiagala, G. (2002) "Implementing the Arusha Peace Agreement on Rwanda," in S. J. Stedman, D. Rothchild, and E. M. Cousens (eds.) *Ending Civil Wars: The Implementation of Peace Agreements* (Boulder, CO: Lynne Rienner Publishers).
Khalidi, R. (1999) "Truth, Justice, and Reconciliation: Elements of a Solution to the Palestinian Refugee Issue," in G. Karmi and E. Cottran (eds.) *The Palestine Exodus, 1948–??* (Reading, UK: Ithaca Press).
Khalidi, W. (1992) *All That Remains: The Palestinian Villages Occupied and Destroyed by Israel* (Washington, DC: Institute for Palestine Studies).
Khasan, H. (1994) "Palestinian Resettlement in Lebanon: Behind the Debate," Palestinian Refugee ReseachNET (April), available online at www.arts.mcgill.ca/mepp/new_prrn/research/papers/khashan_9404.htm (accessed 12 February 2006).
Khatib, G. (2002) *A Palestinian View—Palestinians Have Learned the Lesson*, available online at www.bitterlemons.org/previous/bl210102ed3.html.
Kimmerling, B. (1983) *Zionism and Territory: The Social-Territorial Dimensions of Zionist Politics* (Berkeley: Institute of International Studies, University of California Press).
Klein, M. (2006) "The Palestinian 1948 Refugees—Models of Allowed and Refused Return," in M. Dumper (ed.) *Palestinian Refugee Repatriation: Global Perspectives* (London: Routledge).

Krafft, N., and A. Elwan (2003) "Housing and Infrastructure Scenarios for Refugees and Displaced Persons," presented to the 2nd International Stocktaking Conference on Palestinian Refugee Research, International Development Research Center, Ottawa, June.

Kriesberg, L. (2002) "The Relevance of Reconciliation Actions in the Breakdown of Israeli-Palestinian Negotiations," *Peace and Change*, Vol. 27, No. 4, pp. 546–571.

Kubursi, A. (2000) "Palestinian Losses in 1948: The Quest for Precision," in Palestine Liberation Organization, Department of Refugee Affairs (eds.) *The Final Status Negotiations on the Refugee Issue: Positions and Strategies* (Ramallah: PLO Department of Refugee Affairs).

——— (2001) "Palestinian Losses in 1948: Calculating Refugee Compensation," Center for Policy Analysis on Palestine (Washington, DC) Information Brief No. 81.

Kurosawa, S. (2003) "UNHCR's Contribution to Peace Building," Workshop, Oxford Refugee Studies Centre, March.

Lagos, R., M. Munoz, and A-M. Slaughter (1999) "The Pinochet Dilemma," *Foreign Policy*, No. 114 (Spring), pp. 26–39.

Lean, S. (2003) "Is Truth Enough? Reparations and Reconciliation in Latin America," in J. Torpey (ed.) *Politics and the Past: On Repairing Historical Injustices* (Lanham, MD: Rowman and Littlefield).

Lee, L. (1986) "The Right to Compensation: Refugees and Countries of Asylum," *American Journal of International Law*, No. 80.

——— (1999) "The Issue of Compensation for Palestinian Refugees," paper delivered at the Workshop on Compensation for Palestinian Refugees, International Development Research Centre, Ottawa, 14–15 July.

Lehn, W., and U. Davis (1988) *The Jewish National Fund* (London: Kegan Paul International).

Lemarchand, R. (1998) "Genocide in the Great Lakes: Which Genocide? Whose Genocide?" *African Studies Review*, Vol. 41, No. 1 (April), pp. 3–16.

Lesch, A. M. (1984) "The Gaza Strip: Heading Towards a Dead End," *UFSI Reports*, Part 1, No. 10.

Lesch, A. M., and I. S. Lustick, eds. (2005) *Exile and Return: Predicaments of Palestinians and Jews* (Philadelphia: University of Pennsylvania Press).

Lillich, R. B., and B. H. Weston (1988) "Lump Sum Agreements: Their Continuing Contribution to the Law of International Claims," *American Journal of International Law*, No. 82.

Loescher, G. (1993) *Beyond Charity: International Cooperation and the Global Refugee Crisis* (Oxford: Oxford University Press).

Lustick, I. S. (2005) "Negotiating Truth: The Holocaust, *Lehavdil* and al-Nakba," in A. M. Lesch and I. S. Lustick (eds.) *Exile and Return: Predicaments of Palestinians and Jews* (Philadelphia: University of Pennsylvania Press).

Luxembourg European Council (1997) "Presidency Conclusions," 12 and 13 December, available online at www.consilium.europa.eu.

Lynk, M. (2003) "The Right to Restitution and Compensation in International Law and the Displaced Palestinians," *Refuge*, Vol. 21, No. 2, available online at www.arts.mcgill.ca/MEPP/PRRN/papers/mlink.html.

Maier, C. S. (2003) "Overcoming the Past? Narrative and Negotiation, Remembering and Reparation: Issues at the Interface of History and the Law," in J. Torpey (ed.) *Politics and the Past: On Repairing Historical Injustices* (Lanham, MD: Rowman and Littlefield).

Malkki, L. H. (1992) "National Geographic: The Rooting of Peoples and the Territorialisation of National Identity Among Scholars and Refugees," *Cultural Anthropology*, Vol. 7, No. 1, pp. 13–45.

Mallison, W. T., and S. V. Mallison (1986) *The Palestine Problem in International Law and World Order* (Harlow, UK: Longman).

Ma'oz, M. (2001) "Traditional Positions and New Solutions," in J. Ginat and B. Perkins (eds.) *The Palestinian Refugees: Old Problems, New Solutions* (Brighton: Sussex Academic Press).

Marsden, P. (1999) "Repatriation and Reconstruction: The Case of Afghanistan," in K. Koser and R. Black (eds.) *The End of the Refugee Cycle? Refugee Repatriation and Reconstruction* (Oxford: Berghahn).

—— (2006) "UNHCR Under Duress; The Reducing Power of UNHCR to Influence Outcomes for Afghan Refugees," in M. Dumper (ed.) *Palestinian Refugee Repatriation: Global Perspectives* (London: Routledge).

Martin, S. F. (2000) "Forced Migration and the Evolving Humanitarian Regime," *The Journal of Humanitarian Assistance*, July (part of UNHCR series *New Issues in Refugee Research*), available online at www.jha.ac/articles/u020.htm.

Masalha, N. (1992) *Expulsion of the Palestinians: The Concept of "Transfer" in Zionist Political Thought, 1882–1948* (Washington, DC: Institute for Palestine Studies).

—— (2003) *The Politics of Denial: Israel and the Palestinian Refugee Problem* (London: Pluto Press).

McCaughey, T. (2001) "Northern Ireland: Burying the Hatchet, Not the Past," in N. Biggar (ed.) *Burying the Past: Making Peace and Doing Justice After Civil Conflict* (Washington, DC: Georgetown University Press).

McDowell, C., and R. A. Ariyaratne (2001) *Complex Forced Migration Emergencies: East Timor Case Study* (Oxford: Option for the Reform of the International Humanitarian Regime Project, Refugee Studies Centre).

McDowell, C., and N. Van Hear (2006) "Linking Return and Reintegration to Complex Forced Migration Emergencies: Diversities of Conflict, Patterns of Displacement and Humanitarian Responses—A Comparative Analysis," in M. Dumper (ed.) *Palestinian Refugee Repatriation: Global Perspectives* (London: Routledge).

McDowell, D. (1994) *The Palestinians, The Road to Nationhood* (London: Minority Rights Publications).

MidEastWeb (2000a) *Essentials of the Camp David II Proposals by Israel*, available online at www.mideastweb.org/campdavid2.htm.

—— (2000b) *The Israeli Camp David II Proposals for Final Settlement* (unofficial summary), available online at www.mideastweb.org/campdavid2.htm.

Minow, M. (1998) "In Practice—Between Vengeance and Forgiveness: South Africa's Truth and Reconciliation Commission," *Negotiation Journal*, October, pp. 319–351.

Minster Lovell (2000) *The Final Version Report from the Workshop on the Future of UNRWA*, Minster Lovell, UK, 19–20 February, available online at www.arts.mcgill.ca/MEPP/PRRN/prunrwa3.html.

Moon, C. (2004) "Prelapsarian State: Forgiveness and Reconciliation in Transitional Justice," *International Journal for the Semiotics of Law*, Vol. 17, pp. 185–197.

Morris, B. (1987) *The Birth of the Palestinian Refugee Problem, 1947–1949* (Cambridge: Cambridge University Press).

Muslih, M. Y. (1998) *The Origins of Palestinian Nationalism* (New York: Columbia University Press).

Nabulsi, K. (2006) *Palestinians Register: Laying Foundations and Setting Directions* (Oxford: Nuffield College).

Nasser, M. (2003) "The Palestine Refugee Records Project," paper presented at 2nd Stocktaking Conference on Palestinian Refugee Research, International Development Research Centre, Ottawa, 17–20 June.

Nathanson, R. (2003) "Survey of Palestinian Refugee Real Estate Holding in Israel: Legal Mechanisms After 1948 Which Enable Accurate Identification of Real Estate Owned by Palestinian Refugees and a Proposed Compensation Model Accordingly," paper presented to the 2nd International Stocktaking Conference on Palestinian Refugee Research, International Development Research Centre, Ottawa, 17–20 June.

Nedelsky, N. (2004) "Divergent Responses to a Common Past: Transitional Justice in the Czech Republic and Slovakia," *Theory and Society*, Vol. 33, pp. 65–115.

Nevo, J. (2004) "Transitional Justice Models and Their Applicability to the Zionist-Palestinian Conflict and the Palestinian Refugee Issue," working paper presented to the BADIL Expert Seminar, Haifa, 1–4 July, available online at www.badil.org/Campaign/Expert_Forum/Haifa/WP/WP-5(Jessica-Nevo).html.

Nijem, K. (2003) "Planning in Support of Negotiations: The Refugee Issue," paper presented to the 2nd International Stocktaking Conference on Palestinian Refugee Research, International Development Research Centre, Ottawa, 17–20 June.

Oakley, P. E. (1997) "Humanitarian Affairs in the State Department and Our Relationship with the UN," available online at http://gos.sbc.edu/o/oakley2.html (accessed 10 April 2005).

OCHA (2002) "Internal Displacement: A Consideration of the Issue," UN Office for the Coordination of Humanitarian Affairs published at *IRIN News*, available online at www.irinnews.org/webspecials/idp/bkarticle13.asp.

——— (2004) *Review of the Humanitarian Situation in the Occupied Territory in 2004*, UN Office for the Coordination of Humanitarian Affairs, Occupied Palestinian Territory, available online at www.reliefweb.int/rw/RWB.NSF/db900SID/VBOL-6B7BWQ?OpenDocument.

O'Sullivan, A., and A. Mizroch (2004) "Israel Wants UNRWA Probed," *Jerusalem Post*, 1 October.

Palestine Liberation Organization (PLO) (2000) *The Palestinian Refugees Factfile*, Department of Refugee Affairs (Ramallah and Jerusalem: PLO).

Palestinian Authority/Palestine Liberation Organization (2001) "Palestinian Statement on Refugees," Taba, Egypt, 22 January.

Palestinian Central Bureau of Statistics (2002) "Summary," available online at www.pcbs.org.

Paris, R. (2004) *At War's End: Building Peace After Civil Conflict* (Cambridge: Cambridge University Press).

Parvathaneni, H. (2003) "Who Are the Refugees? Social, Economic, and Legal Conditions," paper presented at 2nd International Stocktaking Conference on Palestinian Refugee Research, International Development Research Centre, Ottawa, 17–20 June, pp. 1–9.

——— (2005) "The Impact of the Oslo Accords on UNRWA's Funding," in M. Keating, A. Le More, and R. Lowe (eds.) *Aid Diplomacy and Facts on the Ground: The Case of Palestine* (London: Royal Institute of International Affairs).

Patel, V. (2003) "A Comparative Analysis of Mass Claims Mechanisms," paper presented at 2nd International Stocktaking Conference on Palestinian Refugee Research, International Development Research Centre, Ottawa, 17–20 June.

Peretz, D. (1958) *Israel and the Palestinian Arabs* (Washington, DC: Middle East Institute).

——— (1993) *Palestinians, Refugees, and the Middle East Peace Process* (Washington, DC: United States Institute of Peace Press).

——— (1995) *Palestinian Refugee Compensation*, Information Paper 3 (May) (Washington, DC: Center for Policy Analysis on Palestine).

——— (2000) "Israel," in P. Mattar (ed.) *The Encyclopaedia of the Palestinians* (Chicago and London: Fitzroy Dearborn).

——— (2001) "Refugee Compensation: Responsibility, Recipients, and Forms and Sources," in J. Ginat and E. Perkins (eds.) *The Palestinian Refugees: Old Problems, New Solutions* (Brighton: Sussex Academic Press).

Peretz, D., and G. Doron (1997) *The Government and Politics of Israel*, 3rd edition (Boulder, CO, and Oxford: Westview Press).

Peters, J. (1996) *Pathways to Peace: The Multilateral Arab-Israeli Talks* (London: Pinter).

Petrin, S. (2002) "Refugee Return and State Reconstruction: A Comparative Analysis," in *New Issues in Refugee Research*, Working Paper No. 66 (Geneva: UNHCR Evaluation and Policy Analysis Unit).

Plascov, A. (1981) *The Palestinian Refugees in Jordan 1948–1957* (London: Cass).

Prettitore, P. (2003) "The Right to Housing and Property Restitution in Bosnia and Herzegovina: A Case Study," unpublished paper presented to the BADIL Expert Forum Seminar on the Role of International Law in Peacemaking and Crafting Durable Solutions for Refugees, University of Ghent, May.

——— (2006) "Refugee Return in Bosnia and Herzegovina," in M. Dumper (ed.) *Palestinian Refugee Repatriation: Global Perspectives* (London: Routledge).

Pugh, M., and A. Cunliffe (1997) "The Lead Agency Concept in Humanitarian Assistance: The Case of the UNHCR," *Security Dialogue*, Vol. 28, No. 1, available online at www.mpr.co.uk/scripts/sweb.dll/li_archive_item?method=GET&object=SD_1997_28_01_MAR.

Quigley, J. (1999) "Compensation for Palestinian Refugees: Initial Comments," paper delivered at the Workshop on Compensation for Palestinian Refugees, International Development Research Centre, Ottawa, 14–15 July.

Radley, K. R. (1978) "The Palestinian Refugees: The Right to Return in International Law," *The American Journal of International Law*, Vol. 72 (July), pp. 586–614.

Refugee Studies Centre (2005) *Developing DFID's Policy Approach to Refugees and Internally Displaced Persons* (Oxford: Refugee Studies Centre).

Rempel, T. (1999) "The Ottowa Process: Workshop on Compensation and Palestinian Refugees," *Journal of Palestine Studies*, Vol. 29, No. 1 (Autumn), pp. 36–49.

Riess, S. (2000) "Return Is Struggle, Not Resignation: Lessons from the Repatriation of Guatemalan Refugees from Mexico," *New Issues in Refugee Research*, Working Paper No. 21 (Geneva: UNHCR Evaluation and Policy Analysis Unit).

Roberts, R. (2005) "The Forgotten People: Palestinian Refugees in Camps in Lebanon," *Refugee Issues Quarterly*, July.

Rodicio, A. G. (2000) *Restoration of Life in Cambodia: 1992–1993 Returnees in Bunteay, Meanchey, and Siem Reap* (Phnom Penh: Jesuit Refugee Service, Cambodia).

——— (2006) "Re-approaching Voluntary Repatriation Within a Reconciliation Framework: A Proposal Drawn from the Cambodian Return Process," in M. Dumper (ed.) *Palestinian Refugee Repatriation: Global Perspectives* (London: Routledge).

Roodt, M. (2003) "Land Restitution in South Africa," paper presented to BADIL Expert Forum for a Rights-Based Approach to the Palestinian Refugee Question, Geneva, 2–5 October, available online at http://www.badil.org/Campaign/Expert_Forum/Geneva/paper09.html.

Rose, R. (1993) *Lesson Drawing in Public Policy* (Chatham, NJ: Chatham House).

Rosenblatt, L., and L. Thompson (1999) "After the Fighting," *Washington Times*, 17 January.
Rouhana, N. (2005) "Truth and Reconciliation: The Right of Return in the Context of Past Injustice," in A. M. Lesch and I. S. Lustick (eds.) *Exile and Return: Predicaments of Palestinians and Jews* (Philadelphia: University of Pennsylvania Press).
Rustow, D. A. (1970) "Transitions to Democracy: Towards a Dynamic Model," *Comparative Politics*, Vol. 2.
Said, E. (1990) "Reflections on Exile," in R. Ferguson et al. (eds.) *Out There: Marginalization and Contemporary Cultures* (Cambridge, MA: MIT Press).
—— (1999) "Truth and Reconciliation," *al-Ahram*, 20 January.
Salam, N. (1994) "Between Repatriation and Resettlement: Palestinian Refugees in Lebanon," *Journal of Palestine Studies*, Vol. 24, No. 1 (Autumn), pp. 18–27.
Sayigh, R. (1979) *Palestinians: From Peasants to Revolutionaries: A People's History, Recorded by Rosemary Sayigh from Interviews with Camp Palestinians in Lebanon* (London: Zed Press).
—— (1994) *Too Many Enemies: The Palestinian Experience in Lebanon* (London: Zed Books).
—— (1995) "Palestinians in Lebanon: Harsh Present, Uncertain Future," in *Journal of Palestine Studies*, Vol. 25, No. 1 (Autumn), pp. 37–53.
Schiff, B. (1995) *Refugees unto the Third Generation: UN Aid to the Palestinians* (Syracuse, NY: Syracuse University Press).
—— (2000) "UNRWA in Transition," paper presented at the PRRN/IDRC/RIIA workshop held at Minster Lovell, UK, 19–20 February, available online at www.arts.mcgill.ca/mepp/prrn/papers/transition.html (accessed 27 May 2005).
Schiff, Z., and E. Yaari (1984) *Intifada: The Palestinian Uprising—Israel's Third Front* (New York: Simon and Schuster).
Schulz, H. L. (2003) *The Palestinian Diaspora: Formation of Identities and Politics of Homeland* (London: Routledge).
Shamir, S., and B. Maddy-Weitzman (2005) *The Camp David Summit—What Went Wrong?* (Brighton: Sussex Academic Press and Tel Aviv University).
Sharif, R. (1979) "The United Nations and Palestinian Rights, 1974–1979," *Journal of Palestine Studies*, Vol. 9 (Autumn), pp. 21–45.
Sharoni, S. (1995) *Gender and the Arab-Israeli Conflict: The Politics of Women's Resistance* (Syracuse: Syracuse University Press).
Sharoni, S., and M. Abu-Nimer (2000) "The Israeli-Palestinian Conflict," in D. Gerner (ed.) *Understanding the Middle East* (Boulder, CO, and London: Lynne Rienner Publishers).
Shiblak, A. (1997) "Palestinians in Lebanon and the PLO," *Journal of Refugee Studies*, Vol. 10, No. 3, pp. 261–274.
Shlaim, A. (1986) "Husni Za'im and the Plan to Resettle Palestinian Refugees in Syria," *Journal of Palestine Studies*, Vol. 16 (Spring), pp. 16–24.
Silverstein, P. (2005) "States of Fragmentation in North Africa," *Middle East Research and Information Project, Middle East Report*, No. 237 (Winter), pp. 26–33.
Slyomovics, S. (2001) "A Truth Commission for Morocco," *Middle East Research and Information Project, Middle East Report*, No. 218, available online at www.merip.org/mer/mer218/218_slyomovics.html.
Smith, C. D. (2004) *Palestine and the Arab-Israeli Conflict: A History with Documents*, 5th edition (Boston: Bedford/St. Martin's).
Smith, P. (1986) "The Palestinian Diaspora, 1948–85," *Journal of Palestine Studies*, Vol. 15, No. 3, pp. 90–108.

Stedman, S. J., D. Rothchild, and E. M. Cousens, eds. (2002) *Ending Civil Wars: The Implementation of Peace Agreements* (Boulder, CO: Lynne Rienner Publishers).

Stein, B. (1983) "The Commitment to Refugee Resettlement," in *The Global Refugee Problem: U.S. and World Response, Annals of the American Academy of Political and Social Science*, Vol. 467, pp. 187–201.

Stepputat, F. (1999) "Repatriation and Everyday Forms of State Formation in Guatemala," in R. Black and K. Koser (eds.) *The End of the Refugee Cycle? Refugee Repatriation and Reconstruction* (Oxford: Berghahn).

——— (2006) "'Sustainable Returns': State, Politics, and Mobile Livelihoods—The Guatemalan Case," in M. Dumper (ed.) *Palestinian Refugee Repatriation: Global Perspectives* (London: Routledge).

Stocktaking I (1997) Stocktaking Conference on Palestinian Refugee Research, Ottawa, 8–9 December, International Development Research Centre (IDRC) and Palestinian Refugee ResearchNet, available online at www.arts.mcgill.ca/MEPP/PRRN/prconference3.html.

Stocktaking II (2003) 2nd Stocktaking Conference on Palestinian Refugee Research, Ottawa, 17–20 June, International Development Research Centre (IDRC), available online at web.idrc.ca/en/ev-32583-201-1-DO_TOPIC.html.

Sutcliffe, C. R. (1974) "Palestinian Refugee Resettlement: Lessons from the East Ghor Canal Project," *Journal of Peace Research*, Vol. 11, pp. 57–62.

Takkenberg, L. (1998) *The Status of Palestinian Refugees in International Law* (Oxford: Clarendon Press).

Talhami, G. (2001) *Palestinian Refugees Pawns to Political Actors* (New York: Nova Science Publishers).

Tamari, S. (1996) "Return, Resettlement, Repatriation: The Future of Palestinian Refugees in the Peace Negotiations," *Final Status Strategic Studies* (Washington, DC: Institute for Palestine Studies).

——— (2003) "Palestinian Refugee Property Claims: Compensation and Restitution," paper presented at the International Conference on Israel and the Palestinian Refugees, Max Plancke Institute, Heidelberg, 11–13 July.

Tamari, S., ed. (1999) *Jerusalem 1948: The Arab Neighbourhoods and Their Fate in the War* (Bethlehem: BADIL).

Tamari, S., and E. Zureik, eds. (2001) *Reinterpreting the Historical Record: The Uses of Palestinian Refugee Archives for Social Science Research and Policy Analysis* (Jerusalem: Institute of Jerusalem Studies).

Tibawi, A. L. (1963) "Visions of the Return: The Palestinian Arab Refugee in Arabic Poetry and Art," *Middle East Journal*, Vol. 17.

Tomeh, G. J. (1974) "When the UN Dropped the Palestinian Question," *Journal of Palestinian Studies*, Vol. 4 (Autumn), pp. 15–30.

Torpey, J., ed. (2003) *Politics and the Past: On Repairing Historical Injustices* (Lanham, MD: Rowman and Littlefield).

Turton, D., and P. Marsden (2002) "Taking Refugees for a Ride? The Politics of Refugee Return to Afghanistan" (London: Afghanistan Research and Evaluation Unit).

UN (1948) United Nations General Assembly Resolution 194 (III) of 11 December 1948, available online at domino.un.org/UNISPAL.NSF.

——— (1951) *Convention Relating to the Status of Refugees*, United Nations Treaty Series 189 UNTS 137, 28 July 1951.

——— (2001) United Nations General Assembly Resolution 55/127, available online at www.cicwebca/UN/pdf/55_127.pdf.

——— (2004) "Basic Facts: Humanitarian Action," available online at www.un.org/ha/moreha.htm (accessed 25 May 2005).

UNCC (2006) "The UNCC at a Glance," available online at www.unog.ch/uncc/ataglance (accessed 23 June 2005 and 20 July 2006).
UNHCR (1993) "Repatriation to Cambodia," extract from *State of the World's Refugees*, available online at www.burmalibrary.org/reg.burma/archives/199703/msg00525.htm.
—— (1996) *Voluntary Repatriation Handbook: International Protection* (Geneva: UNHCR).
—— (2000) *The State of the World's Refugees: Fifty Years of Humanitarian Action* (Oxford: Oxford University Press).
—— (2001) "New Directions for Refugee Resettlement Policy and Practice," available online at www.unhcr.org/cgi-bin/texis/vtx/excom/opendoc.pdf?tbl=EXCOM&id=3b3065f44 (accessed 10 February 2006).
—— (2002) *The Resettlement Handbook*, revised edition (Geneva: UNHCR), available online at www.unhcr.org/cgi-bin/texis/vtx/template?page=publ&src=static/rh2002/rh2002toc.htm (accessed 12 February 2006).
—— (2003a) *Refugees by Numbers*, available online at www.unhcr.org/basics (accessed 14 June 2005).
—— (2003b) *Handbook for Registration* (Geneva: UNHCR).
—— (2004) *RefWorld*, No. 12 (CD-ROM).
—— (2005) "Emergency Food Assistance to Returnees, Refugees and Other War Affected Population in BiH: Joint WFP/UNHCR Evolution Mission," *UNHCR Evaluation Reports*, available online at www.unhcr.ch/cgi-bin/texis/vtx/research/opendoc.htm (accessed 14 June 2005).
UNRWA (1999) *Report of the Commissioner-General of the United Nations Relief and Works Agency for Palestine Refugees in the Near East*, available online at http://domino.un.org/UNISPAL.NSF/0/e0da7117084863418525682b004f8264?OpenDocument.
—— (2003a) *Neirab Rehabilitation Project*, UNRWA Project Briefing, pp. 1–6.
—— (2003b) *UNRWA in Figures (as of 31 December 2002)*. Public Information Office (Gaza), March 2003, and *Interim Report of the Director of UNRWA*, Supplement No. 19 (A/1451/Rev.1), 1951, par. 35 and Table 3.
—— (2004a) *Emergency Appeal, 2004*, available online at www.un.org/unrwa/emergency/appeals/7th-appeal.pdf.
—— (2004b) *The United Nations Relief Works Agency*, available online at www.un.org/unrwa.
—— (2005a) *UNRWA—Finances*, available online at www.un.org/unrwa/finances/index.html (accessed 1 June 2005).
—— (2005b) *West Bank Refugee Camp Profiles*, available online at http://www.un.org/unrwa/refugees/westbank.html (accessed 2 June 2005).
—— (2006) *Pledges to UNRWA for 2006*, available online at www.un.org/unrwa/finances/index.html (accessed 20 December 2006).
—— (2007) *Finances*, available online at www.un.org/unrwa/finances/index.html.
US Committee for Refugees (1999) "Trapped on All Sides: The Marginalization of Palestinian Refugees in Lebanon," June.
US Department of State (2002) Statement by Richard Boucher, Spokesman, Washington, DC, 25 September, available online at www.usembassy.it/file2002_09/alia/a2092505.htm (accessed 1 June 2005).
US General Accounting Office (GAO) (2003) "Department of State (State) and United Nations Relief and Works Agency (UNRWA) Actions to Implement Section 301(c) of the Foreign Assistance Act of 1961," released on 17 November, available online at www.gao.gov/new.items/d04276r.pdf.

van Hear, N. (2003) "From 'Durable Solutions' to 'Transnational Relations': Home and Exile Among Refugee Diasporas," *New Issues in Refugee Research*, Working Paper No. 83. (Geneva: UNHCR Evaluation and Policy Analysis Unit).

Van Selm, J. (2004) "The Strategic Use of Resettlement: Changing the Face of Protection?" *Refuge*, Vol. 22, No. 1, pp. 39–48, available online at www.yorku.ca/crs/Refuge/Abstracts%20and%20Articles/Vol%2022%20No%201/vanselm.pdf (accessed 12 February 2006).

Vayrynen, R. (2001) "Funding Dilemmas in Refugee Assistance: Political Interests and Institutional Reforms in UNHCR," *International Migration Review*, Spring, available online at www.findarticles.com/p/articles/mi_qa3668/is_200104/ai_n8931911.

Vicente, A. (2003) "Justice Against Perpetrators: The Role of Prosecution in Peacemaking and Reconciliation," BADIL Expert Forum: The Role of International Law in Peacemaking and Crafting Durable Solutions for Refugees, Ghent University, 22–23 May, available online at www.badil.org/Publications/Legal_Papers/WorkingPapers/WP-E-02.pdf

Wadie, S. E. (2003) "Palestinian Refugees: Host Countries, Legal Status and the Right of Return," *Refuge*, available online at www.yorku.ca/crs/Refuge/Abstracts%20and%20Articles/Vol%2021%20No%202/said.pdf.

Welchman, L. (2003) *The Role of International Law and Human Rights in Peacemaking and Crafting Durable Solutions for Refugees: Comparative Comment*. BADIL Expert Forum: The Role of International Law in Peacemaking and Crafting Durable Solutions for Refugees, Ghent University, 22–23 May 2003.

Wetzel, J. (2002) "A Meditation on Hell: Lessons from Dante," *Modern Theology*, Vol. 18, No. 3 (July), pp. 375–394.

Wheeler, N. (2000) *Saving Strangers: Humanitarian Intervention in International Society* (Oxford: Oxford University Press).

World Bank (1993) *Developing the Occupied Territories: An Investment in Peace*, Vols. 1–6, No. 12360, available online at http://www-wds.worldbank.org/external/default/main?menuPK=64187510&pagePK=64193027&piPK=64187937&theSitePK=523679&menuPK=64154159&searchMenuPK=64258544&theSitePK=523679&entityID=000009265_3970311123238&searchMenuPK=64258544&theSitePK=523679.

—— (2000a) *Aid Effectiveness in the West Bank and Gaza*. Report prepared (with Japan) at the request of the Ad Hoc Liaison Committee, June.

—— (2000b) "Assessment of the Absorptive Capacity of the West Bank and Gaza in Integrating Returnees and Associated Costs: A Concept Note," unpublished draft.

—— (2003a) *Report on the Impact of Intifada*. Quarterly publication of the West Bank and Gaza office.

—— (2003b) "The Trust Fund for Gaza and West Bank: Status, Strategy, and Request for Replenishment," World Bank Report No. 27094-GZ, November, available online at http://lnweb18.worldbank.org/mna/mena.nsf/Attachments/2003+Strategy/$File/WBG+2003+Strategy.pdf.

Zeager, L., and J. Bascom (1996) "Strategic Behaviour in Refugee Repatriation: A Game-Theoretic Analysis," *Journal of Conflict Resolution*, Vol. 40, No. 3, pp. 460–485.

Zureik, E. (1979) *The Palestinians in Israel: A Study in Internal Colonialism* (London: Routledge and Kegan Paul).

—— (1996) *Palestinian Refugees and the Peace Process* (Washington, DC: Institute for Palestine Studies).

INDEX

Abbas, Mahmood, 34
Abu Mazen–Beilin Plan, 124
Annan Plan, restitution provisions in, 141–142
Al-Aqsa, overt and underlying causes of, 32
Arab states: as host states, 88–91; and refugee compensation, 148–149; refugees' exploitation by, 4
Arab Summit Declaration (2002), and right of return, 33
Arafat, Yassir, 31, 34
Arusha Accords: and refugee right of return, 56; and restitution of property, 140; restorative justice approach in, 177
Ayalon-Nusseibeh Plan: compensation proposal in, 69; and international community role, 63–64; and local integration, 68; references to UN resolutions in, 62; refugee right of return and resettlement in, 58, 63, 66, 69; repatriation in, 63, 67, 95

Balfour Declaration, 23–24
Barak, Ehud, 31, 154, 175
Beirut Declaration: international community involvement in, 63–64; right of return and repatriation in, 63, 94; UN resolutions as reference for, 62, 64
Ben Porat Plan, 92
Berlin Declaration, and creation of Palestinian state, 127

Bilateral agreements, international law based on, 9
Bosnia-Herzegovina: and refugee right of return, 58–59; restitution and compensation in, 140–141, 143–144

Cairo Declaration of Principles of International Law on Compensation to Refugees, 135–136
Cambodia, refugee crisis and repatriation program in, 113–115
Camp David peace talks, 151–152; core issues in, 69, 152; failure of, 32; immigration proposal in, 67; international community involvement in, 63–64; 1978 agreements reached in, 28; refugee property claims in, 150; right of return and repatriation in, 62, 98; UN instruments used in, 62
Casablanca Protocol, 87
Chile's Truth and Reconciliation Commission, 167–168
Civil society: and Middle East peace talks, 174; promotion of truth and justice, 171–172, 173–174; and restorative justice, 177; Track II initiatives of, 33; and transitional justice, 171–172; and two-state solution, 183
Clapp Mission, 87
Clinton, Bill: refugee solutions suggested by, 31–32. *See also* Camp David peace talks
Comay-Michelmore Agreement, 124

223

Commission for Real Property Claims of Refugee and Displaced Persons (CRPC) (Bosnia), 140–141, 143–144
Compensation, 69; alternative mechanisms for, 143; Arab states' argument for, 148–149; Cairo Declaration and, 135–136; calculations of, 137; Canada's role in, 151; Clinton's Camp David efforts for, 152; contentious issues in, 7; and culpability, 137; for displaced persons, 147; and distributive justice, 137; funding, 7–8, 94; for human rights abuse victims, 137; incentives and settlement methods in, 142–143; in international law, 134–135, 147; Israeli preconditions for, 148–149; as problematic solution, 156; and rectification of social and economic problems, 136; and right of return, 137–138; as remedy for reparation, 135; studies, 142–145, 151; and UN Resolution 194, 146–147
Convention Plus consultations, 70
Criminal tribunals, and retributive justice, 165
Cyprus, restitution issue in, 141–142

Dayton Peace Accords: compensation and restitution of property in, 137, 140–141, 143–144; refugee return and repatriation in, 56, 59
Durban Declaration, 136

East Timor, repatriation process in, 112–113
Egypt, refugee resettlement plan in, 91
Egyptian-Israeli peace treaty, Palestinian refugee issue in, 28
Euro-Mediterranean Partnership, as Palestinian repatriation forum, 94
European NGOs, and Middle East peace process, 175
European Union (EU): aid to Palestinians, 1993–1999, 128*tab;* Bosnian refugee compensation, 144; position on Palestinian refugees, 127; UNRWA financing of, 119; and UNRWA's future, 127

Family reunification program, 32; conditionalities in, 97; and Palestinian repatriation, 97–98
Al-FATAH, 26
4Rs concept, and refugee reintegration, 60, 81, 162, 163

Gaza Strip, population saturation in, 100. *See also* Occupied Palestinian Territories
Gaza/Jericho Agreement. *See* Oslo II agreement
Gender issues: incorporated into repatriation programs, 84, 111; and restorative justice, 177–178
Geneva Accord, 124; compensation proposal in, 69; and cross-border coordination, 73; and distinctions between displaced and other affected persons, 72; implementation mechanisms for, 153–154; instruments used in, 62; international community and, 63–64; and local integration, 68; monitoring function in, 74; refugee right of return in, 58, 63, 66; reconciliation issues in, 70, 176; reparation and compensation negotiations in, 152–155; repatriation in, 63, 67, 94, 98, 102; truth, justice, and reconciliation issues in, 175–176; and UNRWA's future, 71, 129
Geneva Initiative: as blueprint for final status agreement, 33; Israel's rejection of, 33
Global Consultations on International Protection (GCIP), 53
Global Palestinian refugees, lack of authoritative information on, 40
Guatemala, refugee repatriation and transitional justice in, 110–112, 170–171

HAMAS-led government: peace process and, 34; UNRWA and, 120, 125, 131–132
Hebron Agreement (1997), 30
Holistic development, as durable solution, 72
Host-country integration: burden-sharing concerns in, 126; as durable solution, 67; *host country* defined,

78; host country's attitudes and policies toward, 88–91. *See also* Local integration

Human rights violations: and perpetrators' rehabilitation, 164; and retributive justice, 160–161; and state responsibility, 135, 137; and straight compensation, 137

Internally displaced persons (IDPs): arbitrary displacement of, 47–48; compensation for, 147; lack of authoritative information on, 40; estimates of, 1950–2003, 41*tab;* Israel's marginalization of, 47–48; noncitizen status of, 47; in the Occupied Territories, 45–48; and UNCHR's lead agency role, 109

International agencies: acting as lead agencies, 108; coordination and cooperation among, 72–73

International community: limited humanitarian responses of, 108–109; Israel supported by, 4; peace process role of, 60; and repatriation, 8, 57; response to Palestinians' plight, 29; Road Map backing of, 176–177; and UNRWA's future, 126–127

International Conference on Central American Refugees (CIREFCA), 111; and voluntary repatriation, 64

International Court of Justice/International Criminal Court, and redress for human rights violations, 136, 161

International Criminal Tribunal of Rwanda (ICTR), 168–169, 170

International Development Research Centre, compensation studies of, 151

International donor community, and neoliberal assistance programs, 60–61

International law: compensation in, 134–135, 147; and Palestinian claims for return and/or compensation, 9; principle of state responsibility in, 135; and refugee right of return, 58, 66; transitional justice concept in, 159; and UN peace processes, 61–62

International practice, 49–75; dual refugee regime in, 80; and durable solutions for refugees, 79–86; and lead agency role, 70–72; and micro-level implementation, 70; Middle East peace process and, 61–74; and operational parameters, 53–56; principles of transparency and refugee choice in, 84; relief-development gaps in, 79; reparations and restitution in, 134–135, 140; repatriation supported by, 82, 93–102; strategic use of resettlement in, 82. *See also specific agency*

International refugee regime, 51, 53, 80

Iran–United States Claims Tribunal, 142

Islamic Resistance Movement (HAMAS). *See* HAMMAS-led government

Israel: aid dependency of, 36–37; Arab and refugee property ownership in, 149; border withdrawals of, 189–190; and moral acknowledgment of refugee suffering, 154, 175; 1949 borders of, 24; and Palestinian refugee claims, 150, 153; southern Lebanon occupation of, 28; US economic support for, 29. *See also* Family reunification program

Israeli civil society, truth-seeking and transitional-justice process of, 181

Israeli Jewish society: collectivist vision of, 22–23; demographics of, 35; "Jewishness" of, 5–6, 155; main features of, 35–37; and mass immigration to new state, 35; rift between Israeli Arabs and Jews in, 35

Israeli-Egyptian peace agreement, 126; reconciliation commitment in, 173

Israeli-Palestinian conflict: "Jewishness" of Israel as core issue in, 5–6, 155; legal and developmental issues in, 9–11; Palestinian displacement as core grievance in, 4; meta-conflict in, 158, 166–167, 180; and transitional justice, 56; and truth commission remedy, 180–181, 182–183

Jordan: and citizen restitution requests, 150; government refugee assistance in, 47; refugee citizenship and rights in, 47, 89–90; restitution requests in, 150

Jordanian-Israeli Peace Agreement, 126, 150, 173–174
Justice: and failure to address the past, 159; forgiveness and, 161, 162; judicial mechanisms for, 160; justice-peace tension in, 159, 163; political context for, 162; post-conflict case studies of, 163–171; through property restitution, 34; and punishment, 161; and refugee reintegration, 162; and repatriation process, 162. *See also* Restorative justice; Retributive justice; Transitional justice; Truth commissions

Kadima Party (Israel), 34–35
Kuwait, Iraqi compensations to, 143

Lead agencies: ad hoc evolution of, 108–109; coordination regime as alternative to, 109; functions and roles of, 106–107; goal and responsibilities of, 105–107; international agencies as, 108–109; NGOs' coordination of, 106; refugee crisis role of, 108; UNHCR role as, 71, 109–115, 131
Lebanon: camps, population of, 46, 47; hostility toward refugees in, 88–89; Israeli occupation in, 28; Sabra and Shatila camp massacres in, 88; secondary Palestinian migration from, 89
Lesson-drawing, comparative research on, 12–13
Local integration: and community absorption capacity, 80; as durable solution, 67–68; and international practice, 67, 86; as limited option, 67–68; UNHCR's role in, 67. *See also* Host-country integration; Resettlement

Madrid Peace Conference, 15, 94; establishment of, 30; failure of, 29–30; and Palestinian state prospect, 118; and reparations, 150; and truth and reconciliation issues, 174
Mandatory Palestine: British support for Jewish homeland in, 23; Great Revolt of 1936–1939 in, 24; as Palestinians' country of origin, 66

McGhee Plan, 86–87
Middle East peace process: acceptable and durable solutions in, 191–192; Arab Summit Declaration (2002) and, 33; asymmetry of power in, 180; and civil society activism, 174; EU position on, 127; HAMAS government as obstacle to, 34; and indigenous conflict resolution, 178–179; and international practice and norms, 60–74, 186; Israeli and PLO concessions in, 30; one-state solution in, 188–189; and Palestinian political rights, 186; Palestinians' participation in, 65; privileging of security issues over resolution in, 172–173; refugee participation and representation in, 60, 65–66; repatriation issues in, 93–102; returnees involvement in, 111; road map for peace in, 33; transitional justice concept applied in, 172–173; truth, justice, and reconciliation issue in, 171–183; two-state solution in, 172, 187; UN agencies involved in, 50; voluntary repatriation and, 58. *See also* Israeli-Palestinian peace negotiations; *specific process and accord*

National courts, and retributive justice, 160–161
1967 War: and demographic concerns, 35–36; displaced persons resulting from, 40; Israel's territorial gains from, 26
Nongovernmental organizations (NGOs): and interagency/intergovernmental coordination, 72–73; refugee aid from, 37; repatriation and property restitution goals of, 34, 111
Northern Ireland conflict: meta-conflict in, 166; nature and roots of, 165–166; transitional justice process in, 165–167

Occupied Palestinian Territories (OPTs): Camp David agreements on, 28; humanitarian assistance to, 119; Israeli settlement policy in, 5, 29, 36; Israeli withdrawal from, 34; local integration in, 91; option of

Palestinian state in, 100–102; Palestinian de facto integration into, 91–92; refugee experiences in, 45–46; UNRWA expenditures in, 123. *See also* Repatriation to Occupied Territories
October 1973 War, 28
Operations Support Officers, 127
Organization for African Unity (OAU) Convention, repatriation in, 64
Oslo Accords: and extended interim phase impact, 32; failure of, 179; interim versus permanent status phases in, 30, 32; lack of enforcement mechanisms in, 30; and 1967 displaced persons, 150; and Palestinian reparations, 150; and Palestinian state prospect, 118; Permanent Status Issue in, 15; PLO-Israeli concessions in, 30; refugee issue postponement in, 151; reconciliation issues in, 174; repatriation issues in, 97–98, 101; security issues privileged in, 172–173
Oslo II agreement, and empowerment of PNA, 97–98
Ottawa process, and UNRWA's replacement, 129–130

Palestine Liberation Organization (PLO): establishment and guerrilla takeover of, 26–27; as military threat, 28–29; and negotiation of refugee return, 10; refugee-related activities of, 95; UNRWA and, 125–126
Palestine Refugee Records Project, 132
Palestine Right to Return Coalition, 34
Palestine: civil war in, 24; historic, Jews' claim to, 21; Jewish population and land ownership in, 1917–1948, 23; 1967 War in, 26; Ottoman rule in, 22–23; partition of, 24; refugee exodus from, 24; and UN Resolution 194, 24–26. *See also* Mandatory Palestine
Palestinian Arab society, bourgeoisie and proletariat nature of, 22
Palestinian intifada, 1987–1991: international community and, 29. *See also* al-Aqsa

Palestinian National Authority (PNA): donor funding to, 118, 119; Geneva Initiative and, 33; as host government, 92; potential UNRWA dismantling and, 123, 128–129; and refugee population in the OPTs, 92; and refugee return to Israel, 98; representation of refugee concerns by, 95
Palestinian national identity: historical development of, 22; UNRWA's support of, 124–125; Zionism and, 23
Palestinian political elite, refugees' exploitation by, 4
Palestinian refugees: defined, 40, 43; global, lack of authoritative information on, 40; Israel's confiscation/transfer of property of, 26; obstacles to safe and dignified treatment of, 114–115; political and historical overview of, 21–48; post–1967 War expulsion of, 26; protection mandate for, 40; registered, entitlements of, 40; viewed as enemies/absentees by Israel, 55. *See also* Internally displaced persons (IDPs); *specific refugee issue*
Palestinian self-determination, return and property rights linked to, 137–138
Palestinian state, future, 118; EU support for, 127; in the Occupied Palestine Territories, 100–102; and right of return concessions, 33–34
Paris Agreement (1991), and refugee right of return, 56
Permanent Status Negotiations, UNWRA's potential role in, 132
Pinheiro Principles, and restitution claims, 138–139

Quick Impact Projects (QIPs), 111, 114

Reconciliation, 157–183; Convention Plus consultations on, 70; as durable solution, 69; and international consensus-building, 162–163; measures, 160; and meta-conflict resolution, 158; in prenegotiations phase, 157; and politicization of law and justice norms, 158; and program

design problems, 157–158; reparations and, 145; restorative justice and, 162; retributive justice and, 160, 161, 165; and stable peace, 8; state-to-state activities for, 9
Refugee: origin of term, 51; as used in the Voluntary Repatriation Handbook, 54
Refugee Affairs Officer program, establishment of, 118
Refugee camps: administration and policing of, 116; conditions and quality of life in, 44–45, 88; infant and maternal mortality rates in, 45; in the OPTs, Israeli approach to, 91–92; reconstruction schemes for, 92; resettlement alternative to, 80
Refugee crises: acceptable and durable solutions for, 77, 191–192; lack of international involvement in, 63–64; and types of conflict, 56–57
Refugee migration, and resettlement in non-neighboring states, 92–93
Refugee population statistics, 39, 41*tab*, 93*tab*, 116
Refugee research: and advancement of Palestinian cause, 14; data collection and case studies in, 15–16; government and agency funding of, 16; methodological problems in, 11–14; and Ottawa conferences, 16; political-realist approach in, 14–15, 16; rights-based approach in, 14–15, 17–18; on socioeconomic conditions, 1
Refugee return: politics and mechanisms of, 1–9; and returnee evaluation and monitoring, 73–74. *See also* Right of return
Refugee status: and personal need for completeness, 3, 4; Jews history of, 4; of refugees' descendants, 43
Refugee Working Group (RWG), 15, 30, 118
Reparations, 145–155; adequate compensation approach to, 136–137; application and lessons learned, 139–145; defined, 6; as durable solution, 69; economic, 135, 165; full restitution approach to, 136, 137, 155; in international law and practice, 134–145; and Israeli culpability, 133–134; for Jews from Arab countries, 154; in Middle East peace process, 145–155; and monetary payment for injury, 135; and property restitution, 186; and reconciliation, 145; research, 139; satisfaction for nonmaterial injuries as, 135; types of, 6–8. *See also* Compensation; Restitution
Repatriation, 82–86, 93–102; absorbing community effects of, 99–100; bottom-up approach to, 84; to country of origin, 67; definitions of, 8; donor demands for transparency in, 85; as durable solution, 78, 82; and economic achievements, 85–86, 95; and exilic bias, 96; gender, age, and disability perspectives in, 84; family reunification as, 93; and forced return, 67; funding needs, 94; holistic development approach to, 85, 96; and host-country integration, 67–68; human resource and capacity-building needs in, 84–86, 96; intergovernmental coordination in, 83; international involvement and support for, 82–83, 94, 103; Israeli support for, 103; large-scale, 84, 114; lead agency established for, 83; and local/regional development, 8, 95; and national reconciliation through return, 70; and networks developed in exile, 95–96; physical and logistical aspects of, 102; planning and execution issues in, 8; programs, 51, 111; prospects for, 93; refugee cooperation and participation, 8, 83, 84, 95; regional framework for, 83; and relief provisions, 108; research and documentary evidence for, 98–99; as resettlement, 8; as return to homeland versus home, 8, 100; and right of return, 93, 95; sequential approach to, 63; technical feasibility of, 99; as third country resettlement, 67; timing of, 63; three-stage road map for, 94; tripartite commissions for, 83; and UNHCR's 4Rs concept, 85; uniqueness of Palestinian case and, 78; world community

experiences of, 94; voluntary, 58, 70, 83–84. *See also* Refugee return; Right of return
Repatriation to Israel, 96–100; family reunification programs and, 97–98; and Jewishness of Israel, 96–97; on limited and ad hoc basis, 98; recent discussions on, 97; and Resolution 194, 96
Repatriation to Occupied Territories: housing and infrastructure requirements for, 101–102; as move to new Palestinian state, 100–102; previous unplanned returns to, 100–101; as right of return to homeland, 100
Resettlement, 69; as alternative to camps, 80; and burden-sharing with host countries, 81; as Cold War option, 79–80; countries, 68; cross-border coordination of, 73; definitions of, 68, 78; and donor countries' foreign policy interests, 80; as durable solution, 79–80, 81; host Arab states' attitudes toward, 87; intentions of, 79; as international protection, 80; local integration as, 78; in non-neighboring state, 92–93; projects, 86–87. *See also* Third-country resettlement
Resettlement Handbook (RH): applicability to Palestinian case, 55–56; and coordination of resettlement activities, 73; international law as reference points for, 61–62; local integration option in, 67–68; overview of, 55; resettlement in, 62, 68–69; right of return in, 66–67; and UNHCR role, 71
Resolution 194. *See* UN General Assembly Resolution 194
Restitution, 140–142; and actual physical return, 7; distinguished from right of return, 139; in international law and practice, 134–135, 140; judicial versus administrative approach to, 140; material and moral damages addressed in, 136, 186–187; possibility and prospects for, 6–7; without rehabitation of properties, 155; and right to return, 142; UN guidelines for, 138–139

Restorative justice, 161–163, 165, 180; apology for harm done and suffering in, 182; civil society's essential role in, 177; concept of, 161; and cultural difference, 178–179; disaggregated process of, 178; and gender balance restoration, 177–178; and punishment, 161; reconciliation and repatriation in, 162; truth commissions, 164–165
Retributive justice: and criminal tribunals, 160, 165; and proportionate harm, 160; in Rwanda's truth and reconciliation process, 169–170
Right of return: and compensation for damage and loss, 137–138; and individual choice, 58; international law on, 58, 66; peace processes and, 58–59, 172–173; repatriation and, 93, 95; and resettlement resistance, 87; restitution and, 142; and "return" to new Palestinian state in the OPTs, 66; and self-determination, 137–138; and UN Resolution 194, 24, 26
Rwanda, failed truth and reconciliation process, 168–169, 170

Sabra and Shatilla refugee camps, massacres in, 28–29
Sadat, Anwar, 28
Sharon, Ariel, 32
South Africa, Truth and Reconciliation Commission (TRC): approaches to justice in, 164–165; forgiveness discourse in, 162; objectives of, 164; restorative justice process in, 177
State institutions: postconflict re-establishment of faith in, 172; and refugees' state-building role, 57
Stocktaking Conferences I and II, 16
Syria: General Authority for Palestine Arab Refugee Affairs (GAPAR), 90; Palestinian integration in, 47, 90–91; refugee literacy in, 47

Taba Talks: "Clinton parameters" in, 31; implementation mechanisms for, 153–154; international community roles in, 64; and Israel's family reunification plan, 32; references to

UN resolutions in, 62–63; and refugee claims, 32, 69–70, 150; reparation and compensation negotiations in, 152–155; repatriation and restitution in, 67, 175–176; resettlement in, 69; and right of return conditions, 62–63; Tripartite Commission proposal in, 65; and UNRWA phase-out, 71, 124, 125–126, 129, 130

Third-country resettlement: asylum and protections goals of, 68; defined, 78; as durable solution, 67; Resettlement Handbook reference to, 68; UNHCR organization of, 52

Transitional justice: alternative model for, 159–160; case studies, 163–171; and civil society, 171–172; defined, 158; Middle East peace process applied to, 172–173

Tribunals: need for international scrutiny of, 178; and retributive justice, 160, 165; in Rwanda, 169, 170

Tripartite Commission, proposed, 65

Truth commissions, 160, 168–168, 177; and criminal trials, 165; and importance of truth-telling in, 161–162; international scrutiny of, 178; and rehabilitation through amnesty and public forgiveness, 164; and restorative justice, 161–162, 171; and transitional justice, 164–165, 168, 171. *See also* South Africa, Truth and Reconciliation Commission (TRC)

UN Conciliation Committee for Palestine (UNCCP): mediator role of, 37; national government oversight of, 147; and refugee compensation, 147–149; and refugee property identification and evaluation, 149; and refugee return, 37–38; resettlement projects of, 86–87; settlement mandate of, 145–146

UN Convention Relating to the Status of Refugees, basis of refugee status in, 43

UN Declaration of Human Rights, right of return in, 9

UN *Draft Basic Principles and Guidelines on the Right to a Remedy and Reparation for Victims and Violations of International Human Rights and Humanitarian Law,* 162–163

UN Economic Survey Mission for the Middle East, 87

UN General Assembly, and partition of Palestine, 24, 25

UN General Assembly Resolution 194, 117; adoption of and goals of, 24–26, 37; Israeli interpretation and response, 26, 151; and refugee repatriation and compensation, 96, 146–147; and refugee right of return, 9; and return based on free choice, 66; Western governments' perspective on, 9

UN High Commission for Refugees (UNHCR): activities and assistance overview, 52–53; budget for refugee return, 51; and Cambodian repatriation program, 113–115; Convention Plus Initiative of, 81, 82; credibility of, 52–53; and East Timor humanitarian crisis, 112–113; evolving mandate and capacity of, 51, 52; concept for refugee reintegration, 60, 81, 162, 163; Framework for Durable Solutions, 81; global consultations and new initiatives of, 81–82; and Guatemalan repatriation, 110–112; implementation of guarantees and amnesties, 63; and international law, 61; lead agency role of, 71, 109–110; and local integration, 67; minimal norms for refugee return, 110; operational framework of, 53–56; Palestinian refugee defined by, 43; reconciliation process envisaged by, 70; refugee consultation mandate, 65; refugee protection function of, 53, 122, 163; and refugee return and repatriation, 52, 58, 59, 63, 83; as research data source, 11; and resettlement option, 80–82; and returnee monitoring, 74; roles of, 37; and third-country resettlement, 52; and voluntary reparation, 64–65

UN Peace Plan for Cyprus, compensation and restitution provisions in, 141–142, 144–145

UN Relief and Works Agency for Palestine Refugees in the Near East

(UNRWA): alternatives to, 129–131; as alternative to HAMAS-led PNA, 120, 125; area of operation, 44*tab*, 45; argument for continued role of, 122; arguments to dismantle, 44, 125; budget and financing, 118, 119; establishment and roles of, 37; expenditures in the OPTs, 123; expenditures by program, 1950–2002, 117*tab*; expenditures per refugee, 1994–2001, 120*tab*; experimental migration policy of, 117; future role of, 10–11, 120–129; human resource development focus of, 116; humanitarian assistance role and operations of, 43–44, 119, 122, 125; Israel's position on, 124–125, 127; as lead agency, 121–122, 130, 131–132; limited or residual role for, 129; and local integration in the Occupied Territories, 91; mandate and functions, 115–116; Medium Term Plan of, 120; official perspectives on future of, 124–127; Palestinian institutions' agreements with, 125; and Palestinian national identity, 44, 124–127; Palestinian refugee defined by, 40; Peace Implementation Programme of, 118; phase-out and replacement of, 71–72; PLO provisional agreement with, 125; political and institutional challenges for, 116–117; and proposed Tripartite Commission, 65; protection mandate of, 40, 50, 117–118; and refugee return, 121; refugees' confidence in, 86; rights-based versus managerial approach to dismantling, 131; service provisions to Palestinian refugees, 45, 116, 117–118; special hardship programs of, 45; and tasks outside its mandate, 130; and transfer of functions to PNA, 123; and UNHCR's coordination, 130; US congressional interference with, 127
UN Resolution 242, as basis for peace efforts, 147
UN Transitional Administration in East Timor (UNTAET), 113
UN Development Programme (UNDP), and UNWRA functions, 122
United States: and Palestinian refugee assimilation, 86; and UNRWA financing, 119, 127
Universal Declaration of Human Rights, and refugee right of return, 58

Voluntary Repatriation Handbook (VRH): applicability to Palestinian case, 55–56; and distinctions between displaced and other affected persons, 72; and interagency and cross-border coordination, 73; and international law, 61; overview of, 54; reconciliation and reparation in, 69; and reference to regional agreements, 64; refugee participation in, 65; repatriation program formulation in, 84; and repatriation timing, 63; responsibility and right of return in, 62, 66–67; and UNHCR mandate, 71; and voluntary repatriation, 66, 67

West Bank. *See* Occupied Palestinian Territories (OPTs)
Women's groups, and restorative justice, 178
Working Group on Resettlement, 73
Wye Memorandum, 30

Zionism: defined as racist ideology, 6; as defining moment for Palestinian nationalism, 23; and immigration to Israel, 35; and settler movement, 5, 35, 36

ABOUT THE BOOK

From the dilapidated camps of Lebanon to the eye of the storm in Gaza, Palestinian refugees continue to be a focus of world attention. *The Future for Palestinian Refugees* addresses in depth this most difficult of the outstanding problems impeding peace in the Middle East.

Michael Dumper maps the contours of the issue, with special reference to wider international practice and its possible bearings on policy options for the Israeli-Palestinian case. Concentrating on topics central to the future of Palestinian refugees—ranging from international involvement in post-conflict agreements, to compensation and resettlement, to justice and reconciliation—he offers an important and positive contribution to thinking on the Middle East peace process.

Michael Dumper is associate professor in Middle East Politics at the University of Exeter. He is author of *The Politics of Sacred Space: The Old City of Jerusalem and the Middle East Conflict.*